NO ONE SPECIAL

CONFESSIONS OF A BADLY-BEHAVED 'BOOMER'

S.W. CAPPS

Book cover design and layout by Ellie Bockert Augsburger of Creative Digital Studios. Cover design features: Photos Provided by Author; 'Welcome to Downey, Future Unlimited' Sign / City of Downey / circa Early 1960s. Interior design features: Roller skates by egokhan / Adobe Stock #137196253; Accordion boy by Paul Moore / Adobe Stock #11831267, cropped to include accordion only; Mood Board Mockup by Kzara Visual / Creative Fabrica.

ISBN

979-8-9907545-3-9 (hardcover)

979-8-9907545-2-2 (paperback)

Also available in eBook

PRAISE FOR S.W. CAPPS

"Capps is adept at capturing all sides of the story and the dilemmas that emerge."
   - *Midwest Book Review*

"His writing keeps me on edge, precarious but in balance."
   - *Thom Rock, Author*
   Silk Pajamas, Tombstone Eyes

"Capps has mastered the art of taking innocent characters and putting them into situations where they have to figure out life anew."
   - *Bill Johnson, Author*
   A Story is a Promise

"His writing is exquisite. He writes with an ease and clarity that wafts you along to the apex of a crescendoing wave."
   - *Nel Rand, Author*
   Mississippi Flyway

"His writing offers exciting twists and turns around every corner!"
   - *Christopher Cook, Journalist,*
   KWTV-9 Oklahoma City

"Capps has a talent for keeping his audience wanting to find out what happens next."
   - *Amazon Customer*

For Mom, Dad, Dennis, and my childhood friends.
You were ALL special to me.

TABLE OF CONTENTS

NO ONE SPECIAL

'Childhood is the one story that stands by itself in every soul.'

— IVAN DOIG

INTRODUCTION

Fourteen years isn't much of a life. That's what I kept thinking as I struggled for air.

Fourteen years of memories. Fourteen years of moments.

All coming to an end, thanks to Dale Lingenfelder.

The Warren Bear football player (who outweighed me by sixty pounds and appeared to be salivating) wrapped his meaty paws around my throat, crushing my trachea like a plastic straw. This must be how asthmatics feel when they forget their inhalers, I thought. Or drowning victims feel when they watch the shoreline slip away. I was on my own, in the pit-black halls of a school I'd yet to attend. Dying. And there wasn't a damn thing...

I'm getting ahead of myself. And besides, the very fact that I'm recounting this story tells you I survived, though not without bruises to body and ego. In truth, I probably deserved this ass beating. And many more, something I'm sure you'll affirm when you read this book.

Until recently, I never thought about writing a memoir. My credentials, which include three less-than-best-selling novels, a string of highly-specialized magazine articles, and a defunct news reporting career, don't exactly merit one. Memoirs, after all, are reserved for the famous or infamous.

I am neither.

Furthermore, I didn't grow up in the Congo, escape from San Quentin, or swim the Bering Strait. In fact, no one has ever thought me remarkable, the word 'vanilla' far too spicy a description.

I am, as the title of this book affirms, *No One Special*.

The phrase, as I sat at the keyboard to begin this project, blipped through my head like a warped game of PONG. What made me think I could write a book about my youth? More important, who'd want to read it? If there's one thing writers do well, besides writing, of course, it's doubt themselves. And I'm the Michael Jordan of self-doubt.

Then it hit me.

We're *all* no one special. From the kid who bags groceries at the Piggly Wiggly to the CEO of General Motors to the Kardashians—*especially* the Kardashians! And death proves it. Its victims are rich, poor, black, white, Democrat, Republican, reminding us with a complete lack of subtlety that we're all on the same 'city bus'.

With that in mind, I began to type, the eventual result this patently-flawed, mostly-true, self-deprecating collection of stories. A sojourn to a place we all hold dear. Not a better place —it's dangerous to believe that—just a different one, a thought worth noting on this short visit.

A little housekeeping...most of the characters in this memoir are amalgamations of people I knew, bits and pieces, if you will, sewn together and often embellished for the good of the story. The names have been changed to protect the innocent. Except for mine, of course. With me, you can presume guilt.

Before we begin, a quick note from William Faulkner, a far better writer than I...or is it me...who really knows? Anyway, he wrote, '*To the man grown, the long-crowded mile of his boyhood becomes less than the throw of a stone.*'

In my case, it was an avocado, but we'll get to that. We'll get to the Lingenfelder incident, too. Both are as much a part of me as my ebbing hairline and aching back. But the stories you're about to read aren't *my* stories. Not really.

They're *ours*.

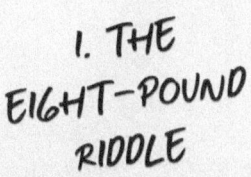

1. THE EIGHT-POUND RIDDLE

1

HOME

We arrive naked and dazed, slimy, screaming harbingers of the people we'll become.

In the irony of ironies, we have no recollection of this event, arguably the most important day of our lives. My big day came with zero fanfare. I was one of 314,798 babies born that day, a member of the last 'Boomer' class, as unexceptional as most of the others. Had I been able to speak, I would've had questions. What do I do now? Where do I go from here? Instead, I just lay there, staring at the ceiling and crapping my pants.

My birth mother, as it turns out, was a kid herself. Seventeen and unmarried, she lacked the means to raise a child, her decision to give me up a blessing for both of us. By doing so, she dodged the burden of rearing a *very* difficult son. And I, for reasons unknown, received the two greatest gifts a man (or baby, in this case) could ask for.

Clarence and Berneice Capps peered through the maternity ward glass in East Los Angeles. My father-to-be had coal-black hair, blue eyes, and shoulders wide as the door. My mother, even on tiptoes, only came to those shoulders, her eyes hazel, her hair an auburn bob. Both stared through thick bifocals, wondering,

I'm sure, what the hell they'd signed up for. They'd already raised a son to within six months of his eighteenth birthday. Why they chose to adopt well into their forties is beyond me. It wasn't like they had piles of cash lying around. My father worked in a factory, ten hours a day, five days a week, to bring home a measly six grand a year. My mother was a housewife who spent most of her time taking care of my brother. Dennis stood on her left, not much taller than Mom, crewcut revealing surgery scars. He was what society called 'handicapped', a term that would one day evolve into 'special needs'. Yes, he was functional, but my parents had their hands full. And Shannon William Capps—that's the name they gave me; more on that later—would only add weight to their cargo.

While they stared at the eight-pound riddle on the other side of the glass, the earth rumbled beneath them. The world was changing in 1964. Gone were the idyllic, post-war '50s, replaced by the volatile, often violent '60s. In the year ahead, President Johnson would escalate military action in Vietnam. Race riots would explode in more than a dozen U.S. cities. And the 'Boston Strangler' would terrorize New England. It would be a year of endings (the aforementioned 'Baby Boom', for one) and beginnings (the Whisky a Go Go would open on Sunset Boulevard). After ten long months, the Warren Commission would determine that Lee Harvey Oswald acted alone. Not to be outdone, the Surgeon General would announce that smoking "may lead" to lung cancer. On TV, *Bonanza* was the ratings king. Cassius Clay became Muhammed Ali. And NASA launched Gemini 1, setting the stage for a dramatic moon landing five years later.

I, of course, knew none of this.

I spent the entire year guzzling milk, which was delivered in glass bottles back then, eating Gerber's—the meat flavors were my favorites—and contributing nothing to the Capps household. I've tried to imagine my parents' thoughts on that chilly spring day. Adopting a child isn't like getting a new puppy. Dogs are easily trained, bark at intruders, and only stick around for a decade or so. A child does none of this.

When my parents arrived at the hospital, Dad had already put in a full day, getting up at four, making himself breakfast while Mom packed lunch, and heading off to the plant for another long shift. My mother and brother, meanwhile, worked feverishly to repaint the nursery (formerly Mom's sewing room), neither worried about the fumes I was soon to inhale. My due date, they'd been told, was still two weeks away. Unfortunately, no one bothered to tell me.

The next day, after sliding their anxious son into an exposed-metal car seat, Dad fired up the Country Squire and headed south. My father was a Ford man, through and through, our station wagon—'Beautifully Built to Take Care of Itself'—a thing of wood-paneled beauty. Southern California was full of them in those days, along with Chevy Impalas, Mercury Comets, Chrysler Imperials, and Buick Electras. As we rumbled into Downey, a bland L.A. suburb and my new hometown, Mom and Dad must've shuddered. They hadn't cared for a newborn since Truman held office. And like the ex-president, they weren't exactly 'spring chickens' anymore. But as parents who'd already survived the trials of raising a child with 'special needs', they had a distinct advantage. They didn't sweat the small stuff. And, trust me, I was about to provide plenty.

Had I been conscious when we turned up Guatemala Avenue, a street I'd soon come to know like the back of my hand, I'd have noticed the cookie-cutter houses. Built in the '50s, there were three models to choose from, all one-story, all three-bedroom/two-bath, all thirty feet apart. They featured pastel paint jobs (pinks, yellows, greens, blues), little front porches (some on the left, some on the right), and manicured front lawns (a few with white picket fences even). The Brinkleys lived on our side of the street, along with the Garvers, Munsons, Friedhoffers, and Lowes. The Andersons lived on the other, next to the Keplers, MacDuffs, Canos, and Langs. Everyone knew each other, and looked out for one another. That's what people did back then when gas was thirty cents a gallon, stamps set you back a nickel, and tickets to the movies cost $1.25. It was a nice neighborhood. In a nice city. In a nice little corner of the country.

A good place to grow up.

As Dad pulled into the drive, I'm sure I cracked my lids. Neighbors had gathered on the sidewalk, some cheering, others gawking at the new arrival. The women of the neighborhood had thrown Mom a shower, as had the ladies at church, netting me a mountain of new diapers to soil, along with a bounty of bibs, booties, bottles, and blankets. Some of the larger gifts, according to Mom's notes, included a layette set (whatever the hell that is), a new rocker (it went nicely with the rest of our mismatched furniture), and a Johnny Jumper (a spring-loaded chair that mounted tenuously to a door frame).

Waving to the crowd, Mom extracted me from the back seat and carried me into the house, a wood/stucco 'ranch' of approximately 1,100 square feet. With the help of a VA loan, my parents had purchased it for $12,500, having been so tapped after the down payment, they slept on the floor for a year. By the time they filled it with furniture, the inflation rate had risen to 1.28 percent, the average cost of a new car was $3,500, and the DOW Jones Industrial Average hovered near 800, not that Dad ever bought a stock. The house on Guatemala was *their* slice of the 'American Dream'. And it meant my parents, like sixty-three percent of their peers in '64, had arrived.

When *we* arrived that day, our normally neat-as-a-pin living room—Mom ran a tight ship—was littered with shower gifts, paint cans, and piles of used sports equipment (bats, balls, racquets, etc.). Dennis had mined the neighborhood the second he heard he was gaining a brother. Beneath the clutter was a cherry wood table and hutch (Mom's pride and joy), a green leather chair (Dad's), a floral-print couch (no one's), and a 20" black-and-white TV. A few feet away, the kitchen bulged with casseroles, neighbors delivering enough food for...well, the entire neighborhood.

After three helpings of wagon-wheel pasta (and a bottle of formula for me), darkness fell. Dad set up camp in his green chair, filling a pipe with Sir Walter Raleigh and scanning the evening paper. Dennis dropped a new record on the turntable, Dean Martin's *Sleep Warm*. And Mom and I swayed back and forth in the new rocker. As fire crackled in the hearth—Dad was one of *three* Angelenos to actually use his fireplace—Dino sang *Dream a Little Dream*, our family spending its first night together.

I'm sure I was beat, having been through the longest and strangest of my two days on Earth, but I'm sure of something else, too. As Dennis lowered the volume, Dad peered over the paper, and Mom leaned down to kiss me on the forehead, I knew unequivocally...

I was home.

2

BORN OF THE SPIRIT

My first actual memory came two years later. Mom told me I could invite two friends to my birthday party. And I knew exactly who to pick. Sean and Seamus O'Leary had moved into the house next door a few months earlier. Their parents, Finn and Betty, were young and hip, drove cool cars, and fought like cats and dogs. Their sons— Sean was a year older than me, Seamus a few months younger —had learned from the masters. Not only did they share a snazzy, red pedal car, but at no time during our fifteen-year friendship did they go more than fifteen minutes without beating the shit out of each other.

Mom baked two cakes in honor of my second birthday, one with white frosting, the other with blue. I might as well get this out of the way now...I was spoiled. Birthdays included not just a party but an embarrassing glut of gifts. And Christmas was worse. Old photographs verify the pillars of presents, often stacked higher than our fake tree. It took hours to rip through them, Mom snapping pictures, Dad recording everything on his Bell & Howell Zoomatic. I don't know how they did it on such meager wages, but my parents refused to let their kids do without, even if it meant doing without themselves. Which it always did.

My father made breakfast that morning—eggs, bacon, hash browns—my mother slapping another coat of icing on the 'twin towers'. They always split kitchen duties, Mom responsible for lunch and dinner, Dad for breakfast. And though he cooked some spectacular meals, I never once saw him do the dishes, even after installing the Dishmaster Imperial III (with 'Jet-Age Velvet-Touch Faucet Valves'). That was Mom's job, they agreed, and later mine.

I woke to the smell of bacon and delirium, having no idea what a birthday party was. But if Dennis could be trusted, it was going to be great! Foregoing my usual T-shirt and shorts, I threw on a plaid jumper, knee-high socks, and patent leather shoes—a solid look, if I do say so myself—then ran to the bathroom. The kid in the mirror had dark, curly hair, blue-gray eyes, and a round, flat face, one that would inspire such nicknames as 'pancake' and 'spoon', along with questions like, "Have you been chasing oncoming trucks?" Two-year-old me also looked like he didn't miss many meals, his arms short and stubby, his legs resembling tree stumps. After checking my hair —still coiled and snarled—I sprinted up the hall, pausing for thirty seconds to wolf down breakfast before making a beeline for the living room. Dad had borrowed a miniature picnic table from a guy at work, placing it in front of the fireplace. I assumed it was both a gift and permanent addition to our Cold War décor. It was neither, just a clever ploy to keep kids off the furniture.

By the time people started arriving, I was coming unglued. Neighbors poured in with presents. Family friends brought gifts. And Betty O'Leary showed up an hour late, Sean and Seamus handing me a lump wrapped in newspaper. The brothers looked nothing alike, Sean's dark hair and high cheekbones matching his dad's, Seamus' blonde locks a copy of his mother's. Only their eyes matched, green and full of hate for each other.

As Mom mingled, Dad fired up the reel-to-reel player, the peppy rhythms of Herb Alpert and the Tijuana Brass filling the room. My father loved electronics. In addition to the Zoomatic and studio-quality tape machine, he'd be the first on the block to score a pocket calculator, 8-track tape player, and VCR (which set him back a cool $900). For a guy who grew up wearing his brother's holey shoes, these were signs of success. And he never failed to splurge on something new and high-tech, whether he could afford it or not.

By noon, everything was running like clockwork. Mom served finger sandwiches while Dad poured Tang and Dennis sliced cake. As our guests chatted and ate, I feverishly opened gifts—a bag of army men, a chrome-plated six-shooter, a new cowboy hat (like the one Eric Fleming wore on *Rawhide*). When I placed it on my head, there was a deafening crash. Everyone turned to find the O'Leary brothers on the floor, Seamus trapped in a headlock, Sean applying pressure. They grappled under the picnic table till their mom stepped in, prying the GI Joe they'd just given me from their sticky fingers. As Betty hoisted them up, a writhing pit bull in each hand, she thanked my parents and headed home.

Truth be told, I hadn't invited Sean and Seamus for the gift. I already had two GI Joes, one with the highly-sought M-1 rifle accessory. The reason they topped my guest list was simple. There was sure to be a fight, and it would be entertaining as hell!

Ask anyone who grew up on Guatemala Avenue in the '60s and '70s, and they'll tell you to a man, no event, Pay-Per-View or otherwise, ever rivaled a Sean-Seamus skirmish. These dustups were legendary, our own fun-size versions of Liston-Clay, Patterson-Johansson, Norton-Holmes, kids sprinting from all directions whenever a donnybrook broke out.

And they broke out often.

Thanks to my front-row-seat status as the kid next door, I was responsible for signaling the neighborhood. "It's on!" I'd yell to Donny Kepler across the street who'd alert his three siblings and the five Cano kids. From there, an intricate sequence of whistles and whoops transmitted word to the Garvers and Brinkleys, zigzagging up Bangle Road to the Watsons and down Alderdale to the Morandinis. In seconds, a standing-room-only mob encircled the warriors, clapping, hollering, and begging for blood.

Sean and Seamus rarely disappointed.

Over the years, the pintsized pugilists clashed over everything from snack allocation to chore division. And the conflicts were epic, words leading to blows, blows leading to weaponry, all in blindingly-short order. The little gladiators would strike each other with all kinds of things—croquet mallets, king-palm fronds, oscillating lawn sprinklers—leaving every wound imaginable in their wake. Some of the battles even garnered their own epithets.

The 'Rumble in the Jungle', stolen from 1974's Ali-Foreman bout, took place on the grassy knoll behind my house. A leisurely game of King of the Hill turned ugly when Seamus, unhappy with his ex-monarch status, plucked a tree limb from the weeds and whacked his brother in the ribcage. The 'Thrilla in Vanilla' began with a dispute over ice cream, escalated to punches, and ended with Sean (ahead on points) taking a potted cactus to the groin. And then there was the 'Fight of the Sinchury'. The brothers had taken on a paper route together—a truly-horrible idea—Seamus folding copies of *The Signal* while Sean sinched them together with rubber bands. When Sean stopped sinching and started shooting, all hell broke loose, a duel with rolled-up newspapers the result. After taking six unanswered blows to the face, Seamus bolted for the house, returning with his brother's lava lamp. "Don't do it!" Sean begged, Seamus slamming it to the concrete in a burst of glass and glop.

Like patrons at a prize fight, we enjoyed every fracas, never once trying to break things up. Looking back, I suppose it was cruel pitting brother against brother—I admit to instigating more than a few conflicts myself—but it was also sheer spectacle, our own life-size Rock'em Sock'em Robots. Who needed video games—Super Smash Bros. was still four decades away—when we had Sean and Seamus?

"Time to clean up, Shannon," Mom called from the kitchen with a faint Oklahoma twang. Our guests had gone, Dad slipping off to the garage when he saw an opening, Dennis watching a ballgame. Basking in the glow of my new acquisitions, I wound up two Frantic Frogs and watched them hop down the hall. It wasn't nearly as riveting as the 'Punch-Out Under the Picnic Table', but at two, I was easily entertained. Cleaning up nothing, I donned my new cowboy hat and walked to the kitchen. Mom had already scrubbed the counter and was now taking steel wool to the range.

"Why do Sean and Seamus fight?" I asked.

She dabbed her brow with a Playtex glove. "They're brothers." Mom had four of her own, six sisters, too. The question, to her, must've seemed ridiculous. I walked to the window and peered through the curtain. Seamus was steering the little, red car while Sean pushed him up the driveway, both cackling with glee.

It suddenly hit me. The O'Leary brothers didn't *hate* each other. They fought because they shared space, struggled for individuality, vied for the same 'piece of the pie'. They were no different than Dennis and me, really. Or the other kids in the neighborhood. Or the friends I'd make when I started school a few years later. We were *all* brothers, '*born of the spirit*', to quote Lailah Gifty Akita. Bound together by common ground, collective experience, and love of place. Yes, there'd be fights. Our parents even encouraged them from time to time. But when our tussles ended, we'd patch things up and move on. Because that's what brothers do.

Of all the gifts I received that day, this was the greatest.

And I had two shrunken Irishmen to thank.

As I turned to go, I glanced through the curtain again. A pair of metal trashcans had been turned over. The pedal car was flipped on its side. And Sean was on top of Seamus, banging his head against the cement.

3

MAGIC HANDS

It didn't take long to discover how little talent I had. I couldn't turn junk into toys like Hobo Kelly on TV. Or juggle like Bozo. Or invent stuff like Mr. Green Jeans. And hard as I tried, I couldn't change leaves into money. My father could. I watched him do it dozens of times. He'd pluck a sprig of ivy from the back yard, stuff it in his big, clenched fist, and pull out a dollar bill.

At age three, I was convinced this was real, my only question...why didn't he do it more often? If you think about it, Dad's trick wasn't *that* unbelievable, especially when you consider the other stuff three-year-olds believe in, like a bird delivering babies, a bunny breaking into houses, or a fairy collecting human teeth. Although he was glad to perform the 'leaf to loot' routine whenever asked, I wanted witnesses. Our dogs, Tim and Crackers, were unreliable, so I gathered kids from the neighborhood. As expected, their jaws dropped on cue, convinced like I was that my father's hands were magic.

Surviving his dirt-poor childhood was a feat of magic itself. Born in a crumbling shack on the Missouri-Kansas border, Clarence was the second of six rough-and-tumble boys, each as 'full of piss and vinegar' as the next. Their father was a horse-trader, a sharecropper, a logger, and a barkeep (the vocations he *admitted* to), their mother the only 'hen' in the house.

They survived the Great Depression by hunting, fishing, farming, whatever it took to put food on the table, food that included possum, carp, and the occasional squirrel. It wasn't the carefree childhood he'd later give me, but it was all he had. And it made him tough as nails. By the time Dad reached his teens, he'd dropped out of school, gone to work at the sawmill, and fought every man in the county, rarely suffering defeat.

When work dried up in the 'Show Me State', he headed west, hitchhiking, hopping trains, and hoofing it to California, where he picked fruit (a la *Grapes of Wrath*) in the San Joaquin Valley. It was brutal work that left his hands blistered and bloodied, but he survived. He *always* survived. Migrating south, Dad found work coiling springs at one of the countless factories buttressing the war effort. That's where he met my mother, a real-life 'Rosie the Riveter', and truth be told, a woman *way* out of his league.

It would take more than magic to land her.

Their first date was a drive to the country—in those days, you could still find open spaces in L.A.—Mom packing a picnic basket, Dad bringing his guns. That always seemed a strange proposition to me. "Care to join me for a delightful afternoon of shooting tin cans in the desert?" But Dad's 'sorcery' won out again. Mom fell hard, and three months later, they walked down the aisle in Yuma, Arizona, a spaghetti-thin wedding band sealing the deal.

Three months after that, Dad left for New Guinea, drafted as a tech sergeant in the U.S. Army. He and his fellow recruits survived for a year there (with no ammunition, if you can believe that) before shipping out to the Philippines. While they awaited orders—rumors of an amphibious invasion of Japan were circulating, a tack that would've made Normandy look like a training exercise—my father put his magic hands to work again. Taking a break from the flamethrowers he serviced, Dad built the equivalent of a modern-day Jet Ski (thirty years prior to the real deal) out of two belly tanks and an old propeller. He and the other GIs took turns riding it through the breakwater, his invention bringing a little light to an otherwise-dark situation.

When the war finally ended, Dad returned home, two years, four months, and thirteen days after kissing Mom goodbye. She didn't recognize him when he arrived on Christmas Eve, 1945, the man on the porch fifty pounds lighter than the one she'd married. But my war-ravaged father convinced her to let him in, my brother, Dennis, born (as Dad liked to say) nine months and five minutes after she opened the door.

It would be another seventeen-and-a-half years before 'son number two' came along.

When I met Dad, he was still in the prime of life, hard jaw, firm chin, and built like the guy on the Oscar. He also had the biggest hands I've ever seen. Those hands routinely gathered me up when I was crying, steadied me when I took my first steps, and held me when I needed comfort. They also, when Mom wasn't looking, offered me the occasional swig of beer or puff on his pipe. And every night after work when I ran out to greet him, those magic hands would pick me up and stuff me down the front of his coveralls, making my legs disappear as we walked up the driveway.

The first 'real' magic I saw him perform was in the garage. Over the course of a month, he transformed a beat-up, old lawn-mower into a minibike, complete with rubber grips, padded seat, and a working stick shift. I was too young to ride it myself, but Dad made me his copilot, holding me as we rumbled down our street to the cheers of neighbors, his enormous hands guiding mine.

He spent a lifetime providing joy with those hands, whether it was strumming his old guitar, making the world's best blueberry waffles, or tossing a ball with his sons. A tool and die maker by trade, he could fix or build anything, his reputation as a 'wrench turner' unparalleled. As a result, an endless river of cars, trucks, and motorcycles flowed into our driveway, each with a conundrum its owner couldn't solve.

Dad never turned anyone away. And he never charged a penny.

Don't get me wrong, my father was no saint. He was a hard-headed Missourian, proving it once by taking a ricocheted bullet to the forehead. The slug entered over his right eye, caromed off his granite-hard skull, and exited behind his ear. "If that bullet had landed a half-inch to the right," the doctor chastised him, "you'd be dead!"

"A half-inch to the left," Dad responded, "and I'd still be hunting!"

He had a temper, too, a bad one at times, and cussed like Gordon Ramsay, "Je-*sus* Christ!" and "Son of a bitch!" his two favorite expletives. But angry as he got, he never raised a hand to his wife or kids. And he never hit a man who hadn't earned it.

When I was ten, I begged him for a motorcycle. After months of scrimping, saving, and working side jobs, he brought home a shiny, gray Honda XR-75. It was the first *new* vehicle he'd ever purchased, and the day it arrived was the best of my life— still ranks in the top ten, by the way. I put thousands of miles on that little bike, from dirt roads in the San Bernardino mountains to sand-covered trails in the Mojave Desert. When I dumped it, his hands were there to pick me up. When it broke down, they were there to fix it.

It was Dad's idea to take our one and only motorcycle road trip. In the summer of '77, he suggested we take our bikes to

Tombstone, Arizona. "Bikes?" I questioned. Grinning like a fox, he showed me a crate of old parts.

"I'll have this son of a bitch running in a month!"

Thirty days later, we rolled down I-10, bikes strapped to a borrowed trailer. We'd never taken a father-son trip before, but Dad had somehow finagled a week off work. Magic! We stayed in cheap motels, ate at roadside diners, and visited every tourist trap along the way. When we made it to Tombstone, my father was in heaven. A lifelong Western fan, he'd dreamed of gunfights at the O.K. Corral, seats at the Birdcage Theater, and walks through Boot Hill Cemetery. We did it all. And we rode the wheels off those motorbikes! We were more than a father and son that week. We were partners. Riding buddies. Best friends.

I lost my best friend on Veterans Day, 2005. Cancer had ravaged his 87-year-old body, turning his trophy-like physique into a withered shell. A few days before his death, he stared at the mirror. "This isn't me," he whispered. And he was right, save for one thing. Though cancer had taken his body, it hadn't touched his hands.

No, sir. On the day he died, those hands looked stronger than ever.

Ten years later, nearly to the day, I found myself at a Harley dealer. As I signed the papers on a new Ultra Classic, I caught sight of my own hands. They weren't my father's, not by a long shot. There was no dirt under the fingernails. No scars from the sawmill. No calluses on the palms. And there was certainly no magic in them. Never had been. But since his passing, I *had* figured out a few chords on the guitar. Learned to make blueberry waffles, though they paled in comparison to his. Even fixed a few things in the garage. At best, I was a bad carbon copy.

But I was trying.

When I hopped on the bike, I had no idea Dad's long-departed hands had a little magic left in them. As I fired up the engine and took off, I did what most riders do...smiled uncontrollably and stopped for photos. One of them leaped off the camera screen. My new bike sat in a stand of towering firs, a single beam of heavenly light illuminating the passenger seat. My smile grew. After all these years, Dad was still with me. I'd been his copilot once. Now he was mine.

As I rode home that day, I thought of all the sacrifices he made, the things he taught my brother and me, the joy he brought to our lives. And I swear, I felt those magic hands. Resting on my shoulders. Guiding me down the road.

4

NOISE IN THE 'HOOD

Of all the sports we watched on TV, Roller Derby was my favorite. That's why I begged for skates the minute I learned to walk. Every kid in the neighborhood skated. Or rode bikes with cards in the spokes. Or bounced balls. Sometimes all three at once. It made for a cacophony of clamor on our otherwise-quiet street. And not a single grownup —except for Mrs. Noid who lived six doors down, had no kids, and was universally-hated—ever complained.

Our little dot on the map was anything but unique. My street, like virtually every other strip of California blacktop, was lined with homogenous houses, postage-stamp yards, and evenly-spaced trees, from Sweetgums and their prickly seedpods (a serious skating hazard) to Crape Myrtles and their peeling trunks. Every house had a flag holder, and on Labor Day, Veterans Day, Memorial Day, and the Fourth of July, it damn sure held a flag!

Neighborhoods like this sprouted up all over America in the 1950s, ours the byproduct of Downey's exploding aerospace industry. Vultee Aircraft, eventually known as North American Rockwell, built 13,000 planes for WWII here, adding thousands of employees to the workforce. These blue-collar factory workers needed homes, and with Downey's population tripling, builders raised them by the hundreds, our modest little abode on Guatemala Avenue one of them.

Long before then, Downey was one massive orange grove. Irish immigrant John Downey purchased seventeen thousand acres of fertile Los Nietos Valley land back in 1873, carving it up to sell lots for ten bucks an acre. Known as the 'Pioneer of the Modern Subdivision'—his parents must've been proud!—he introduced not only oranges to homesteaders but corn, beets, sugar, and castor beans. Fast forward a hundred years and Downey's little hamlet would become the 'Home of the Apollo', the birthplace of The Carpenters, and the site of Taco Bell number one.

I grew up in northwest Downey, nine houses from the freeway, traffic noise, along with the aforementioned skate, bike, and ball racket, the music of my youth. Bland but never boring, our neighborhood ran from I-5—we used to stand on the overpass and beg truckers to honk—to the end of the sidewalk at Danvers, home to more bicycle skid marks than a velodrome. Middle-class families lived here, along with their dogs, cats, lawns of St. Augustine, and streetlamps that blazed at seven o'clock sharp.

Guatemala Avenue, an odd name for a street void of Mayan ruins, stretched far beyond our little neighborhood, a mile-long belt of arrow-straight asphalt that paralleled the Rio Hondo River. A quick aside...rivers in L.A. bear no resemblance to their bucolic brethren. For one thing, they're made of concrete. Built by the Army Corps of Engineers, these uncomely flood channels usher industrial and residential waste to the Pacific Ocean. No one dared raft down one, or go for a swim, or, God forbid, take a drink! But these waterways did provide an unintended benefit to the kids who lived nearby—a huge, grassy easement on either side.

The riverbed, as we called it, was a football field, sandlot diamond, and motocross track, all rolled into one. We played every game we knew—Tag, Hide-and-Seek, Steal the Bacon, etc. —on this unsupervised swath of Nirvana. Never mind the high-voltage power lines, ankle-deep chuckholes, or occasional coyote. It was our personal playground, though setting foot on the property, according to NO TRESPASSING signs, was PUNISH-ABLE BY LAW. Over the years, we pretended it was Iwo Jima, the Sahara Desert, or the loam of another planet. 'Make believe' was a bona fide pastime in those days, and when I got my first motor-cycle, I was Evel Kneivel, jumping the Snake River Canyon...at least till Mrs. Noid spread broken plaster over the track.

When we weren't blazing trails in the riverbed, we were gathering in our driveways and yards. At least fifty kids lived in our neighborhood, 76 million in neighborhoods like it across the country, all looking for something to do. Fortunately for us, the weather always cooperated—in soCal, it's sunny and seventy, seven days a week—allowing us to play outside year-round. Our parents loved this concept, able to ditch us for hours on end without worrying about our 'safety', a word that held little meaning back then.

In the shadow of the smog-veiled San Gabriels, we rode bikes without helmets, skipped rope in bare feet, and wrestled on asphalt. When I learned to skate, it was with plastic wheels strapped to my Keds. And though I graduated to metal, they weren't much better, stopping instantly when I hit a crack, pebble, or prickly damn seedpod. None of that stopped us, however. We skated through traffic and 'skied' behind bikes, every activity, from skating to the now-politically-incorrect Smear the Queer, leading to injury.

And these were just the 'made-up' games

The manufactured ones were worse.

Toy companies offered all sorts of lethal playthings. There was Wham-O's Super Elastic Bubble Plastic, which allowed kids to blow bubbles with polyvinyl-acetate (just don't inhale). The Water Wiggle attached to a garden hose, transforming the innocent, green tube into an African Bush Viper (I still have 'bite' marks to prove it). And then there was the sadistic Swing Wing, a sort of Hula Hoop for the head (I'm pretty sure my arthritic neck began there). Not to be outdone, Town & Country gave us Rocket Lawn Darts, a set of steel spikes to be tossed at targets across the yard (six thousand kids visited the E.R. as a result). And if that wasn't enough, one could purchase the Little Lady Stove—*offensive?*—granting girls license to bake cookies in a six-hundred-degree oven (without Mom and all her dumb rules). At one time or another, we played with all of these things, never once worrying about laceration, disfigurement, or trips to the burn unit.

That's what Mercurochrome was for. And we wore it like a badge of honor.

Through it all, not a single kid in the neighborhood died. Yes, we maimed ourselves from time to time, but scars seemed an equitable tradeoff for the fun we were having. And of all the fun (and near-death) experiences we had, our favorite, by far, was Roller Derby.

The neighborhood track happened to be in *my* driveway. One of the older kids chalked an oval, the metal-on-concrete skate noise unbearable. Dad drowned it out by pounding and sanding in the garage. Mom hiked the setting on her mixer. We skated around and around, from morning till night, elbowing each other, whipping teammates around corners, knocking each other down. We tried to keep score, but no one *really* understood how. So, for us, the game was about staying upright. And sending everyone else sprawling.

Skaters ranged in age from four to fourteen, in size from three to six feet, and in zeal from 'wanting everyone dead' to 'hoping to survive'. Billy Friedhoffer was the oldest (and coolest), often skating with a lit cigarette in his mouth. Donny Kepler was the fastest. And Sean and Seamus O'Leary were the meanest. My style could best be described as 'head on a swivel', years of Swing Winging a tremendous asset. To identify teams, we wore jerseys cut from old T-shirts, colored markers providing names, numbers, and bold shoulder striping. Though we juggled our rosters, the matchup was always the same, the L.A. T-Birds vs. the Texas Outlaws, each of us representing our favorite skating star—Danny Reilly, 'Big John' Hall, Ronny 'Psycho' Raines.

Only two things could stop a match in progress. The first was the Helms man. Five days a week, fifty-two weeks a year, a little, yellow truck, one of three hundred in the Helms bakery fleet, rolled through our neighborhood, offering candy, sweet rolls, and yesterday's donuts. When the white-capped driver came to a stop, kids swarmed like flies on dung. I can still hear the whoosh of the heavy, wooden drawers. Still get a whiff of the fresh-baked bread. A dime would buy almost anything in the vehicle, a dollar the entire inventory. These were the final days of home delivery, the ice man already dead, the milk man on life support. Even diaper trucks had gone the way of the Pig-Footed Bandicoot. Somehow we knew, even then, that time was fleeting, so we never missed an opportunity to savor a maple bar or candy necklace. But not for too long. The Derby was waiting.

The second thing to stop a match, or *any* activity, really, was blood. We were fine with scrapes and scratches. They were part of life. But when blood gushed, poured, or flowed, we stopped in our tracks (no pun intended). One Saturday afternoon, in the final days of the Johnson administration, our 'league' officially folded. Hector Cano, after surviving an unexpected ambush from the O'Leary brothers, whipped Tad Brinkley forward, past the jostling pack and into the side of our house. The result for the would-be 'jammer' was a gash the size of a Raspberry Fruit Slice. As he screamed in pain, we did what all kids do in times of crisis. We just stood there.

"Je-*sus* Christ!" my dad thundered. It wasn't the injury that upset him. He was pissed at having to power down the belt sander. Grabbing a rag, he walked to the fallen skater and pressed it to his forehead. "Hold it there till you get home." The kid walked off crying, Dad turning to the rest of us. "You know this shit's fake, right?"

We all stared, dumfounded. Even Billy Friedhoffer looked dazed. As he lit another Camel, our eyes moved to the pavement, settling on the blood. If Roller Derby was phony, what else was? Santa Claus? *The National Enquirer*? How many other disappointments did life have in store?

Seeing our spirits sag, Dad backpedaled a bit. "I don't mean *fake* exactly, just...you know...*rehearsed*." We continued to stare at the puddle, Dad massaging the back of his neck. "Look, fellas, these guys have gear, training, hell, even the track has padded rails!" A few of us looked up. "Let's find something else to do, huh? Something a little *safer*."

Ten minutes later, he had us all in the back yard.

Playing a rousing game of Rocket Lawn Darts.

5

SUMMER OF LOVE

When I was four, I discovered with great pomp and circumstance that I was heterosexual. Until then, I hadn't given the matter much thought. Sure, there were girls who caught my eye. Elly May Clampett of *The Beverly Hillbillies*. Betty Jo Bradley on *Petticoat Junction*. And Cora Lee Stevens who lived three doors down, had the prettiest smile I'd ever seen, and threw a football like Roman Gabriel. But her family moved in '68. And I was too young to fret over such things.

1968, as it turned out, was a tumultuous year. Not only did the Stevenses leave, but on the other side of the globe, North Vietnam launched the 'Tet Offensive', causing mass casualties in an already-unpopular war. At home, civil rights leader Martin Luther King, Jr. was shot and killed, Robert F. Kennedy meeting the same fate two months later. As Apollo 8 became the first manned spacecraft to orbit the moon, people on Earth were in turmoil, the violence reaching its apex when demonstrators clashed with Chicago police at the Democratic National Convention. None of it mattered, however, as Republican nominee Richard Milhous Nixon from nearby Yorba Linda won the election, becoming the thirty-seventh president of the United States.

Mom, Dad, and Dennis watched it all on our new Admiral color TV while I, in blissful ignorance, played Kerplunk on the living room floor. I didn't know it then, but I'd soon be playing a *different* game.

It all started innocently enough. Emily Wexler, a much older woman of five from around the corner, was three months away from her first day of kindergarten. Until then, her mother, one of two women in the neighborhood who worked, needed someone to watch her. Mom, as always, stepped up to help, agreeing to babysit twice a week. No big deal. I liked Emily enough. She was good at sports, wasn't afraid of spiders, and had a decent sense of humor. For a girl. And she wasn't ugly or anything, her blonde hair secured in pigtails, her nose a spray of freckles. Since we were close in age, we could entertain one another while Mom did...whatever it is moms do.

Over the first few weeks, we tossed a Frisbee in the back yard. Dug holes in the riverbed. Played Cootie on the patio. All in all, we had a pretty good time together. But when July arrived, the heat index soared, limiting our outdoor activities. "Come inside, you two!" Mom would holler from the back door, convinced we were seconds away from heat stroke. "I've got sandwiches!"

Bribing me with food worked then and now.

Sprinting into the kitchen, we'd find two PB&Js on Wonder bread, a handful of Fritos, and a pair of Shasta Colas. Despite taking the time to spread her napkin, Emily always finished before me. I marveled at the way she sipped through a straw without spilling and chewed with her mouth closed, talents I'd yet to master. Then again, she *was* a year older. And a girl. Though I mostly hadn't noticed.

"Go play in your room," Mom told us, already rinsing plates.

"I need to run the vacuum." My mother was always running the vacuum, or sweeping the linoleum, or hanging clothes on the backyard line. I had no idea why she created so much work for herself.

After downing our sodas, Emily and I took out for the bedroom. Having joined the family last, I was assigned the smallest cubicle. It featured a trundle bed, a desk, and a window that faced the street. Two years later, I'd try to escape through it after being sent to my room, receiving not freedom but a spanking for my efforts. Today, like most days, there was crap everywhere—dirty clothes, Tonka trucks, half-played games— my days of anal retentiveness still eons away. Kicking stuffed animals aside, I exposed my Uncle Wiggily board. While I searched for the cards, I heard stirring behind me. Emily was apparently creating space, too. It took several minutes, but I found all the Rabbit Cards. When I turned to show her, I dropped the stack.

Standing there, a mere two feet away, was my little neighbor. Naked as the truth.

I was rarely speechless, even back then. But I had no idea what to say. Or do. Or feel. I just stood there—catatonic—staring. A minute passed. Maybe it was five. I swear to God, my Ronald McDonald clock stopped ticking. I'd never seen a naked girl before. Not in a magazine. Not in the movies. And sure as hell not in person! I noticed one thing right away. Her 'plumbing' didn't match mine, not by a long shot. As I continued to stare, Mom fired up the vacuum, shaking me from my stupor. But the noise had no effect on Emily. She continued to pose, 'au naturel', her eyes expressing neither solicitude nor guilt. I moved to the door, instinctively shutting it.

This felt wrong. *Very* wrong. But it also felt right.

Not the last time I'd pair those two warring sensations.

Needless to say, nothing happened. Four- and five-year-olds

aren't very inventive. I stared for a while longer, till Emily put
her clothes back on. And then we played Uncle Wiggily, making
our way to Dr. Possum's house without further incident. When
she left that day, I was naturally confused. How could I not be...
what in the world had just happened?

When Dad got home, I forgot to run out and greet him.
When Mom asked about my day, I grew defensive. "What does
that mean?" I snapped, eyes moving around the dinner table.
Did she know something? Did they *all* know something? I
unfurled my napkin to buy more time, then mumbled something about Lawn Bowling and Old Maid. It seemed to appease
them.

Two days later, Emily came over again. We played with my
dogs in the yard, ate PB&Js, then headed to my room when Mom
started cleaning the oven. Nothing unusual had taken place that
morning, Emily making no mention of the Uncle Wiggily incident. But I was on edge, shaking even, and silently wondering if
it could happen again.

I wouldn't have to wonder long.

As I shut the door, Emily slipped out of her romper. And just
like that, I lost the ability to move, speak, or exhibit brain function. I was a toy whose batteries had died. A caveman frozen in
tundra. A frame of 8mm film, paused near the bulb and melting.
As my mouth hung ajar, my neighbor just stood there, expressionless, naked as the day she was born. After a beat, she threw
her clothes back on and sat. It was apparently Uncle Wiggily
time. And like the other day, she made short work of me,
avoiding all orange spaces as she slipped past the Rabbit Hole, a
phrase that had taken on new meaning.

This, I'm ashamed to say, went on all summer.

Like clockwork, we'd play outside together, eat lunch, then
go to my bedroom, where she'd shed her clothes and school me
at Uncle Wiggily. That was our routine, not a word spoken about

it. Mercifully, while she was 'showing me hers', I never thought to 'show her mine'. What interest could she possibly have in that? But I also never averted my gaze, asked her to stop, or, God forbid, told my parents.

Truth is, I liked it. It made me feel...*funny*.

And before long, that funny feeling was all I could think about.

When Mom brought me to Gemco for new socks, I thought about Emily. When Dad took me to Fedco for training wheels, I thought about Emily. When Dennis walked me to church...well, you get the idea. The feelings she produced in me were complex and confounding. Inexplicable and inescapable. Was this love? I had no idea. But I did know this...the time between Emily's visits passed like sludge through the Rio Hondo.

And then, as quickly as it started, it stopped.

September brought cooler weather, and school for the five-and-over crowd. Mrs. Wexler no longer needed Mom's services. And Emily no longer needed mine. Chest aching, I'd stare out my window, watching her leave with the older kids and never once looking my way. When I felt particularly blue, I'd set up the Uncle Wiggily board and play by myself, imagining her on the other side, trouncing me yet again. For me, the game had been the 'Exciting Adventure' the box promised. And I started carrying Rabbit Cards in my pocket to remind me of better days.

In late October, the foam factory on the other side of the river caught fire. This happened every five years or so and was a huge neighborhood event. Once the pads succumbed to flames, there was no stopping them, firefighters manning useless hoses as the blaze reached dizzying heights. Since our house backed up to the riverbed (and had a three-foot fence), our yard was a prime gathering spot. Families from every house nearby poured through our gate, jockeying for position to get a better view. My father, without fail, would ask, "Who brought the goddamn marshmallows?" the crowd offering a nervous ripple. The heat, even at a quarter-mile away, made us sweat. And the smell was a thousand times worse than burning trash.

God knows what we were breathing!

As I watched the inferno, I felt a tap on my shoulder. Emily had come up behind me, my knees buckling. I had no idea what to think, her expression matching the one that accompanied garment removal. As I stared, my mouth turned to ash, my heart exploding like the transformers behind me. I hadn't seen her in a month. When I summoned the strength to speak, she slipped past me, taking my spot at the fence.

Face baking, I stood there in thought. I wish I could tell you that everything fell into focus, or that, like Siddhartha, I stared at the river and experienced enlightenment. But as most of us slow-witted males know, women—even the five-year-old ones— are a mystery, as enigmatic as the stone heads on Easter Island or the ghost lights of Marfa. When the fire died out, I watched my little neighbor file out with the others.

She didn't look my way. She didn't say, "Goodbye."

Over the next few months, we saw each other less and less. She had school friends now, and I went back to being the 'kid around the corner'. The Wexlers divorced a few years later, and Emily moved with her father. A few years after that, we had a garage sale, peddling everything from Dad's tools to Mom's crafts to my old toys and clothes. A woman in a housecoat handed me a five, gathering up a stack of little pants. As she turned to leave, she stopped herself. "I almost forgot..." She reached in the folds and grabbed something. "I found this in one of the pockets."

She handed me a Rabbit Card.

I stared at the dog-eared rectangle, the long-forgotten artwork featuring a dancing hare with top hat and cane, then flipped it over. There was a giant 6 on top, followed by the words,

'*Move Uncle Wiggily forward by six. The clever rabbit knows all the tricks.*'

When I looked up, the woman and her five-year-old daughter were gone.

I nodded knowingly, then shoved the card in my pocket and walked inside.

6

FEED YOUR HEAD

W hile Woodstock unfolded on the other side of the country, I stood in line, 2,758 miles away, waiting for my Kiddie Kollege diploma.

Fourteen people came to our preschool commencement ceremony. Four hundred thousand attended Woodstock, with millions more talking about it, dreaming about it, or trying to get there in their beat-up VW vans. Perhaps the only two people in America who didn't know (or care) about the iconic event were my parents. Clarence and Berneice were in their early fifties by 1969, a generation removed from festival attendees. Both thought rock-and-roll music and the 'hippie culture' that went with it were deplorable. "This is what *real* music sounds like!" Dad would boast, dropping a Woody Herman LP on the turntable.

And he was right. Woody Herman and his Big Band buddies —Benny Goodman, Tommy Dorsey, etc.—did play 'real music'. But so did Joe Cocker, Janis Joplin, and The Who, not that I'd heard a single note from any of them. Our house, as you may have guessed, was a desert island in the '60s ocean, a safe haven, if you will, from the 'Tune in, Turn on, Drop out' crowd, its stereo system featuring far more clarinets than electric guitars.

Regardless, this *was* the 'Psychedelic Era', a time of musical, social, and civil upheaval, all influenced by the burgeoning drug culture. Around the world, young people experimented with marijuana, 'magic mushrooms', and LSD, an estimated nine of ten Woodstock-goers high on at least one of them. While Santana performed *Evil Ways*, hallucinating fans marveled at the kaleidoscope of color, texture, and sound in front of them.

I was experiencing the same thing at my graduation, my empty stomach largely to blame. I'd refused to eat breakfast that morning, having worked myself into a frenzy over the upcoming event. I had a tendency to stress over such things—like being the ring-bearer in a friend's wedding (I was sure I'd drop the pillow), picking out Keds at the Uniroyal factory (there were only two choices, high-top and low), or delivering my one and only line in the church pageant (what if young Jesus accidentally said, "Shit?").

These things rattled me, as did the Kiddie Kollege building itself, a bright yellow edifice with giant lollipops lining the walkway. Talk about 'acid trips'! The first time Mom dropped me off there, I feared I'd never see her again, convinced as an adoptee that I'd somehow failed my 'tryout'. "This place is an orphanage!" I told myself, where Mr. Bumble (the guy from *Oliver!*) would make me eat gruel, then sell me to an undertaker. Turns out the lady in charge was actually our neighbor. The food was crackers and cheese. And Mom picked me up in an hour. Still, almost two years later, as I waited for my name to be called, my mind spun out of control.

According to scientists, humans start forming explicit memories around the age of two, those memories growing stronger and more detailed with age. These early recollections, for most of us anyway, come in flashes, the preschool years a turning point in both development and long-term recall. *I* was thinking in flashes that hot August day, my food-deprived brain bouncing from memory to memory.

As Mom looked on, I thought of the times we'd spent together—licking Green Stamps at the kitchen table, building sandcastles at Junipero Beach. I thought about Dad who was working that Saturday, probably to pay for my new shirt and tie —showing me stuff in the garage, teaching me how to pitch a tent. I thought of my brother, Dennis—letting me win at Don't Spill the Beans, watching *Jonny Quest* with me. As flashbulbs flashed, more memories came—a helicopter ride to Catalina, the crunch of Jack in the Box onion rings, the smell of my cap gun going off. Though I was only five, I'd already lived a full life. And as lame as this graduation was, it did feel, even then, like a genuine rite of passage.

"Shannon William Capps," Miss Applewhite announced. She was a part-time helper who wore miniskirts and go go boots. An image of Emily Wexler flashed. I shook it away, scaling the riser. After a sweaty handshake, Miss Applewhite handed me my diploma, Mom managing to clap *and* snap a photo while wiping back tears.

"I'm so proud of you, Shannon!" she wheezed on the way home. Staring at the crumpled paper in my hand, I had no idea why. It wasn't like I'd finished a list of requirements or aced a bunch of tests. This was *preschool*. For the past twenty-four months, I'd finger-painted, played with blocks, and given Mom a break. That being said, I did enjoy the attention. Maybe I could parlay it into some oatmeal cookies or a new comic book. "I'm dropping you off at the Andersons," Mom announced. "Your brother needs shoes."

The news was a gut punch. It was bad enough Dennis had weaseled out of my graduation, a deft move that only a twenty-one-year-old veteran of moments like this could pull off, but now he was stealing my 'praise and reward' time. "I don't like the Andersons," I growled.

"Of course, you do." Mom eased to a stop at their house, 'curb feelers' scraping concrete. "Nancy watches you all the time." Nancy Anderson was fifteen, gangly, and smelled like cabbage. In addition, she refused to watch *Atom Ant* with me and listened to AM radio constantly.

Still, if I was forced to admit it, her company was better than shopping for footwear.

Head down, I peeled myself from the seat and climbed outside. "Can I at least change?"

"Oh, dear..." Mom's face said she hadn't considered it. "Just...play nice, okay? I'll be back in an hour." She smiled as she dropped the shifter in gear, eyes still glinting. "I'm *so* proud of you, Shannon," she repeated, voice wavering as she drove off.

"Nice duds!" Nancy jeered, squeezing a fresh pimple. As I moved inside, her mother, Madge, barely looked up from her coupons, her father, Del, shrinking behind a newspaper. "I hope you know I only do this for the money."

I knew. I also knew someone should be paying *me*.

After tossing me an orange, she led me to the back yard, grabbing her radio along the way. Fiddling with the knobs, she yammered on about something called Woodstock. "If I wasn't stuck here with *you*," she whined, "I'd be there right now. Swear to *God*, I would!" It was a bold claim for someone who lived twelve states away and didn't have a driver's license.

"I don't like oranges," I groused, refusing to make this easy.

"Beggars can't be choosers, *flat*-face!" she fired back—one point for Nancy—setting her radio down. As she claimed a chaise lounge, she doused herself with baby oil, the summer sun baking her skin.

An hour passed, the radio blaring nonstop. After an

Excedrin ad, Grace Slick sang, '*One pill makes you larger, and one pill makes you small...*'

"I don't like this music, *oil*-face," I shouted—one point for Shannon. I was determined to ruin her afternoon, too. And why not? An hour ago, I was basking in the glow of Mom's adoration. Now I was stuck here with this glistening git, listening to noise on a crappy transistor.

"You don't, huh?" She hiked the volume, applying more oil.

"I want a *sandwich!*" I demanded.

She ignored me, singing at the top of her lungs—"*You've just had some kind of mushroom, and your mind is moving low...*"

"I'm *hungry!*"

"*When logic and proportion*—eat your orange—*have fallen sloppy dead...*"

"I will *not!*"

"Then have an *avocado!*" she sniped, pointing to the shriveled orbs on the lawn. In late-'60s Los Angeles, everyone had an avocado tree (or an orange, lemon, or kumquat), fruit more plentiful than traffic and smog.

As the music built to a crescendo, I reached down and grabbed one.

"*Remember what the dormouse said,*" she sang with feeling, eyes closed. "*Feed your head. Feed your head...*" She and Slick repeated the phrase over and over. I couldn't take any more. I wound up like Dizzy Dean and launched the avocado across the patio. It soared in slow motion, like the ball Roy Hobbs would hit in *The Natural* fifteen years later. No one was more surprised than me when it found its mark—Nancy's eye—her recital coming to an abrupt and painful halt. In shock, she covered her face, wondering what hit her, then bolted inside, crying as she fled.

I was in big trouble and knew it. In those days, parents routinely spanked children. So did aunts, uncles, grandparents, and friends. I'd committed a violent crime, one that merited equally-violent punishment. As Mrs. Anderson stormed out the back door, she seemed to agree.

"What in the *world* did you do?" she wailed, flanked by her police-sergeant husband and black-eyed daughter. I'd given Nancy a real shiner—her eye looked like the fruit I'd just tossed —tears streaming down both cheeks and hanging like icicles on her quaking jaw.

"Do you have *anything* to say for yourself?" Mr. Anderson probed. He should have read me my Mirandas, but with a Schlitz in his hand and shorts battling his gut, he was clearly off duty. "Well, *do* you?"

I stared at the ground, bracing myself for the inevitable flogging. Mom used a flyswatter, soon to be replaced by the wooden spoon. I wondered what the Andersons employed. A belt? Mr. Anderson's police baton? Maybe a switch from the avocado tree for poetic justice? Before I could find out, the doorbell rang.

Mrs. Anderson marched me to the door, where my still-smiling mother waited. In a grating voice, the woman recounted the incident like someone who'd seen it, introducing a mountain of evidence: 1) the dented avocado; 2) her still-sobbing daughter; and 3) my hangdog expression. Mr. Anderson backed her testimony, adding that I couldn't be "trusted around fruits or vegetables". Their case was damning. When offered a chance for rebuttal, I looked up momentarily, then shook my head, refusing to take the stand.

As Mom offered apologies, promising to drop off a casserole, I sauntered to the car. When we climbed inside, the silence was deafening, save for Dennis' snoring. "Shannon...how could you?" my mother whispered, her sweet, little voice cracking.

In truth, I didn't know. That's the thing about five-year-olds. They do stupid things and can't tell you why. And they do them often. What I *did* know was there'd be no comic books or oatmeal cookies. No pats on the back when Dad unfurled my diploma. No 'Three Days of Peace and Music' like the kids in New York were experiencing.

There was only a date with the flyswatter. And hours of time in my room.

A mother's pride, it seemed, was a fleeting thing.

11. WAITING FOR THE AXE TO FALL

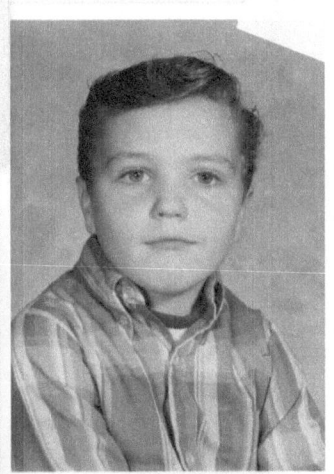

7

ONE GIANT LEAP

Fifty days after Neil Armstrong took 'one small step for man', I took 'one giant leap' into kindergarten. Like the much-anticipated Apollo mission, it was time. I'd learned everything there was to learn at home, from speaking in semi-coherent sentences to no longer wearing my Batman costume as casual attire. "You're growing up," Mom insisted, and that meant swapping *Highlights* magazine for 'higher education'.

When the first day of school arrived, my skin prickled. I was a 'Late Bird', Mom explained, which meant I didn't report to class till one o'clock. "You're kidding!" I bellowed, already dressed in my Sears shirt and khakis. I'd even combed my hair!

It was six a.m.

"We talked about this," Mom said, her tone that of a SWAT team negotiator. "Half the kids go in the morning, half in the afternoon." She handed me a Pop-Tart. "Mrs. Garo's your teacher. She's very excited to meet you." As an adult (and one-time substitute), I know this was bullshit. No teacher at any school was ever 'excited' to meet his/her students. But the words seemed to pacify me, Mom navigating the next six hours without need of a sniper.

Even with the extra time, we managed to be late. The roll of film Mom shot in front of the house was partly to blame, along with the grocery list she compiled and the floor that needed waxing. When we arrived at Roger Casier Elementary, 'Early Birds' had taken flight, 'Late Birds' lined up and tagged like cattle. At 3'9" and 45 pounds, I had no shot at becoming the class bully. My plan was to lay low, blend in till I got the lay of the land. Mom made that impossible when she parked me under the *KINDERGARTEN* sign for another twelve photos. When the shoot finally ended, the other 'bovines' had filed inside.

Moments later, Mom introduced me to my teacher as every kid stared. A few of them looked more frightened than me. Most snickered at the late (and now-clearly-identified) class buffoon. After swapping a few pleasantries, Mrs. Garo slapped a nametag on my chest and led me away. If I didn't know better, I'd swear Mom was crying, but I couldn't worry about that. There were thirty sets of eyes on me. The thermostat was set at roughly a million degrees. And the floor felt like quicksand.

"Welcome, kindergartners," my teacher greeted us. She was frumpy, forty-something, and smelled of mimeograph paper. She pointed to a spot on the rug, where I sat 'Indian-style' with the others. "This is your first day at Roger Casier!" I glanced around. Most of the kids had lost interest in me, one shoving a finger up his nose. "We'll learn our letters." I glanced at the charts over her shoulder, one for capitals, one for lowercase. "Our colors." A pie chart showed slices of red, blue, and yellow. "And our numbers, from one to ten." Neatly-written numerals lined the top of the chalkboard, the area below blank. Relief washed over me. Between Kiddie Kollege and Mom's early instruction, I knew all this stuff. "We'll also have snack, nap time, and recess."

My confidence was growing.

After a ten-minute discussion on big *A*, followed by another on little *a*, Mrs. Garo released the 'inmates' into the yard. Our playground featured a jungle gym and swings, the grassy square cordoned off via chain-link from the general population. Almost immediately, the girls flocked to the swings, the boys to the jungle gym. I looked for familiar faces, finding one in the crowd —Kyle Blount from my preschool class. We weren't exactly close, but he'd do in a pinch. As I latched onto him, a voice came from behind, "Hey, *you!*" I turned to find a burly, blonde kid with an *a*-shaped nose and tag that read *KEITH*. "He's *my* friend, not yours!" Before I could respond, he had me in a headlock, a recess aide doing her best to pry us apart.

In the 'waxing phase' of my thirteen-year public education cycle, I'd arrived late, rumbled with the school ruffian, and was now being lectured by a woman with a Brooklyn accent. All in all, not a bad first day.

By the time the next Apollo crew landed on the moon, I'd survived two full months of this. Not only had Mrs. Garo flipped our letter chart from *Aa* to *Ff*, but we were counting from *1* to *4* and finger-painting with primary colors, well on our way to becoming NASA scientists. I'd even made a few friends: Keith Budro, the kid who'd jumped me (turns out Kyle wasn't worth fighting over); Benny Sherman who liked to swing standing up till the aide screamed his name (*"Shoiman!"*); Nils Svensson, a Swedish lad who dressed in Native American garb (it was highly-confusing); and Jerry Flax who collected red and black ants (housing them in separate pockets).

I was also learning that rules, most arbitrary, were made to be broken. Why did I need to raise my hand? Or line up for recess? Or stay in my seat for more than two minutes? These dictums were unreasonable. And if reason didn't exist, neither should compliance. Mrs. Garo felt differently: '*Shannon is inattentive to the group*,' she cited on my first report card, '*and his attitude is not the best*.' The assessment could've—and should've—

been worse. In my first eight weeks 'on the job', I'd been chastised for making inappropriate comments about the 'Early Bird' teacher (a younger, more attractive version of Mrs. Garo), for placing my nap mat next to the Girls' bathroom (and laughing when the toilet flushed), and for shirking my 'fatherly' duties while playing house (how should I know the baby didn't sleep in the oven?).

When confronted with these charges, I either blamed someone else...or lied.

Not ideal for a kid who listed *'policeman'* as *'what I want to be when I grow up'* on the kindergarten questionnaire.

But not everything I did was bad. I sat perfectly still while Mrs. Garo traced my profile, hoping she'd add a chin (she didn't). When vandals trashed our classroom, I was quick to finger Billy Friedhoffer (I had no idea if my neighbor did it, but he smoked and rode a motorcycle). And when acts were needed for the talent show, I signed up immediately (talent TBD).

Most of the acts, as it turned out, involved singing, dancing, or acrobatics. Since I stunk at all three, I opted for standup comedy, presuming (incorrectly) that I was funny. Having no material of my own, I stole it from a children's record—*The Adventures of Little Orley*. I must've practiced that routine a thousand times, memorized the words, even mimicked the delivery. When the big night arrived, three hundred people filled the auditorium. I was scheduled to 'close', having to sit through fifty horrible acts before mine. There was baton twirling—Katy Knesskie shattered a light. Singing—Keith Budro killed (and not in a good way) *The Bear Went Over the Mountain*. Musical interpretation—Nils Svensson, in full war bonnet, did hand gestures to *This Land Is Your Land*. And finally, a bit of 'comic genius' that no one was in the mood for.

As I waited in the wings, the sixth-grade MC manned the microphone. "And now for the final act of the night..." The announcement yielded cheeky applause. "…Shannon *Craps*." In one fail swoop, he'd not only slaughtered my name but constructed a concise, vulgar sentence that destroyed any chance I had of success, the place erupting with laughter.

It was the only laugh I got all night.

With a failed standup gig behind me, I headed for the home stretch.

April brought the long-awaited discussions of *Xx*, *Yy*, and *Zz*, the introduction of secondary colors, and another trip to the moon, NASA's third in less than a year. But Apollo 13 proved unlucky, running into serious trouble when an oxygen tank failed. At the same time, I found my own trouble on the playground. Vernon Nessler, a kid I'd barely spoken to, approached me with a proposition. He had two older brothers, he explained, one in junior high, the other in high school. I had no idea how this concerned me. "Watch this," he murmured, hoisting a middle finger.

I stared, waiting for an explanation. None came. As I turned to go, he grabbed my arm.

"Hold on…" His finger was still raised. "They say if we do this, people'll get mad."

"*We?*" He nodded, eyes narrowing. Before I could argue, the three o'clock bell sounded, sending the older kids home. "Come on," he ordered, dragging me to the fence. As a gaggle of third-grade girls passed, Vernon flipped them the bird.

"That's not nice!" one of them chided, my new pal grinning at me.

I grinned back, lifting my finger like Vernon's, my first bout with peer pressure ending in failure. "You're naughty!" three more third graders scolded, Vernon and I cackling. "I'm telling your mother!" a girl from my neighborhood swore, the two of us in stitches.

For the next ten minutes, we greeted every passerby with the same salute, soliciting shock, reproach, and outright threats. We were Neanderthals with fire. The Wright Brothers at Kitty Hawk. And if the high-five had been invented—

"Go inside," Mrs. Garo interrupted.

We turned, digits erect.

"*Go inside!*" she repeated, teeth clenched. We lowered our fingers and shuffled to class, spending the last half-hour in separate corners. When we left for home, it was with handwritten notes.

"*Why*, Shannon?" By now, Mom could've trademarked the question, Dad conspicuously absent. He and Dennis were glued to the Apollo coverage in the other room.

"It was Vernon's idea," I responded in knee-jerk fashion.

"If Vernon asked you to jump off..." No need to expand on Mom's tactic here.

"But..." I squirmed in my chair, eyeing the wooden spoon on the counter. "...I don't even know what that finger means!"

Mom peered over her shoulder for help, Dad nowhere to be found. "Well, I..." She raised a hand to her collar, looking more uncomfortable than ever. My poor mother! How on Earth was she going to explain 'Fuck you!' to a five-year-old? "...it's not... very..." I watched her wheels spin, then land on something. "...it means stick your finger up your butt."

Somehow in her sweet Oklahoma innocence, she'd found the only explanation worse than the real one. But it was on the table. And staying there.

"Why would—"

"The point is," she cut me off, "it's a *very bad* thing." She took my plate, still full of lima beans, and carried it to the sink. "Please don't do it again."

"I won't," I lied, just glad she'd bypassed the wooden spoon.

After sharing this new and questionable information with every kid in school, I went about my business, avoiding Vernon, my teacher, and the entire third grade. The Apollo 13 astronauts, meanwhile, made it home safely. And I, somehow, made it to the end of the year.

On the last day of school, Mrs. Garo handed out report cards. When I got home, Mom read her final note—'*I enjoyed having Shannon in class.*'

That's when it hit me. I *had* learned something in kindergarten.

Five-year-olds aren't the only ones who lie.

8

NO BURDEN

In the summer of 1970, Dennis moved out, making me a de facto 'only child'. I can't say I was happy or sad about this event. I just remember wondering why. I mean, we had it pretty good, he and I. There was free food, air-conditioning, a color TV.

What more could anyone want?

Dennis wanted to be a man. He wanted to work, to live in his own place, and to provide for himself. Simple goals. But my brother was a victim of bad timing. There were no programs for kids like him back then, no para-educators to help him in school, no jobs set aside for people with 'special needs'. Success and independence were pipedreams. And as much as he longed for both, he never had a chance.

Born in '46, Dennis was a member of the first 'Baby Boomer' class, the survivors of World War II anxious to start families. My mother and father, as mentioned earlier, wasted little time in this endeavor, Mom pregnant before Dad's army duffel bag hit the floor. The pregnancy itself was uneventful. Mom, retired from 'Rosie the Riveter' duties, stayed home in Huntington Park, no doubt cleaning the apartment daily, while

Dad went back to work, hoping to never be shot at again. Dennis was born in September, a seemingly-healthy, six-pound baby boy.

But Mom sensed trouble immediately, certain her newborn child was losing consciousness. When she told the doctor, he laughed between puffs on his Lucky Strike, calling her a "nervous, first-time mom". The would-be-seizures continued through her hospital stay, nurses imploring her to "relax". When my parents took Dennis home, the 'attacks', as they came to be known in our house, worsened. Mom rushed him back to the doctor, begging the man to listen. He responded with a few more "nervous mother" cracks and sent her home.

A week later, she returned, this time with Dad who was in no mood for jokes. The doctor agreed to run tests—apparently, he liked the way his face was arranged—finding that Dennis had indeed suffered a birth injury. The forceps used to extract him, 'Dr. Mengele' explained, caused fluid to accumulate, damaging his brain. "I'm afraid it's too late for surgery," he informed them, leafing through files on his desk. "But I'd be glad to refer a specialist."

There were no apologies. Just a bill for the extra appointment.

Mom and Dad left the doctor's office, devastated. If this had happened a few years later, there'd be lawsuits and payouts. As it stood, Clarence and Berneice took their child home, locked arms, and faced the world alone, a world that had changed dramatically in the last few hours, and one they'd never fully comprehend again.

As a result of the injury, Dennis suffered permanent paralysis to the right side of his body, leaving him with a curled hand. In addition, he was afflicted with epileptic seizures, and his learning capacity was greatly compromised, 'slow' or 'feeble-minded' the words used to describe him. A neurologist recommended treatment, prescribed medication, and made a sobering forecast. "He won't see his thirteenth birthday."

My parents refused to accept that. They did everything in their power to give my brother a normal life. There were toys, camping trips, ballgames—my brother might've been the only kid in soCal to love the Dodgers and Angels equally—and when he turned five, they enrolled him in public school, Mom helping with his letters and numbers, Dad teaching him to defend himself. I can't imagine the angst they felt, dropping him off for kindergarten. Turns out, it was warranted. The new elementary school was still under construction, a backhoe excavating dirt outside Dennis' classroom. My brother, like any red-blooded American five-year-old boy, wanted to watch, so he walked to the door and peered outside. For this, he was expelled. "Your son," the principal told my parents, "can't handle the rigors of public education. You'll need to make other arrangements."

When I think of the rules *I* broke in kindergarten, receiving nothing for my efforts but a slap on the wrist, it boggles the mind. But forty years before the Americans With Disabilities Act guaranteed people like my brother the same rights and opportunities as everyone else, my parents had little recourse. They took their son home. And taught him themselves.

Over the next few years, his seizures worsened, prompting my parents to shuttle Dennis from one specialist to another. Although recommendations varied, doctors agreed on one thing...there was no hope. *No hope?* They might as well have questioned my father's manhood, more than one MD getting an earful from an angry ex-drill sergeant. Dad, you see, was no quitter. And he'd do anything for his boy, even if it meant loading him in his '53 Mercury and driving twenty-eight straight hours to the Mayo Clinic. My parents did this on two occasions, Dennis undergoing life-saving operations both times.

While recovering from one surgery, my brother celebrated

Christmas in the hospital. There was no money for gifts. My parents had spent everything they had on doctor bills and travel expenses, not sure how they were going to get home. But on Christmas Eve, an agent from the Salvation Army delivered two presents. Mom swears it was the only time she ever saw Dad cry. To this day, I can't pass a Salvation Army bucket without emptying my pockets.

Three months later, an even greater gift arrived—a letter from the Seventh Day Adventist school. '*Although you're not church members,*' the principal wrote, '*we'd be honored to have Dennis as a student.*' Now it was Mom's turn to cry. Despite his limitations, my brother passed every test, navigating a slow but steady course through the end of eighth grade. Along the way, he made friends, enjoyed school activities, and experienced life the way other kids experienced it.

Except for one thing.

"I want a brother." The announcement came on his thirteenth birthday, a day doctors said would never arrive. Having just turned forty, Mom and Dad stared blankly. "I know," he read their minds, "but you could adopt!" They were against it at first. But, like our dad, my brother was no quitter. He hounded them for years—four, to be exact—till they finally gave in. Dennis would forever call my adoption his "greatest blessing". And having a baby brother, it turned out, was the perfect medicine for a young man beginning to question his place in the order of things. He fed me formula and changed my diapers. Pushed my stroller and rocked me to sleep. But these activities, though wonderful, were only a placebo for what ailed him.

Dennis had grown into a man, with Mom's easy smile and Dad's hairy chest. At eighteen, he'd begun scouring the city for work, every employer taking his info and promising to call. No one did. A few guys at the market befriended him, even let him help out every now and again. But they grew tired of his company and started dropping pills in his sodas, a dangerous prank for someone on heavy medication.

It all weighed on Dennis, disappointment turning to defeat, defeat to depression. On his nineteenth birthday, he got up in the middle of the night and took every pill in the medicine cabinet. My father found him an hour later, lying face-down in the riverbed, unconscious. Flushed with adrenaline, Dad threw Dennis over his shoulder and sprinted for the car, doctors pumping his stomach at the last possible moment.

It was the worst night of my parents' lives. And it happened again a year later.

These events brought Mom and Dad to their knees, my parents having no idea how to deal with a child who wanted to die. They did their best to hide it from me, but we spent a lot of time in hospitals. And police stations. After the suicide attempts, Dennis snuck out again, making his way to the local bank, where he kicked the door in and began trashing the place. When Downey PD arrived, he made no attempt to elude them. He *wanted* to go to jail, telling Dad to leave him there when we came to pick him up.

For years—a *lot* of years—I resented Dennis for the anguish he put my parents through. They didn't deserve it, their only crime loving him without condition. But the torment Dennis was going through himself was worse. I know that now. When he moved out, Mom and Dad did what they always did. They offered support and told him they loved him. I remember his first apartment, a decaying rat-hole in north Pasadena, one of several he'd call home for the next decade. They were halfway houses. Today's PC crowd would call them 'rehabilitation centers'. Whatever the name, they were scary places for a six-year-old to visit, filled with drug addicts, ex-cons, and people with disabilities.

I hated it there. My brother loved it.

For the first time in his life, he was living alone, paying his bills (via state disability checks), and fending for himself. He was a man, in every sense of the word. No, he'd never hold a job, or marry the love of his life, or buy a house in the suburbs. But he was okay with that, content to play the hand life dealt him. On *his* terms.

I wish I could say his troubles ended there. In the ensuing years, Dennis would disappear for days on end, traveling by bus all over the southland, my parents having no idea if he was alive or dead. When he'd turn up, he looked like a stray dog, tired, hungry, and filthy to the bone. Over time, his health declined— he smoked two packs a day and often skipped his meds— landing him in a state-run assisted living facility. The place was far worse than the halfway houses he'd lived in, and it killed my parents to see him there. It killed me, too, but for different reasons. Shameful as this sounds—and it *is* shameful—I had better things to do. As I hit my teen years, I visited less and less. And eventually not at all. I was angry at Dennis, angry for what he'd done to my parents, angry at what he was *still* doing. And I let it fester, to the point of infection. For ten years, I didn't speak to my brother. Didn't phone him. Didn't write.

And for that, I'm ashamed.

I got the call on a Monday morning. It was January, 2004, and Dennis had recently moved into a nursing home. He and I had reconciled by then. I'd even gone to see him, his once-brown crewcut a wild shock of gray. The man on the phone sounded matter-of-fact. He'd found Dennis dead—eyes closed, hand curled at his side. "He look peaceful," he spoke in broken English. In the end, it wasn't the brain trauma, or the epilepsy, or any of his other ailments. His heart simply stopped beating. He was fifty-seven years old, having celebrated forty-five more birthdays than doctors predicted.

On the heels of his death came a massive winter storm. The

airport in Tulsa, where Dad lived after Mom passed, was closed. The one in Portland, twenty miles from my home, was iffy at best. My father was too old to drive to California, and I wasn't willing to put my family at risk.

So I went alone.

Dennis had made all the arrangements, buying a casket and plot, even hiring the chaplain. All I had to do was show up, something I'd seldom done when he was alive. It was a gorgeous southern California day, the air crisp, the sun hanging low in the eastern sky. I climbed from the car, making my way to the fresh mound of earth. "Are you Shannon?" a man in a dark robe asked. I nodded, shaking his hand. "Expecting more guests?"

I looked at the empty seats. I'd assumed *someone* would be here. A rep from the nursing home. An orderly. Maybe even a friend.

It was just me.

"If you'd like to forego—"

"No," I stopped him. "He deserves a full sendoff."

For the next twenty minutes, the clergyman spoke, in loving terms, about a man he'd never met. The emptiness of the setting was tough, the sheer loneliness unbearable. I felt so many things—sadness, anger, hurt—but guilt won out. Guilt for being a lousy brother. For being anything but the 'blessing' Dennis once called me. Sitting here alone—with no family to support me, no friends at my side—*that* was my punishment. My penance.

But as the sermon wore on, the guilt began to fade, replaced by memories. I saw my brother, dancing to his Elvis records. Heard him singing along, forever off-key. Smelled his Old Spice cologne, overpowering the flowers. Tasted smoke on his lips as he kissed me goodnight. And I heard our mother's voice. '*I hope we weren't selfish, Shannon, adopting you when your brother had so many needs.*' The chaplain finished his homily, nodding as he walked off. '*I pray Dennis wasn't a burden,*' she finished her thought.

I stood there for a moment, then walked to the casket. A ruby-crowned kinglet sang in the distance. A breeze stirred the overhead oak. I placed my hand on the lid and held it there.

Dennis was no burden, Mom.

He was my brother.

9

GROWING UP WHITE

Everyone I knew was white—my neighbors, the kids in school, our teachers. When Mom took me to the doctor, he and his nurses were white. When we went to the market, the checkers were white, too. So was our mailman, barber, pastor, and garbage collector.

I don't remember thinking it was a good thing. Or a bad thing. It just was.

I'd seen black people, of course, mostly on TV. Bill Cosby played a secret agent on *I Spy*, the first television show to feature a black lead actor. And Diahann Carroll won a Golden Globe for her portrayal of *Julia*. But that was about it.

My home town of Downey, known colloquially as the 'White Island', was of little help. In 1960, the census painted a colorless portrait. Almost a hundred percent of the population was white. A decade later, little had changed. There were several reasons for this lack of diversity. For one, home deeds in the '30s and '40s actually included language that prohibited owners from selling to blacks or Hispanics. The U.S. Supreme Court ruled these race-restrictive clauses 'legally unenforceable' in 1948. In addition, these same homeowners stood pat after the Watts riots of

'65, neighboring residents fleeing to Orange County, a phenomenon known as 'White Flight'. Reasons for the *non*-exodus in
Downey were twofold: 1) residents felt geographically and
socially removed from the unrest, retaining control of their own
municipalities; and 2) by having their own school district, officials were able to resist the mandatory integration that *Brown vs.
Board of Education*, a 1954 ruling that declared segregation uncon-
stitutional, called for.

As a six-year-old eating fish sticks in the school cafeteria, I
knew none of this. I'd not only slept through the Civil Rights Act
of '64, I'd missed Rosa Parks, the 'Black Power' movement, and
the life and death of Jimi Hendrix. I really was on an island. We
all were.

But that was about to change.

Wanda Harris walked into our classroom on a Wednesday
morning, escorted by Principal Creed. We looked up from our
Janet and Mark books to find Mrs. DeWitt smiling. "Children,"
our teacher addressed us, "this is Wanda. She's a new student at
Roger Casier. Please make her feel welcome." We stared at the
new arrival like dimwitted first graders, which, of course, we
were. Wanda was tall for her age, with long arms and longer
legs. And she was dressed to the nines—patent leather shoes,
eyelet-lace socks, and a frilly, pink dress.

Oh, and one more thing.

She was black.

Most of us, myself included, continued to stare long after she
sat. I don't remember feeling anything but curiosity that day.
After all, she was the first black person my age I'd ever seen. And
she was the only black student in our school, perhaps the first
one ever. In a perfect world, we shouldn't see color, but we sure
saw it then. Her skin was extremely dark, her hair darker. And
her big, brown eyes rested under a bulbous forehead. If she was
scared—and let's face it, she had to be—it didn't show. She sat at

her table and followed along in the book, its two main characters white as the paper they were printed on.

Spurning Mrs. DeWitt's instructions, I didn't welcome
Wanda that day. None of the boys did. I can't speak for the
others, but for me it had nothing to do with skin color. She was a
girl. And as a boy in first grade, if you didn't *hate* girls, there was
something seriously wrong with you. At recess, our new classmate drew even more stares. The other kids had yet to see
Wanda, and they were just as intrigued as we were. None of it
seemed to bother her, however. In no time, she worked her way
into a foursquare game, beating her opponents handily.

"There's a black girl in my class," I told my parents at dinner.
They glanced at each other, then back at me. I was staring at my
plate, segregating the mixed vegetables, hoping the diversion
would save me from them.

"Well, be nice to her, Shannon," Mom responded, scraping
my veggies back in a pile.

"Why would I do that?" I groused, Dad chuffing as he ate a
spoonful for me.

I've often wondered how other dinner conversations went
that night. In my brief time on Earth, I'd witnessed plenty of
slurs. A lot of adults I knew still used terms like 'colored' or
'negro' to describe blacks, despite the civil rights movement's
pronouncement that both were no longer acceptable. And more
than one old person had offered me "nigger toes". When I told
Mom about this, she suggested the alternate Brazil nuts.

If parents did, at the table that night, tell their kids to avoid
Wanda, I saw no signs of it. She was back the next day, in a
yellow dress and matching hair bobbles, smiling and chatting
with classmates. As our first-grade class struggled with addition
—the Math kind—we stared less and less, eventually not at all.
Before long, Wanda found favor with a group of girls. We boys,
lacking couth and sensitivity, bestowed names on all of them.

There was 'Donna the Dumb', 'Shari the Short', 'Mule-Face Mona', and 'Four-Eyed Fawn'. It never occurred to us that these names were offensive. We thought they were clever, our way of acknowledging the girls without saying we liked them. Over time, the name calling became ritual, as did the recess activity that went with it.

That activity went something like this...shortly after recess began, one of us—myself, Keith Budro, Benny Sherman, Norbert Barker (all blonde and blue-eyed but me)—would venture into the female fold, pretending to retrieve a ball. As the girls ignored him, he'd single one out, then yell, "'Toothless Tammy'!" for example, forcing Tammy Lebowitz (who'd recently found a nickel under her pillow) to give chase. She and the other girls rarely caught the fleeing offender, having no idea what to do if they did.

This went on for weeks, each of us insulting a 'girl du jour', then escaping to the safety of our all-male muster. On rare occasions, one of us would challenge Wanda. It had nothing to do with race. We stopped noticing her skin the day after she got there. The reason we didn't test 'Wanda the Wicked' (the name we'd chosen when no one could think of another *W* word) was that she was faster than all of us. With young Miss Harris in pursuit, we rarely made it back to our squadron unscathed. She'd cut off our escape routes, catch us by the shirttails, or shove us playfully to the ground. She was a bona fide weapon, the girls' UZI submachine gun to the boys' one-shot muskets.

And she seemed to enjoy every minute of it.

Till one fateful day, when Budro, the fastest and most athletic among us, volunteered for a 'suicide mission'. No one had challenged Wanda in a month, and we were getting tired of easy targets like 'Pudgy Paula' or 'Lucy the Lame'. After some deep knee bends, Budro made his way to the hopscotch game, shouting Wanda's now-familiar nickname. As he bolted, she took out after him, closing the gap immediately. Despite our fervent coaching, he had no chance. There was too much real estate to cover. That's when he made a fatal error, changing his course for the Boys' bathroom. We knew what he was thinking —no girl would *ever* set foot inside—but Wanda was too close to concede. As Budro lunged for the urinals, she grabbed a fistful of jacket, altering his trajectory and sending him into the wall. I was the first to see blood. As our battered comrade stood, it trickled from his forehead, then gushed like a waterfall.

We were shocked—horrified—no one more so than Wanda herself. A recess aide, seeing what happened, collected the wounded and walked him to the office, returning a minute later for Wanda. "You killed our friend!" Norbert yelled, the rest of us hollering support. But when we returned to class, Budro was already there (looking surprisingly-fit for a dead man), as was his 'assailant'. Both were smiling, the only sign of trauma a Band-Aid over the injured eyebrow. The relief we felt was palpable, that relief extending to Wanda, too. We knew she didn't mean to hurt him, and we were glad, at least privately, that she wasn't expelled.

Or was she?

Two weeks later, Wanda went missing, never to be seen again. Conspiracy theorists pointed to the bloodletting episode. Rational thinkers assumed her parents had moved. Although we'd never know the truth—the adults around us weren't talking—I sincerely hope it was the latter. Either way, it would be five long years before we had another black classmate.

During that time, we gleaned our information on black culture from the mass media. We watched *The Flip Wilson Show* every week—*TIME* called him '*TV's first black superstar*'—along with *The Jeffersons* and *Room 222*. At the movies, 'Blaxploitation' films like *Shaft* and *Superfly* were hits, presenting black characters as heroes for the first time. And the birth of disco elevated artists like Donna Summer and Kool & the Gang to mainstream stardom. But nothing had more influence on us than sports. Thirty years after Jackie Robinson broke the color barrier, black athletes like Walter Payton, Kareem Abdul-Jabbar, and Reggie Jackson were dominating. We watched their games, practiced their moves, and wore their jerseys.

I don't remember a lot of negativity during this period, but there *were* missteps along the way. It was common to quote lines from *Blazing Saddles*, imitate Fred Sanford, or retell Richard Pryor jokes (with the racially-charged words included). In the fourth grade, our Abe Lincoln play featured an empty stage when the president, played by yours truly, spoke of "freeing the slaves". And in sixth grade, a group of friends dressed up like *Fat Albert and the Cosby Kids*, donning 'blackface' for Halloween.

In sports, we mostly played other all-white teams but on occasion traveled to cities like Lynwood or Compton, both predominantly-black. Our coaches would often share horror stories along the way. I remember one about chains flying through a bus window in Crenshaw, another involving gangs in the stands at Rancho Dominguez. But in all my years of participation, I never experienced one episode of maltreatment, unless you count the drubbings we received on the gridiron and court.

With no black teammates, friends, or classmates, we inevitably bought into stereotypes. Most of us, for instance, believed all black males were cooler and funnier than whites, each with his own catch phrase, like Jimmy Walker's "Dy-*no*-mite!" or Haywood Nelson's "Hey, *hey*, hey!" In addition, they could all dance—*Soul Train* proved that—and each was an amazing athlete, Laker games the only evidence we needed.

For those reasons and more, we were ecstatic when Austin Waters arrived. Like Wanda five years earlier, he was the only black kid in school, this time Griffiths Middle. Rumors began circulating immediately: Austin was a seventh grader (possibly an ex-con) who'd been kicked out of every school in Inglewood; he was also huge, charismatic, smooth with the ladies, and carried a football everywhere he went. We couldn't wait to meet him! By mere association, he'd up our 'cool rating' considerably, entertain us in class, maybe even teach us to boogie! More importantly, our football team, after years of futility, was now a shoo-in for the title.

I saw Austin for the first time a few days later, standing in the corner at an all-school dance. He wasn't particularly-large, nor was he at present entertaining the fellas *or* wooing the ladies. He wore glasses, had a short-cropped afro, and looked bored—a little sad even—moving to the beat of *Disco Inferno* like a newborn colt. And he was definitely *not* carrying a football.

As we got to know Austin, he showed a little more personality, but he was nothing like J.J. on *Good Times* or 'Rerun' from *What's Happening?* That's not to say he didn't have a sense of humor. On Dress-Up Day, he and powder-white Craig Dempski came to school as salt-and-pepper shakers. And we did, on occasion, catch him chuckling at one of our low-brow attempts at comedy.

But the real test was yet to come.

Flag football tryouts were scheduled for the first Monday in October. Austin, like the rest of us, showed up in a T-shirt and gym shorts, ready to run Coach Fredrickson's drills. All eyes were on him as he stretched, squatting on bandy legs and windmilling pole-thin arms. But looks can be deceiving, we reminded ourselves, more than one spindly, black kid having wiped the court with us. "Passing line!" Coach Fredrickson barked, Austin moving to the front. "Ready." He knelt in his stance, the rest of us holding our breaths. "Hut-hut!" He broke downfield—not all that swiftly—then cut to his left, Coach lofting a perfect pass.

It clanked off his hands and fell to the grass.

Benny and I traded glances. Everyone drops a pass now and

then, we rationalized. The line moved quickly, Benny catching his pass, me dropping mine. Before long, Austin was back in the pole position. He crouched again—"Hut-hut!"—hurtling forward, then cutting right. Coach hit him in stride, the ball slipping through his outstretched fingers. Two passes, two drops. And things went downhill from there. In total, Austin got eight opportunities, muffing six of them. His forty-yard dash time was below average. And he failed to pull a single flag on defense.

It wasn't the tryout we'd envisioned, nor was Austin the superstar we'd unfairly imagined. But he did make the team, as did most of the kids who tried out, propelling us to another trophy-less season. Along the way, he dropped multiple passes, rarely covered his man, and became our friend. Not the friend we'd concocted in our minds—I don't think he ever 'moonwalked', delivered a good wisecrack, or dated triplets—but a friend nonetheless.

Most important, he taught us a lesson. As more black and Hispanic kids trickled into our classrooms, changing the landscape of Downey forever, we'd never trust the stereotypes again.

Except the one about Asians being good at Math.

10

BY ANY OTHER NAME

N o one dreaded the first day of school more than me.
Every year—and I mean *every damn year!*—the
'Einsteins' in the front office put my name on the
Girls' List. Back then, we not only recognized gender, we catego-
rized it. Boys were placed on the Boys' List, girls on the Girls'
List. Simple. Straightforward. What could go wrong?

Everything, if you answered to Shannon.

My mother had chosen the name, claiming to have several
male cousins with that moniker, all handsome, all successful.
"One's a lawyer!" she boasted. What difference did *that* make?
I'd never met any of these guys. Still haven't. And I hated them
for not stopping her. They had to know life was *hell* with a name
that screamed estrogen.

"Alan Adkins?" my second-grade teacher queried.

"Here," a doe-eyed boy with a flattop answered. He didn't
have a care in the world. Girls named Alan didn't exist!

As Mrs. Reoch, a meaty woman with cat-woman glasses and
a scowl, went down the list, I squirmed in my seat. I knew what
was coming. It was my third go-around with opening day roll
call, kindergarten and first grade both ending in disgrace. Still, I

offered up prayers—you could pray in school in 1971—hoping this was the year they'd be answered.

"Norbert Barker?"

My mind drifted back to my second summer. I was two years old, with long, coiled ringlets that looked like Shirley Temple's. Mom had refused to cut them on principle alone. "Wouldn't you just kill for that hair?" she'd ask strangers at the store, women at the post office, tellers at the bank. They'd all respond the same way—"What a beautiful girl!"—my mother correcting them with a giggle. The greatest day of my life, at least up to that point, was when Mom finally broke down and took me to Bullock's for a haircut. We both cried that day, her tears from sorrow, mine from relief.

"Herman Caldwell?" As the kid raised his hand, my sphincter tightened, everyone but me engrossed in their shiny, new desks. We'd graduated from the miniature tables of *K* through *I*, proud owners of individual work stations now, with swiveling chairs, built-in pencil trays, and lids. Those lids would conceal everything from books and paper to wadded-up sweaters, bubble-gum wrappers, and notes from girls. They were the greatest thing—

"Michael Dittman?"

Dammit! The lists were *always* in alphabetical order. Even in second grade, I knew *D* came after *C*, which meant it was all happening again! As Mrs. Reoch made her way down the register, I shook my head in disgust, waiting for the axe to fall.

My cousin, Rowan, was the first person to question my masculinity. Four years older and twice my size, he anointed me the "little sister" he never had, making fun of my name, my curls, and just about everything else. I saw him once a year, along with most of my other relatives, when we visited family in Oklahoma, his first words to me, "Are you a boy or a girl?"

Our relationship worsened from there.

Staring down from her lectern, eyes magnified, Mrs. Reoch chugged through more names, "Roger Wilson", "Brian Young", a runaway train on her way to "Zack Zrelli".

This was it. The bottom of the Boys' List. The end of inner peace.

There were typically two or three names on the Girls' List before mine. Not much time to prepare. I thought about diversions, my brother's epilepsy an option. I'd watched hundreds of seizures over the years and could fake one to perfection. But that would bring the school nurse, a scary, old woman who smelled of ammonia and refused to sanitize her thermometer.

"Mary Sue Abbott?" A girl clutching a *Bambi* lunchbox responded, looking more nervous than me. I could start a fire, I thought to myself, but no one carried matches, not till we started lighting farts a few years later.

"Carolyn Bidwell?" I swiveled in desperation. The kid next to me looked frail. If I landed a haymaker— "Shannon Capps?"

And...*action!*

The laughter that followed was louder than last year's, lasting twice as long as the year before. Nothing was funnier to a group of seven-year-olds than a blatant misidentification of sex. Staring down at the floor, I waited for the laugh track to fade, face redder than the nearby fire extinguisher. "I'm...here," I mumbled, another wicked chorus following. When I finally looked up, no one was laughing harder than the teacher I'd met five minutes earlier.

W.C. Fields once said, "It ain't what they call you, it's what you answer to." For me, they were one and the same. I tried everything through the years, from inventing cool nicknames like 'Ace' or 'Rocky'—not surprisingly, none of them stuck—to going by my middle name, William or Bill. They were *all* upgrades, but my parents refused to use them. And my friends just laughed. They knew my name was a prison sentence. And had no desire to commute it.

When our school closed in '72, we moved en masse to the primary across town. Although my surroundings had changed, the routine had not. First day of school. *Check.* Name on Girls' List. *Check.* Humiliating laughter. *Check.*

It would be another long year. And the phenomenon was spreading.

Unwanted mail began to arrive, some of it admittedly my own fault. In the '60s and '70s, ads targeted every underage dolt in the country, appearing on cereal boxes and kids' magazines by the thousands. A voracious saver and halfwitted consumer, I ordered everything—X-ray glasses, Kung Fu lessons, miniature submarines, Fool-Your-Friends vomit. I even sent off for a live squirrel monkey once, Mom canceling the purchase as I licked the stamp. Every order I placed took four to six weeks—you think the postal service is slow *now*?—and, unbeknownst to me, added my name to another mailing list.

The first feminine hygiene sample, addressed to '*Miss Shannon Capps*', arrived in '74. "What's this, Mom?" I asked innocently.

"Oh...I..." Her face turned crimson. "...it's...for...*ladies*," she managed, taking the box and slipping it into her apron. "I'm sure it was a mistake, Shannon."

It wasn't.

In the days (and years) to follow, a river of Kotex, Playtex, and Tampax flowed into our house, all addressed to the pre-pubescent boy who lived there. There were mini pads, maxi pads, sanitary napkins—as opposed to *un*sanitary?—cramp remedies and more. And they promised everything from 'Complete Freedom' to 'Extra Confidence', providing neither.

Mom felt terrible for me. Dad seemed to enjoy it.

Back at school, things began to settle down. After two more

Girls' List episodes for the now-somewhat-jaded fourth- and fifth-grade crowds, I looked forward to junior high. A reliable source, Keith Budro's older brother, Kit, told me humiliating roll calls were a thing of the past there. Thankfully, he was right. I breezed through sixth grade, even took a summer school course with my newfound confidence.

Yes, I still had a girl's name, but it would never burn me again. Or so I thought.

On September 13, 1976, our mail dropped through the slot at three p.m. No tampons on this warm summer day—*thank God!*—just an oversized envelope with my name in black ink. I tore it open, revealing my fall schedule. I was excited about seventh grade, my friends and I no longer the youngest kids in school. A fresh crop of 'rookies' was on the way. And we were going to haze the hell out of them! I glanced at my class list. Period one—Chorus.

What the hell?

I hadn't signed up for Chorus. I didn't even *like* singing! I grabbed the phone and dialed a friend. No answer. I pulled back the curtain and scanned my street. Deserted. On the last day of summer, every mom in town had dragged her child to Zodys, forcing him/her into corduroy or denim.

I was on my own.

When the alarm sounded at six the next morning, I shot out of bed. No one was going to beat me to school. If I had to take Chorus, it would be from the best seat in the house, the one in the far back corner! And the only way to insure this was to get there first. Joe the custodian unlocked the room at seven. I was in my seat by 7:01. From there, time passed like sour milk through a straw. A girl entered at 7:40, followed by another at 7:45. I needed a male face. Just one. Another 'dude' to help me weather the storm.

By 7:50, there were ten kids in the music room—nine girls

and me. I sat in the shadows, heart beating like the adjacent snare drum. At 7:55, a flock of females filed in, followed by a bubbly teacher in a blue jumper.

The room was full now. And I was the only one there with a penis.

"Weren't you in my Math class last year?" I jerked to the voice, staring at Kim Rozini, the prettiest girl at Griffiths Middle. "Funny," she tittered. "I thought you were a boy!"

I leaped to my feet, chair banging the wall. Everyone turned, forty eyes on me at once. Thirty-nine actually—one girl had an eyepatch. Thanks to me, no one noticed. As I made my way to the front, the accompanying laughter was familiar. It was, after all, the first day of school.

"I need a counselor!" I screamed—boy, did I!—laughs spreading like flames.

Cackling with everyone else, the teacher grabbed a pass. "You mean, you don't like *Girls'* Chorus?" she heckled, the crowd howling now.

I did not.

On the way out, I bumped into the chimes, causing more hysterics. By the time I reached the office, it was a dull, painful roar. The guidance counselor, smirking as I pled my case, agreed to reassign me, Metal Shop—was there anything more *manly*?— replacing Chorus. In truth, I was a better singer than welder, but I kept my mouth shut.

"How was your day, Shannon?" Mom asked when I shambled home. I looked up, staring at the woman who'd caused all this trouble. She'd burdened me with an albatross, one I'd be forced to carry the rest of my life. I might as well have a harelip, or a missing ear, or a wart on the tip of my nose. I looked deep in her eyes, eyes so filled with love it hurt.

This woman would die for me!

"It was fine, Mom," I answered, the hug that followed curing everything.

"Special delivery, bud." I turned, Dad tossing me a box of Vagisil. "No yeast infections for you," he snickered, making his way up the hall.

I stared at my name on the label and sighed.

'Ace' Capps would never put up with this.

11

NO ONE SPECIAL

Seven-year-olds rarely stand up for one another. And even when they do, a swarm of 'angry gnats' isn't exactly intimidating. I could've used some support—crowd *or* moral—when my second-grade teacher dressed me down in front of the class.

But none came.

Allow me to back up a bit. By the time most of us reach second grade, we've figured out where we fit in the school hierarchy. There's the 'athlete', graced by the gods with a chiseled body and ability to use it. The 'nerd', ignored by those same deities but blessed with an oversized brain. The 'bully' who combines sheer brawn with sluggish brain function. And the 'clown', the role *I* chose to embrace, who relies on average intelligence at best, using it to entertain the masses and hide his own shortcomings.

The first laughs I remember getting came as a three-year-old. We were visiting Dad's folks in Missouri, octogenarians who mostly ignored me. One of the neighbor kids, an overweight bumpkin who rarely spoke, came over to play. As luck would have it, we found paint in the garage, and I decided, for reasons unknown, to use 'Jethro' as canvas. When my parents and grandparents emerged from the house, they doubled over, guffawing at my work. But for the whites of his eyes, the kid was blue from head to toe!

The laughter I received was intoxicating. Like a drug, I wanted more. *Needed* more. But learning what's funny and what isn't was an education in itself. I watched cartoons, Little Rascals comedies, reruns of *F Troop*. I eavesdropped on my parents' conversations, not just with each other but with neighbors and friends. One thing became apparent immediately. Humor is subjective. As I crowed at Heckle and Jeckle, Mom leafed through a magazine. As Dad howled at 'Polack' jokes, I shrugged with indifference. And my brother, Dennis, was no help. He laughed at everything.

Still, hard as comedy seemed to master, I was determined. I bought Spike Jones records and mimicked the songs. Memorized Allan Sherman's *My Son the Nut*. Marveled at the insults on Don Rickles' *Hello, Dummy!* Slowly and deliberately, a style emerged—part music parody, part funny voices, part defamation of character. Once I'd honed my material, it was ready for school, much to the chagrin of Alice Reoch and every teacher thereafter. One thing I'd failed to realize is that teachers *hate* the class clown. It's hard enough to 'herd cats' for six hours, even harder to compete with one for their attention.

But as I said before, I needed a fix!

It all started at recess. I found I could entertain second graders with little to no effort. A song about underwear would do it. So would a silly noise, holding a banana near my crotch, or an impression of Gomer Pyle. Before long, however, my twenty-minute 'sets' just didn't suffice. I needed more time—and more laughs! Why not take my act indoors? If my audience liked me at recess, they'd *love* me in class!

And so began my endless torrent of office visits.

In those days, a trip to the principal's office was no walk in the park. Corporal punishment was alive and well in '71, Mr. Creed's prowess with the paddle legendary. But in most cases, teachers at Casier handled discipline themselves, either with admonishment ("Shut your trap, young man!") or a trip to the corner (where we'd stare at the wall for up to an hour). On rare occasions—not *that* rare, in my case—a frustrated instructor would pass the buck. I found myself, on one such day, trudging up the main hallway to the office. I'd fired off a dopey comment, made fun of a girl's voice, or simulated farts during an earthquake drill. Whatever the offense, I was in no hurry for punishment.

Until I heard what sounded like buffalo hooves behind me.

Peering over my shoulder, I saw them in the distance—twenty students from the MR wing. That's what we called children with Down syndrome, MR an abbreviation for 'mentally retarded'. Our school had four classes of them, divided, I assume, by age and ability. They were located on the north side of campus, fenced off like kindergarteners from the rest of the population. From a distance, they seemed nice enough. But they were also a little scary. They were older than we were. Larger, too. And they talked with strange inflections, did weird things with their hands, and sometimes drooled. These are the observations of a seven-year-old. In retrospect, they seem (and are) a bit wide of scope. But the fear they invoked was real.

I turned back and quickened my pace, checking their progress every few seconds. As I walked faster, *they* walked faster, their huge strides swallowing my own. I broke into a half-jog. They narrowed the gap. I upped it to a full-jog. They gained more ground. The office was still several halls away. *I'd never make it!* In a panic, I dove into a rosebush, squatting among thorns. The first row of massive marchers passed without incident, as did the second and third. From the safety of the shrubs,

I watched their movements, studied their mannerisms. An idea blossomed. A *horrible* idea. I considered myself adept at impressions—Maxwell Smart, Ricky Ricardo, Aunt Bea from *The Andy Griffith Show*. Why not add these guys to my arsenal?

Without warning, a door opened. As I turned, the principal's secretary emerged, eyes moving from the note in her hand to the prat in the plants, expression one of disgust. "You again?" I nodded, following her to Mr. Creed's office.

Over the next few days, I used every recess to study my new 'subjects'. There was Edna who danced in circles and talked to trees. Ronald who kicked soccer balls higher than our best sixth-grade athletes. And Frankie who told little jokes and kissed the girls' hands. They were sweet kids. And despite our fears, we liked watching them. Of course, watching them and *teasing* them were two different things.

I began to imitate their quirks, to the delight (and laughs) of friends. Before long, everyone was doing it, all as poorly and distastefully as me. In my peers' defense, they didn't know better. But I did. My own brother was a 'special needs' kid. No, he wasn't 'mentally retarded', but there was plenty to make fun of. And it pained me when people did.

Yet here I was, doing the same thing.

"That's enough!" a shrill voice interrupted. As I turned, Mrs. Reoch's black eyes bore a hole through me. She was seething and pointing to the office!

It was the first time I walked there feeling guilt. What I was doing, ample as the laughter was, just didn't feel right. And after a ruthless scolding from Mr. Creed, I resigned myself to look elsewhere for laughs. My classmates, however, made no such commitment. They continued to beg for impressions, do their own, and invent despicable new ones. I'd created a monster and had no idea how to stop it.

Fortunately—and I use the term loosely—Mrs. Reoch did.

One afternoon, during a third-degree smog alert, a condition that canceled every recess in L.A., she lined us up at the door. "We're going to a party," she announced, far more cheerful than usual. As a general rule, there was *nothing* cheerful about Alice Reoch, having taught clods like us for thirty years. As she led us north, I smelled a rat. We'd never left class for a 'party' before, never left class for anything but an assembly or film. And based on our behavior lately—specifically *mine*—we sure hadn't earned one.

When she unlatched the gate, I knew we were in trouble. She was leading us straight into the MR wing. A hush fell over the pack, save for an anxious ripple of whispers. On the way there, I'd cut six places in line. I now found myself directly behind Mrs. Reoch, sweat oozing from every pore. As we entered the room, I heard my heart thrum. But Don Ho and the Ali'is drowned it out. There was a luau going on, with music, cupcakes, and—*oh, Jesus!*—dancing.

As the teachers chatted, we huddled in the corner, trying desperately to keep a low profile. Frankie was the first to see us, waving a cake-smeared hand. A few more partiers moved in after that, some in grass skirts, others wearing leis. We clustered like penguins, nervous and ignorant, hoping and praying the luau would end. As an aide dropped a needle on Bobby Darrin's *Dream Lover*, Edna locked eyes with me. *Oh, God!* I looked away, but when I looked back, she was heading my way. Instinctively, I shoved Nils Svensson forward, his moccasins about to be mobile! Edna dragged him onto the dancefloor, the rest of us watching in both fear and delight. No one liked Nils. And if someone had to be sacrificed, we were glad it was him.

On the way back to class, silence turned to giggles. We couldn't get the image—Edna, at sixteen, stood a foot taller than her reluctant dance partner—out of our heads. Mrs. Reoch's plan, though noble, had failed. She'd hoped to portray these students in a whole new light, to present them as *kids*, with the same likes, hopes, and dreams that we had.

Instead, she'd just given us more material.

"Sit down and shut up!" she snarled. We glanced at the clock, its plodding hands far from the final hour. As we sat, she stomped on high heels between us, pacing the room like a bull.

No one was laughing now.

When she passed nearby, I felt her stare, hot on my neck. Smelled her perfume, that of the rosebush. Tasted saliva, my own. "Those children," she began, tramping to the front of the room, "didn't ask to be different." She turned to look at us, her face an angry mask. Two rows behind me, Norbert Barker gulped, Benny Sherman dropping his pencil. "But they're kind." She stepped forward. "Warm." Another step. "Affectionate." Two more steps...she was heading straight for me! "And caring." She stopped at my desk, addressing the class. "Those kids are special." Her voice cracked as she turned to face me. "*You*, on the other hand..." She dropped down to my level, breath stinking of coffee. "...are *NO ONE SPECIAL!*"

Her eyes—cavernous, black pits—held their stare for eternity.

As I stared back, at a rare loss for words, no one came to my aid.

I don't blame them. Harsh as the admonishment was, I deserved it. We *all* did.

There are lines in comedy that shouldn't be crossed. And Mrs. Reoch made that abundantly clear. These kids, she'd pointed out artfully, hadn't asked for this, no more than I'd asked for curls, Norbert had wished for pink skin, or Benny had wanted trichotillomania (the nonstop urge to pluck his own hair).

Years later—Benny was no doubt bald by then—I learned from a friend that Alice Reoch had died. She was survived by a daughter, he told me, a daughter with 'special needs'. The girl's name was Edna. And she loved to dance.

I'd like to say that Mrs. Reoch taught me a lesson, that her words, though vicious, changed me forever. But over the years, I'd fail again and again in my pursuit of laughter.

That's the thing about comedy. And *life*, really.

Sometimes it's funny. Sometimes it isn't.

Perhaps Joan Rivers put it best. "Comedy's a very rough beat."

Indeed it is, Joan. Indeed it is.

12

SICK-ISH

I wouldn't describe myself as a sickly kid. More like sick-*ish*. But I did miss a lot of school, the notes on my report cards confirming it. Bacteria and viruses weren't the problem. I've already chronicled Mom's insatiable cleaning habits.

The problem was daytime television.

Back then, TV stations signed off at night, playing the national anthem before going dark. At six a.m., the iconic 'Indian Head' test pattern would emerge, signaling the dawn of a new day. When I was up that early, it was to watch sci-fi puppet shows like *Thunderbirds* or heavy-handed moral tales like *Davey and Goliath*, the 'sharing' and 'caring' themes soaring right over my head. *Captain Kangaroo* started at eight. But so did school.

And therein lay the dilemma.

If I was truly sick, the choice was easy. Stay home, drink Jell-O water—the mere thought of this clotted concoction still makes me retch—and watch TV all day. But if I was just feeling a little off, or in fact never felt better in my life, it was more complicated than that. Telling Mom I was ill meant the immediate appearance of the rectal thermometer. And there was nothing I hated worse. The decision was torturous...turn off the

TV and get ready for school or suffer the indignity of anal pene-
tration with a medical device? The sheer fact that I *ever* chose
the latter tells you how much I loved television.

With three networks, four local channels, and several UHF
stations to choose from, options for a kid with the sniffles were
ample. When *Captain Kangaroo* ended, I'd switch to local legend
Sheriff John who began every show with a song—'*Laugh and be
happy, and the world will laugh with you*'—followed by the Pledge
of Allegiance and a host of cartoons. From there, it was back to
network for reruns of *That Girl*, *Bewitched*, and *The Beverly Hillbillies*. As I curled up on the couch, I remember feeling sorry for
the kids in school. While they 'concentrated' in class, I was
watching *Concentration*, coughing to 'sell my illness' through *Sale
of the Century*.

At noon, Mom would bring me lunch, a bowl of tomato soup
on a TV tray. There was no chicken noodle in our house. No
chicken *anything*. My father despised poultry, tolerating turkey
on Thanksgiving but banning everything with feathers the rest
of the year. I grew to love tomato soup with soggy crackers and a
7-Up chaser. But I never finished a meal. That would tell Mom I
felt better. I learned this the hard way once. After wolfing down
lunch, I was marched to the car, shoved inside, and dropped off
at Casier mid-day.

As a result, I missed the entire 'afternoon block'!

That block began with *Search for Tomorrow*, one of five
straight soap operas Mom tuned in for, and ended with *The Edge
of Night*, which it damn near was by then. Along the way, we'd
find ourselves nailed to the sofa for such earthshaking develop-
ments as Bob leaving Myrna, Tom confronting Sarah, or Ed
meeting his long-lost, illegitimate son. Someone was always
showing up on someone's doorstep (which included the obligatory zoom, music swell, and cut to commercial). Actors were
swapped for other actors (with their own husbands and wives

failing to notice). And everyone eventually came down with amnesia (a condition I suffered whenever Mom asked about school). Though totally-implausible, the storylines were riveting, my addiction to them far more genuine than the infirmities I faked. It took every ounce of strength to tear myself away.

Full disclosure...there were times of *actual* illness. I got the mumps when I was five, jowls swelling to the size of Raymond Burr's. I followed that up with chicken pox, unable to walk when blisters covered my feet. Peppered in between were the customary sore throats, headaches, and bouts with the runs, the belching humidifier in my room creating an ersatz Ecuador. In addition, I once threw up an entire sausage pizza, Mom scrubbing the rug till three a.m. But these afflictions, though traumatic, were fleeting. So you can imagine my surprise when one of them lingered.

After a pain-filled week of puking and pissing, Mom took me to Dr. Dormer's office. The kindly, old physician had treated me since birth, my brother before that. He always smiled, which wiggled his unshorn nostril hairs, and shook my hand like a friend. As I sat on the exam table that day, air ripe with disinfectant, he wasn't smiling. "I'd like to run some tests, Berneice." What more could he do to me? I'd already weathered *his* rectal thermometer, had a stick the size of a surfboard shoved down my throat, and been forced to pee in a plastic bottle, all in front of his nurse (who happened to be our neighbor). It was beyond humiliating, but I barely put up a fight, even when they stuck a needle in my arm to draw blood.

"Go lie down, Shannon," my mother insisted when we got home, already mixing more Jell-O water. "*The Guiding Light* starts in—" The phone rang, Mom grabbing the receiver. I watched through yellow eyes as she steadied herself. "I understand, doctor...yes...right away." When she hung up, she turned to face me. "Doctor Dormer thinks...we should go to the hospital." Before I could get clarification, she was back on the phone. "May I speak to Clarence Capps, please?"

Uh-oh! Mom never called Dad at work. It was his sanctuary, his brick-and-mortar foxhole when shit hit the fan everywhere else. In three decades of toiling away at the same company, he'd never missed a day. Not when he threw his back out. Or broke a bone. Or donned the 'blue robe', a garment he only wore when vomiting all night and sweating out fever.

"He thinks..." Mom choked up, a tear betraying her. "...it's nephritis." More tears spilled, her voice striking an unfamiliar tone. I had no idea why a word that sounded so— "We'll meet you at Downey Community." *Wait...what?* Dad was leaving work early?

Sweet Jesus, I was doomed!

As we checked into the hospital, I tried to look healthy, but it felt like our station wagon had dragged me there. Mom trembled as she filled out paperwork, Dad's expression dire. Making our way up the hall, I thought of a recent field trip. My class, for some reason, had visited a cattle farm, a few of us sneaking off to the slaughterhouse next door. As we looked on, one naive cow after another lumbered up the chute, where a guy with a stun gun waited to cap them. I knew how they felt now, about to be 'ground chuck', too!

A nurse with devious eyebrows pointed to a door. After checking her for weapons, I moved inside, Mom and Dad behind me. "You'll need to put this on," she announced, handing me a gown. I was confused. Even with the ties secured, my scared, little wiener would poke through the front, the gap making it look even smaller. "It ties in *back*," she clarified. That made more sense, but I'd still be exposed, not to mention cold! Mom tied the strings for me, Dad helping me into bed.

If this wasn't the worst day of my life, it was certainly 'top five'.

That's when I saw it. Bolted to the ceiling and angled just so, a color TV with its own—*wait for it*—hard-wired remote control! I'd never used one before. Up to that point, *I* was the remote, Dad barking orders like "Turn that shit off" or "Switch it to *Wild Kingdom*". I grabbed the unit and began flipping channels. As *Three on a Match* cut to commercial, I switched to *As the World Turns*, no longer caring about my imminent death. If I had to meet my maker, I was damn sure going to do it watching *The Newlywed Game*!

The door wheezed open, and a ninety-year-old nurse shuffled in. Smelling like gauze, she clutched a clattering tray in one hand, a hypodermic needle in the other. "Time for your shot," she croaked. Mom and Dad parted, leaving me vulnerable. As she approached, I saw her liver-spotted hands, shaking more than mine. Noticed her fingernails, dirtier than Dad's. Glanced at her nylons, gathered like Slinkys around two bony ankles. "Roll over!" Nothing about this woman instilled confidence. And she was about to gore me with a six-inch needle! Turning away, I closed my eyes, feeling the touch of cold, wet cotton, followed by the stab of a bayonet. And like a soldier in battle, she skewered me again and again, the pain mind-numbing. "See you tomorrow," she rasped, doddering off (sans apology) to her next helpless victim.

As I lay there—ass throbbing, remote forgotten—I wondered how much more I could take. The answer was two weeks' worth. That's how long I'd be in the hospital, suffering 'Nurse Ratched's' shiv attacks, untold temperature checks, and the worst food on the planet!

With my diagnosis—nephritis can often lead to renal failure, even death—doctors insisted on a 'bland diet', featuring unsalted vegetables, mystifying meats, and pudding that looked (and tasted) like shaving cream. In addition, I was forced to drink six hundred gallons of water a day, pissing into a jug every three minutes. All fine and dandy during the daytime, but when I awoke at night, room blacker than a coal mine, I could rarely find the receptacle, opting for my soon-to-be-yellow sheets instead.

Needless to say, the graveyard shift hated me.

Despite unlimited access to TV, I grew bored. An eight-year-old can only take so much *Jeopardy*—that show will never last!—before begging for anesthetic. Furthermore, I actually missed school. The feeling was intensified when Mom dropped off a stack of get-well cards. Every kid in class had sent one, my closest friends adding a few unsanctioned comments. Even Mrs. Reoch penned a note. Now I *knew* I was dying!

But on my thirteenth day of captivity, Dr. Dormer arrived, smiling from ear to ear. "Good news," he announced, Mom and Dad hopeful for the first time since check-in. "The diagnosis was inaccurate." As my parents stood, I grabbed the jug to relieve myself. "He doesn't have nephritis." I stopped midstream...then what the *hell* do I have? "He's got strep throat." Although it sounded far worse, I knew it wasn't, Mom and Dad hugging like amnesia survivors.

"So we can go home, doctor?" Mom asked through tears.

"First thing tomorrow." He grinned, shaking my hand. We were apparently friends again.

As joy filled the room, I had but one question. "Can someone get me a *damn* McDonald's hamburger?"

A few days later, I was back in school, homework crushing my desk. Norbert Barker patted me on the back. Benny Sherman gave me his dough-dog at lunch. And Nils Svensson returned my lucky pencil—"Sorry, man, I thought you were a goner!" So did I. Only Mrs. Reoch seemed indifferent, sending me to the corner when I showed Nils my punctured ass.

The attention eventually faded, but so did my desire to stay home from school. In the end, it wasn't the shots, the terrible food, or the bedwetting that did it.

It was politics.

While doctors investigated my puzzling illness, the Justice Department was investigating Richard M. Nixon. The results of the probe were the Watergate Hearings of 1973, the proceedings airing live on every channel for weeks. As a kid who'd survived a bout with nephritis...well, *strep throat* anyway...I had no interest in the president's role in a DNC break-in. Nor did I care what the Select Committee on Presidential Campaign Activities had to say about it.

I just wanted to watch *Password*, dammit!

13

108 STITCHES

I met my soulmate when I was seven. She was small for her age, with rounded features and skin the hue of cream. When I held her, my heart raced—still does—and when I caught her scent, it was of fresh-cut grass. I fell in love with her the moment we met. And five decades later, that emotion is still raw. My wife understands. She's in love with her, too.

My soulmate, you see, is baseball.

My father loved the game before I did. Growing up in Missouri, he listened to France Laux on KMOX, the Cardinals his favorite team. When I was born in '64, they hadn't won a title in two decades. But I was "their lucky charm", Dad said, Lou Brock and company taking the pennant by one game that year, then slaying the hated Yankees to win the World Series.

Six-and-a-half years later, my father, hoping for the next Stan Musial, signed me up for Little League. Tryouts, from what I remember, went poorly. As a result, all eight teams passed on my 'talents', sending me to the 'Instructional League' (aka Tee Ball). When I showed up that first day, wearing jeans, sneakers, and my cousin's tattered mitt, I fit right in. There were thirteen of us, a sad collection of booger-eating dullards, each as poorly-skilled as the next. In lieu of unis—we apparently didn't merit them—they handed out maroon T-shirts and hats, then lined us up for a team photo. My pal, Keith Budro, stood tall in back next to Raymond 'Stretch' Wurtz while I slumped in front, alongside 'Wee Willie' Haskins and a kid who'd survived polio.

After the picture, a phlegmatic Coach Barnes—the poor bastard had clearly drawn the short straw—emptied an equipment bag near home plate. "Warm up," he ordered, sparking a Winston. We looked at each other like lost souls. One kid was crying. Coach told him to "knock it off", then paired us up on opposite sides of the baseline, handing out six balls. I found myself on the end, facing two slack-jawed partners, our odd numbers an affront to symmetry.

"Play catch!" one of the dads bellowed. On cue, balls began flying, none hitting leather.

As I chased mine down, I noticed the field next to ours, dirt perfectly-groomed, grass so green it hurt my eyes. Boys a year older were dressed in full uniform, white-and-blue on one side, gray-and-red on the other, whipping balls back and forth like choreographed ballet. It was beautiful—*perfect*—a Norman Rockwell painting come to life. In that exact moment, with the sounds, scents, and colors of Furman Park filling my senses, I reached down and grabbed the baseball.

And it grabbed back.

"You gonna pick daisies all day?" Coach Barnes yelled, lighting another fag. I shook my head and hurried back to the line, setting my feet like Dad had shown me and firing a strike to the kid on the end. It hit him in the chest—literally.

It wasn't the first time I'd played catch. From the moment I could stand, my father put a glove on my hand and tossed me a baseball. He was a lefty, using an ancient, three-fingered first-baseman's mitt. And he could hit from both sides of the plate, though he never played an organized game. Some of my earliest memories are of him pitching to me in the back yard, the bat taller than I was. When I actually made contact, he'd call it like the radio voice of his youth—"There's a double down the line!" or "That one's out of the park!" As I rounded the imaginary bases, I felt like a Hall of Famer.

Dad and I played as much as we could. And when we weren't playing, we were watching. Dodger games aired on Channel 11, with Vin Scully and Jerry Doggett on the call. Our preferred Angels played on Channel 5, where Dick Enberg lauded great plays—there weren't many—with an "Oh, my!" On rare occasions, Dad would score tickets to Chavez Ravine, where I could sit in the pavilion and watch visiting stars like Willie Mays and Hank Aaron, or to the 'Big A' for a close-up look at hometown hero Jim Fregosi. Seeing these Big Leaguers master the game gave me hope. Maybe *they* struggled like I did when they were young. And maybe, just maybe, *I'd* be playing under the lights someday.

"Two hands!" Coach Barnes screamed. I glanced down the line, not a single maroon-clad teammate resembling a ball-player. Even Budro (whose brother was an All-Star and dad a Major League scout) was overthrowing his partner. We were awful. Worse than trained chimps. Worse than *un*trained chimps. And I had no faith we'd get better.

But we did.

Over the course of the gameless season, we learned to field ground balls, hit off a tee, catch the occasional fly, and run the bases, all in the shadow of the real contests going on next door. It was painful at times, seeing those flashes of color, smelling the hot dogs, hearing the roar of the crowd as we rolled balls across the pasture. But it gave us hope. Made us dream of days to come.

Less than a year later, I was drafted by my first actual team, the Northwest Downey Little League—*gulp*—Yankees. I'll never forget that first uniform. It was ancient, made of wool or tent canvas, I'm not sure which, the piping threadbare or missing. As I held it to my face, I smelled mildew, the pants and jersey a mismatch of grays. When we assembled for our first game, I noticed three iterations of worn Yankee duds, some with block letters, others with script, still others with numbers on the moth-eaten sleeves. None of that mattered. When I put that uniform on, I felt like a genuine baseball player.

If only I'd played like one.

I hit .000 my first year in Minors while playing a much-less-than-stellar left field. Don't get me wrong, I *could* hit. I just refused to. Much to my father's chagrin, I discovered early on that if I parked the bat on my shoulder and waited, the bored umpire would eventually award me first base, via the 'fan-favorite' walk. This strategy, thanks to horrible pitching, worked most of the time, but it kept me from experiencing one of the game's pure joys—squaring up a baseball. Dad tried everything to make me swing. So did my coaches. But I just wouldn't do it, leaving the heavy lifting to older players like Gavin Broomfield and Matty Yankevich. As a result, the Bub's Daddy gum we received after wins (even the watermelon flavor) tasted bitter-sweet.

Over the winter, I practiced every day. Dad fashioned a 'pitch simulator'—a leg of Mom's nylons with a tennis ball in the foot —and hung it from the garage. It worked like a charm, the pendulum moving forward, back, forward, back, till I was ready to swing. And swing, I did. I must've hit the ball a thousand times that winter, eventually sending it (along with half of Mom's stocking) over the O'Learys' roof. No one saw the majestic clout, but I broke into a home run trot anyway, grinning like Manny Sanguillen.

I was ready.

Having been traded in the offseason for a 'player to be named later', I showed up in Reds camp, raring to go. Along

with new teammates and a new uniform, I had a new mantra...
swing the damn bat! I'd soon get my chance. Batting leadoff, I
lined the first pitch of the '73 season off the right field wall, no
one more surprised than I was. We *all* hit that year. And fielded.
And threw. Like the 'Big Red Machine' of the '70s (with Rose,
Bench, and Morgan), our 'Little Red Machine' (with Wurtz,
Capps, and Budro) won back-to-back titles, bringing home
trophies bigger than Willie Haskins.

Winning, it turns out, felt good. And so did being part of a
team.

I played on a lot of them over the years, the Senators, Cubs,
Twins, Giants, Bears—worse than our *Bad News* counterparts—
Pirates, 49ers, Blue Sox, White Sox, Red Sox—why do they
name teams after footwear?—Dodgers, Expos, and Hops. I was
no Stan Musial, nor did I ever play 'under the lights', but I
outlasted most who did. In a career that spanned forty years, I
won a batting title in high school, played a little in college, and
was part of three World Championship teams in the adult
leagues, surviving on minimal talent and sheer determination.
Along the way, I wore out gloves, busted bats, watched more
games than Connie Mack, and collected every Topps baseball
card made.

Through it all, there was one constant. My boundless love of
the game.

When I met my wife in 1990, I was playing in Orange County.
I knew she was different. For one thing, she always beat me to
the sports page. For another, her idea of a perfect date was
watching a game on TV. Turns out she grew up ten minutes
from Anaheim Stadium, her father introducing her to baseball
before she could walk. Her heroes, like mine, wore uniforms.
And her love of the game was unrivaled. Till she met her future
husband.

When I asked her to marry me, I wrote it on a baseball. And

when our son was born three years later, there was already a ball in his crib. The minute he could stand, I was tossing it to him, adjusting his shoulders, showing him how to set his feet. When he got older, I pitched to him in the yard, mimicking the calls of Jack Buck—"Go crazy, folks!" and "I don't believe what I just saw!" As he rounded the bases, I saw in his sparkling eyes the same love of the game my dad saw in mine. I saw it in my daughter's, too, every time she and her mom watched *Web Gems* on ESPN.

That's the beauty of this game. It's passed down, like an heirloom, from one generation to the next, father to son, mother to daughter, the perfect legacy. And though I no longer play, I still feel the magic when I hold a baseball. It's such a simple thing, really. A wad of yarn, wrapped in horsehide, held together by 108 stitches. But those stitches connect us, bind us together through experience and memory. The memory of a father and his three-fingered mitt. Of a son who plays the game better than his old man. And of a wide-eyed seven-year-old who reached into the weeds one day to pick up a baseball.

And never let go.

III. SHIFTING INTO THIRD

14

5′ 1¾″

T hanks to me, Mom knew everyone in the principal's office, most on a first-name basis. As a result, our phone got more calls than KHJ's request line. One of those calls, on a stormy spring day, turned my world upside down. "Don't repeat this, Berneice," the woman whispered—I was listening on the line Dad installed in the bathroom—"but Roger Casier is closing."

I nearly dropped the receiver. This was fantastic, *better* than fantastic! I didn't have to go to school anymore! By noon that day, the secret was out, the 'mole' an eight-year-old kid who'd timed his morning poop perfectly.

What I'd failed to realize, of course, is that we'd all be flushed (like said poop) to Maude Price Elementary, the school that kicked my brother out for acting like a kindergartener. Keep in mind, he was *in* kindergarten at the time. Mom wasn't happy about this. And neither was I.

A new school meant new rules, new classes, and new class-mates. Yes, my friends were coming with me, but we'd be forced to make other friends, meet strange teachers, learn all kinds of different stuff. Hell, I didn't even know where the bathrooms were!

When the first day arrived, I was admittedly wary. Dressed in a Hang Ten and Toughskins, I checked my hair—by then, I was trying to straighten it with clips and Mom's dryer—then headed off to school. As I scouted the new playground, another third grader (a girl in pigtails and pink tights) began to make fun of me. *"You're on the girls' swing!"* she sang, face twisted in a self-righteous snarl. This 'chick' had no idea who she was messing with. I was the Don Rickles of Roger Casier, dammit! I countered with two vicious zingers, one targeting gender, the other intellect, but she ignored them, upping her attack with a series of dance moves. Already anxious, and now angry, I leaped forward and swung. I'd never hit a girl before—unless you count the avocado incident—and had no intention of hitting *this* one. I swear on a stack of hotel Bibles, I just wanted to scare her. In hindsight, not a great idea. Since my aim was off, I clipped her chin, loosening a baby tooth and shocking us both.

"Nice to meet you, Mrs. Capps," my new principal greeted Mom. She sat beside me in his office, an hour into my first day at Price, dressed in a pantsuit and nodding. As she listened to the man's mostly-true recap, her expression was one of disappointment. I'd seen it before. And, like always, it hurt.

My mother was the sweetest, kindest, gentlest soul I've ever known.

And she deserved better than me.

Born in Coyle, Oklahoma in 1918, Berneice was the tenth of eleven children. Her father owned the general store. Her mother ran the household, no easy task with thirteen occupants. Mom's childhood was the flipside of Dad's. Before the Great Depression, her family had money, enough to build the largest house in Logan County, on the highest plateau, overlooking the meandering Cimarron River. But as the economy tanked, so did the family store, her father's good nature (so much like Mom's) doing them in. He refused to let customers suffer, extending them credit till there was none left to give, the Coyle Mercantile folding like a napkin.

For the rest of his life, Mom's father, with the help of his four boys and seven girls, survived on farming. Mom raised chickens (which meant ringing the occasional neck for Sunday dinner), cleaned house (till she could see her reflection in the mahogany), and rarely found trouble (she was caught smoking a grapevine once, apologizing forever). I don't know what she dreamed of back then. Or what she hoped to do or be one day. I never thought to ask.

But I do know she was happy.

In school, she studied without prompting, played the clarinet in band, and made the girls' basketball team, never once at 5'1¼" sinking a basket. Her toy stature wasn't solely to blame. Mom always put others in front of herself, whether at home, in class, or on the hardwood. Why *wouldn't* she pass the ball every time she touched it?

At eighteen, she'd seen all of Coyle she was going to see, so she hitched a ride with friends and headed to California. It's hard for me to picture her, eyes open, smile huge, in the back seat of that '32 Essex, rumbling down Route 66 with an unwritten future. But that's what she did, moving in with girlfriends and enjoying the nouveau playground of mid-'30s L.A. She ate lunch at the Brown Derby, soaked up the sun at Hermosa, listened to Big Band music at the Cocoanut Grove, her favorite artists Glenn Miller and Harry James. And she went to church on Sundays, her Christian upbringing as much a part of her as her miniature stature and sweet, little voice. She was even engaged once, to a young attorney in Hollywood, but broke it off, refusing to settle for less-than-true love.

When the war broke out, she and her roommates filled

factory jobs vacated by men in the service. I've seen pictures of Mom from her time on the assembly line. She really did favor the iconic J. Howard Miller 'We Can Do It' model (minus the flexing muscles). Dad's muscles—he worked at the same plant till his orders arrived—caught her attention immediately, along with his quiet confidence and boyish smile. But she feigned disinterest, waiting "like a lady" for him to make the first move. It didn't take long. Their first date ended without a kiss. As did their second. But the love Mom was waiting on had arrived.

Ten weeks later, Dad asked her to marry him.

And she said, "Yes."

They took out for the 'Sooner State', planning a wedding in front of Mom's family. But four hours in, she panicked near Yuma. What would folks think of a woman driving cross-country with a man she wasn't married to? Dad solved the problem by rousting the Justice of the Peace. The man married them in his bathrobe, his wife and the desert stars the only witnesses.

When Dad left for New Guinea three months later, Mom counted the days till his return—866 in all—the couple reuniting as President Truman lit the 'National Christmas Tree', the first time since Pearl Harbor. As noted previously, Mom gave birth to Dennis nine months later, adding me to the fold seventeen years after that, her little family complete.

Despite the massive age gap, Mom and I were close. With Dad at work and Dennis grown, we did everything together. In the early years, there was potty training—I refused to squat till Mom read me a book—and nap time, my favorite spot wherever she was vacuuming. As I got older, there were trips to the beach (where sandwiches included real sand), visits to the bank, post office, and store (I can still smell the fetor of Don's Market cheese), and outings to church (time in those pews moved slower than erosion). In all the hours we spent together, there was never a lull in conversation. Nor were any subjects off limits. Mom always listened, or at least pretended to, and gave me sound advice in return, though I seldom took it.

She was both a modern woman, by 1970s standards, and a throwback to the past. She and Dad shared household tasks like fifty-fifty partners, my father ruling the outside of our home, Mom governing the inside. Her duties included all housework, most of the cooking, and total control of the finances. She also made her own clothes, coiled springs for extra income, and did the books for our church missionaries. She wasn't exactly a 'Women's Libber', identifying more with Phyllis Schlafly than Gloria Steinem, even rooting for Bobby Riggs in the 'Battle of the Sexes', but she sympathized with the movement, believing women could do anything men could, if given the opportunity.

More than anything else, Mom loved people. In all her years on the planet, she never met a stranger, striking up conversations with everyone from the filling station attendant to the paper boy. She even liked Mrs. Noid, and stranger yet, Mrs. Noid liked *her*! Hell, everyone did. Neighbors. Women at the hair salon. Ladies at church. It drove me nuts, especially when we were late for baseball practice, but I couldn't blame them. Neither could Dad. After all, he was the one who loved her most.

They were inseparable, my mother and father. Like bread and butter. Two peas in a pod. Choose your own cliché, but if it connotes love, respect, and companionship, all rolled into one, it would be apt. I swear on the same stack of Bibles I used earlier that I never saw them fight or raise their voices to one another. And the hugs, kisses, and affection—Dad patted Mom on the rump every chance he got—were never-ending. I even caught them with their bedroom door locked one afternoon, Mom offering an out-of-breath "Don't come in, Shannon...we're... talking about your Christmas presents."

It was July.

The love I felt growing up was palpable. Mom loved Dad and her kids more than life itself, to employ another cliché. And she'd do anything to protect them, even if it meant going to bat for a sinner who'd clearly sinned, which described *me* most of the time. Oh, and one more thing...

As sweet as she was, it was never a good idea to piss her off.

"I'm sure you agree, Mrs. Capps," the principal asserted, tone dripping with condescension, "that Shannon's actions deserve punishment." My eyes moved from the oil painting behind him —a listing schooner on an angry sea—to Mom's face. She was no longer nodding, looking comically small in the wingback chair. Mr. Phelps had no way of knowing this, but underestimating Mom's might based on her Lilliputian stature was a huge mistake. She'd survived the Depression, World War II, and the birth of a son with 'special needs'.

By comparison, the troubles *I* caused were a cakewalk.

"I looked at Shannon's file this morning," the man prattled on, scouring the contents of a thick manila folder. "Is there a reason you didn't sign the Corporal Punishment permission slip?" He shot me a dagger, then smiled at Mom through half-moon spectacles.

"I'm glad you brought that up," she answered.

This might be a good time to point out that I've always done my mom's impression with a high-pitched Hungarian accent. She wasn't born in Hungary, nor had she ever visited, the imitation making no sense whatsoever. Yet by all accounts, including those of multiple eyewitnesses, it's spot on. Feel free to apply it to all future 'Mom dialogue'.

"I've seen vat kind of deescipline you people dole out." That should get you started. "And if it's all the same to you..." She stood, making her appear only slightly taller. "...when it comes to disciplining my son, *I'll* do the spanking." With that, she grabbed my arm and led me out of the room, pausing at the front desk to compliment the secretary on her blouse and sign up for a bake sale.

On the way home, we stopped for lunch at Bob's, Mom ordering a salad, me tackling the Big Boy Combo. As I dipped fries in my chocolate shake, we reviewed the events of the day, from my angst at attending a new school to my all-too-accurate punch to Mom standing up for me in the principal's office. I thanked her for coming to my aid. She made me promise to never hit a girl again. "Don't even *pretend* to!"

I told her I wouldn't. She patted me on the hand.

"You're a good boy, Shannon..." She nabbed a fry and popped it in her mouth, feeling guilty for the extra calories. "But you sure know how to hide it!"

She winked a loving eye at me. And we headed home.

Thirty seconds after we arrived, Mom made good on her promise to Mr. Phelps.

And spanked the shit out of me.

15

OH, TANNENBAUM!

On Christmas Day of 1972, my world got a little larger. I woke up that morning to find a Schwinn Lemon Peeler parked next to our tree. The blindingly-yellow bike, one of four Stingray Krates offered that year, featured a banana seat, rear-disc brakes, and a six-inch shifter on the frame. It was the first new bicycle I'd ever owned, Dad dropping $113.95 on the shiny five-speed. "Worth every penny, Pops!" I assured him.

Easy for me to say. It wasn't *my* week's salary.

One of the perks of growing up in soCal was a complete lack of winter. Christmas morning looked like every other, sun shining in the blue-brown sky, thermometer pushing eighty. My unfortunate peers in the Northeast had to wait months for a jaunt on *their* new bicycles. I had to wait minutes, the time it took for the rest of my family to open their sad trickle of presents. The bike had apparently decimated our gift budget.

"Merry Christmas, everyone!" I hollered, pedaling away. Mom told me to be careful. Dad hurried off to the garage. And Dennis, home for the holidays, stared after me, holding his new slippers like a pair of turds.

Up to that moment, my entire world had been a one-block rhombus of concrete, grass, and asphalt. Now it stretched as far as five gears would take me. I headed west, houses on both sides of the street quiet, cool morning wind in my hair. It smelled of fresh-baked bread—the Langendorf Bakery sat just across the river—and of freedom. Sweet freedom!

'Helicopter parents' didn't exist back then. Our moms and dads allowed us to explore and solve the problems we created in the process. After a certain age (five or six maybe), we were 'handed the keys', independence the perfect challenge, experience the greatest teacher. From that point on, I can't remember a single parent watching us play, ride our bikes, or, hell, even swim! As a result, the kids of our generation learned to navigate the world. Without GPS.

Of course, Global Positioning Service wasn't the only thing we did without. There was no cable TV—HBO launched national subscription television in '72, but no one knew what the hell it was. Cellular technology was a good decade away, unless you counted *Get Smart*'s shoe phones. And PONG, also introduced in '72, was only available in bars and bowling alleys.

So if we wanted escapism, it came on two wheels.

Shifting into second gear, I rolled past the Tudors' house. The family, which included twin daughters my age, had moved into the neighborhood months earlier. But the parents were British, so we avoided them like cholera. They also lived next to Mrs. Noid, an even better reason to bypass the area. Unless it was eight a.m. on Christmas morning. Which it was.

I slowed to a crawl and checked for movement. No sign of the Noids, their curtains drawn. A mischievous thought crossed my mind, followed by a wicked smile. I was riding a *new* bicycle and wearing a *new* T-shirt, a gift (and obvious hand-me-down) from Dennis. That meant I was totally incognito!

Veering across the drive, I cut back left, digging my tires into the Noids' lawn. Snaking back and forth, I carved a huge *S* in the velvet Dichondra, then jumped the walkway, taking out two Floradoras in the process.

"*Heeeeeeeeeeeeeeyyyy!*" I heard Mrs. Noid scream. But I was long gone, pumping hard and shifting into third.

Normally, the end of the sidewalk meant the end of my ride. But not today. I hopped the curb at Danvers and kept pedaling, shifting into fourth as I passed Bairnsdale and Allengrove. My buddy, Bart Kinsey, lived up that street, as did Mitch and Curtis Dobbs. I could visit them all now, along with Keith Budro who lived on Finevale, Dickie Hamner who lived up Smallwood— we'd yet to make fun of either name—and Norbert Barker and Benny Sherman who called the other end of Guatemala home. This was fantastic! If I kept going, Vernon Nessler lived on Calm-crest, Trig Bechtler on Suva, and baseball teammates Willie Haskins and Raymond 'Stretch' Wurtz on the oddly-named Island (which wasn't even a peninsula).

This was the best Christmas ever! Maybe even the best—

Someone sprang into the street, frantically waving me down. I spun my nonexistent brakes, remembering they were *hand* levers now, then squeezed hard, swerving to a halt in front of Saul Tannenbaum. He had plastered bangs and the face of a marionette, the most annoying kid at Price, perhaps the most annoying kid in Downey!

"What the *hell*, Saul?"

"I thaw you from a dithtanth," he lisped, the impediment caused by slow-growing teeth. Saul was the first sign of life, beyond Mrs. Noid's Yeti-like howl, that I'd experienced all morn-ing. I looked him up and down—he was filthy—then noticed his parents in the yard.

They were *gardening*, for God's sake!

"What are you doing?" I asked incredulously. "It's Christmas!"

"We're Jewith," he responded, checking out my new bike. "Hey, nithe wheelth!"

"Saul," his mother shouted, oblivious to the hour. "Introduce us to your friend."

He pulled me out of the street, my new Stingray skidding beneath me. When we reached the drive, I set the kickstand and sauntered over. Mrs. Tannenbaum beamed like I'd handed her a cardboard check, Mr. Tannenbaum ignoring me altogether. "Thith ith Thannon," Saul made the spit-soaked introductions, his mother removing gloves. "He thitth nextht to me in clath."

"Nice to meet you, Shannon." She shook my hand like Ed McMahon's, then turned to her husband. "Saul's worked long enough today, don't you think, dear?" The man grunted, clipping a Bird of Paradise. She turned and smiled, grabbing me by the shoulders. "You two go play." *What...NO!* "Our son got some marvy toys for Hannukah." I shook my head, but no words came. "You boys'll have a wonderful time playing with them."

Saul dragged me to the back yard, my shiny Schwinn shrinking behind me. "Wait till you thee my Adventhure Tunnel!" he spluttered. "It'th a hundred incheth long and hath picthureth of Winnie the Pooh on the thideth!" *Jesus,* I thought to myself, feeling immediately guilty for the slur on His birthday. "Thpeaking of Pooh," he droned on, spittle flying everywhere, "I altho got a new Thee 'n Thay!" My *God,* those were for *three-year-olds!*

For the next hour, we crawled through the tunnel again and again, Saul cackling every time he pulled the string on his Pooh-themed See 'n Say. It was the longest hour of my life, up there with trying on new clothes, Vacation Bible School, and dental X-rays. So when his mother showed up with a pitcher of lemonade, I seized opportunity. "My...uh...mom wants me home," I excused myself, sounding like Eeyore. "I mean..." I looked from one to the other, hoping this wouldn't offend them. "...it's Christmas."

Mrs. Tannenbaum smiled again. "Of course, dear." As Saul walked me back to my bike, she thanked me repeatedly for stopping by. Did I have a choice? "Please come again." I told her I would, already calculating a different route for next time, one that would circumvent their house completely. "And maybe Saul can visit *you* someday?"

"I...uh...sure." At that point, I'd have said anything to get out of there. Head pounding, I hopped on the Peeler and took off, forced to turn home as they watched me ride away. I felt a little guilty, having just lied to an adult, a big 'no-no' at age eight, but after spending an hour with the Tannenbaums, who could blame me? Hell, I'd lie under oath if it meant shedding Saul's company! The torturous visit had not only killed my spirits but destroyed my wanderlust. Seeing them in the yard, digging up weeds on Christmas morning, had also, in a weird way, made me miss my *own* holiday traditions. By now, Dad was surely sawing something in the garage. Mom was vacuuming the carpet. And Dennis was watching *Miracle on 34th Street*, muttering about the gifts I'd received.

I could explore on my new bike anytime. And would.

In the years ahead, my world would expand again and again. I'd visit the guys I mentioned often, bouncing from house to house, yard to yard, neighborhood to neighborhood. When summer arrived, we'd ride to the dairy (sharing a Big Stick till it felt wrong to do so), cruise to Sav-On (for Sea Monkeys and monster models), or build ramps in the riverbed (jumping and laughing till Mrs. Noid screamed). When I outgrew the five-speed, I upgraded to ten, broadening my horizons even further. There were trips to Furman Park for Pickle, excursions to The Meralta for B-movies, and outings to Stonewood for loitering at the mall. As we got older, we visited Farrell's for ice cream,

House of Humor for 'stink bombs', Skate-O-Rama for girls. Downey offered twelve square miles of unsupervised adventure. And by the time we left for college, we'd explored every inch, each little voyage a step closer to adulthood.

But there'd be time for all that. Today was about family.

I rolled up our driveway and parked in the garage. Dad was indeed at the saw table—no gloves, no safety glasses—cussing over the racket. I waved and headed inside, where Mom put the Kirby away and Dennis devoured cookies. No one did what *Sing Along with Mitch* encouraged, but the iconic album was playing on the stereo, the house smelling of ham. "How was your ride, sweetheart?" Instead of answering, I hugged her, happy to be home and not wanting the hug, the feeling, or the day to ever end.

On Christmas and Thanksgiving, we ate at four o'clock sharp. That gave me time to watch football with my brother, shoot the breeze with Dad, and watch Mom make twice-baked potatoes. Holidays at the Capps house were low-key affairs. There was no hurrying off to Grandma's. No preparations for company. No friends dropping by with cutlets or Cold Duck.

It was just us. And that's how we liked it.

"Shannon?" Mom placed the last plate on the dining room table, a slab of cranberry sauce shaped like the can. She was wearing the scarf I bought her, a great find from the 99-cent bin at Gemco. As we all sat, Bing Crosby sang *White Christmas*, a heatless fire crackling in the hearth. I looked from face to face. Everything was perfect. We were together. Safe. About to break bread on the greatest holiday ever. "Would you like to say grace?"

The question took me aback. Prayers at Christmas dinner had always been Dennis' job, Mom bequeathing the honor years ago, Dad avoiding church like the IRS. I glanced at Dennis—he was already pissed about the bike; now he was seething—then back at Mom. Did this mean I was growing up? I quivered like the cranberry log in front of me, then turned to Dad, his expression saying, 'Make this quick!'

I brought my hands together and bowed. "Dear God, thank you for—"

A knock at the door stopped me.

When I looked up, Dad was staring back, his expression now saying, 'Answer the goddamn door!' I dropped my napkin and walked to the foyer, a quick peek through the eyehole revealing the caller. *Dear God, NO!* I couldn't move, waiting, hoping—*praying*—he'd go away. But the knock came again, louder this time. Out of options, I eased the door back. "Who is it, Shannon?" Mom called out.

The intruder barreled past. "Thaul Tannenbaum," he introduced himself, marching straight to the table. "I can only thtay for half-an-hour." My mother, God bless her, greeted Saul warmly, offering him a chair and plate. Dad and Dennis, after matching dirty looks, ignored him, attacking their food. And I, in 'dead man walking' fashion, made my way back over.

The 'half-an-hour' Saul promised turned to three. Over the course of his visit, he lectured us on the evils of ham, scratched one of my brother's records, dropped a piece of pie on the rug, and walked in on my dad showering. In the process, he talked nonstop, leaving traces of saliva everywhere.

When he finally left, it was pitch-black outside, and we all agreed...

Worst Christmas ever.

16

DORKS ON FILM

My best friend and I were dorks. I know this because Marcy McTavish said so, the rest of her third-grade posse agreeing. The assessment, if I'm forced to admit it, was accurate. But I prefer the term 'misunderstood'.

Arthur C. Fitch and I met in Kiddie Kollege, starting preschool on the same day. Although we looked nothing alike— he had straight, red hair, pallid skin, and the ears of Clark Gable; I had wavy, brown hair, olive skin, and the ears of a Russian doll —our lives were remarkably parallel. We were both born in '64. Our parents were the same age. And our brothers were seventeen years older. *Weird*, right? And there's more. Each of us could draw. Both spent hours writing short stories. And we were enamored with old movies.

How could a pair of dorks like this *not* be friends?

The friendship began when our mothers bumped into each other, years after sharing mutual adventures with their firstborn sons. If the older boys were friends, why not the younger? From that point on, Fitch and I spent untold hours together, most of them at his house. Going to the Fitches was like visiting another world. They had more new gadgets and cutting-edge electronics than anyone I knew (including Dad). As a result, we never left the house.

I take that back. We did venture out on one occasion. I'd gotten a new toy for my birthday, some sort of 'death wish' known as the Zippy Brick. It consisted of two long rubber bands, a set of handles, and a foam rectangle with a hole in it. The idea was to stand on opposite ends of the yard, pull your hands apart, and zip the brick across to your partner who would then zip it back in like fashion. After a good deal of coaxing, Fitch agreed to the outdoor activity, even seemed to be enjoying himself, till one of the bands broke and cracked him in the eye, scratching his cornea and sending him back inside forever (the first two weeks in sunglasses).

From that point on, our pursuits were 'roof-covered' only. We drew pictures of monsters, using felt-tip markers and colored pencils. We wrote stories together, our favorite character a kid named Irving Kumquat who, despite his 'dorkdom', was always the hero. I have yellowing copies of both, the drawings surprisingly decent, the writing not-surprisingly awful.

When our creative juices ebbed, we turned to our *favorite* activity—watching Our Gang and Three Stooges comedies on KBSC. After memorizing all the lines, we'd search the rest of UHF for Charlie Chaplin or Laurel & Hardy, mixing in equal parts of Buster Keaton, Abbott & Costello, and the Marx Brothers. Like two hungry wolf cubs, we couldn't get enough. And we weren't just watching. We were studying these films. How did the characters interact? What made the writing funny? Why was the timing crucial?

Dungeons & Dragons hadn't been invented yet. This is what dorks did in 1973.

And we didn't stop at comedies. Our love of cinema extended to all genres, from dramas and Hitchcock thrillers to Westerns, musicals, and horror. One minute, we'd be singing

Bless Yore Beautiful Hide from *Seven Brides for Seven Brothers*, the next frozen stiff as Bela Lugosi climbed from a coffin. Before long, it wasn't enough to merely view these films. We had to *collect* them! The VCR was still four years away, so we used our tape recorders to capture them on audio-cassette, hitting the *PAUSE* button for commercials and staying up till two a.m. for the credits. We recorded dozens of films this way, though I must admit, nothing was more tedious than listening to *Psycho* or *Brigadoon* on tape!

But that's what we did. Till we discovered Blackhawk Films.

The Davenport, Iowa company peddled vintage motion pictures on 8mm and Super 8, its catalog offering titles from Chaplin's *Easy Street* to Michael Landon's *I Was a Teenage Were-wolf*. We bought them all, every cent of our allowance converted to celluloid, every stamp in the house earmarked for mail orders. When the films arrived, months after we sent in for them, we held viewing parties on our twin Eumig projectors, Laurel & Hardy becoming more a part of our lives than our own big brothers.

And we didn't stop there.

For Show and Tell, we begged our teachers for more time, lugging our projectors to school for matinees of *Blockheads* or *Saps at Sea*, our bored viewers longing for the simpler pleasures of pet frogs and Skipper dolls. As we amassed more movies, we made more appearances, showing reels at Indian Guides meetings, Kiwanis Club gatherings, Ladies' Auxiliary luncheons. Along the way, we stockpiled memorabilia as well, buying vinyl soundtracks, hanging posters in our rooms, and collecting rubber masks.

After seeing Edgar Bergen and Charlie McCarthy in *You Can't Cheat an Honest Man*, we bought ventriloquist dolls, practicing with material so bad the dummies wouldn't laugh. On our birthdays, we visited Universal Studios, where Fitch corrected the tour guides. And on Halloween, we dressed as Stan and Ollie, our friends trick-or-treating without us.

At nine years old, we were addicted to film. But like *all* addicts, we needed more!

Steven Spielberg once said, "All good ideas start out as bad ideas." Well, we had a doozy! Instead of devoting our time to watching movies, why not *make* one? Spielberg produced his first film at seventeen, a year less than our combined ages. If he could do it, so could we.

We pooled our resources and bought a five-minute canister of film, then pounded out a script longer than *Spartacus*. It had to be scrapped, of course, the minute we remembered Dad's camera featured no audio. With pre-production going 'smoothly', we picked our location. The riverbed was perfect, requiring no sets and no lights. And since Fitch was already scheduled for a Friday night sleepover, we had our shoot date, too, which gave us a full day-and-a-half for production meetings.

In addition to dual roles as producer and actor, we agreed that I would direct and Fitch would assistant direct, sharing costume design, prop master, and cinematography duties. We soon realized, however, that most of the scenes involved both of us on screen, so we hired Mom (who was busy with the laundry) as director of photography. With time and money wasting, we rifled through wardrobe options, selecting a football jersey and helmet for my character, a rubber mask and hat for Fitch's. The premise of our film was simple. An injured football player finds himself in the middle of nowhere, where an evil ghoul (wearing a stylish derby with built-in hair) emerges from the shadows to kill him.

Not the worst idea ever pitched in Hollywood but right up there.

"What should we call it?" I asked, grabbing some butcher paper. In our haste to get started, we'd neglected a title. Fitch thought for a moment, then grabbed a Sharpie, scrawling *THE LOST FOOTBALL PLAYER* in black ink. Smiling, I added *MCMLXXIII* for credibility.

And we were ready to roll.

As luck would have it, Friday, April 13th was the windiest day in recorded history. We tried again and again to shoot our title sheet, the wind launching it every time. In desperation, I taped our poster to a cinderblock wall, then crouched beneath it, securing the corners with my fingers. Our DP (clearly still thinking about the 'spin cycle') shot the entire thing in wide angle, my hands—and arms—in frame.

"Cut," I hollered, moving the crew to our next location.

Without editing equipment, we were forced to shoot the film in sequence. We'd envisioned a high-angle establishing shot for the open, one that would define the starkness of the terrain and reinforce the isolation of our protagonist, the 'lost football play-er'. Exactly why he was lost, or how he got there, or what he was doing in full uniform in the middle of the desert was a mystery. But those details seemed trivial. *We were making a movie, dammit!* A movie, as it turns out, with no dolly, long lens, or crane. Which is why we opted for an eye-level medium shot instead, one that included not just a bad actor with a fake limp but power lines, houses, and a busy freeway a short walk away.

Scene two looked remarkably-similar to scene one. Mom moved three steps closer to film the same limp-hampered walk up the same path from the same angle. For reasons unknown, my character now clutched his left arm—the new injury went nicely with the limp—and began falling every step or two for effect. We had no idea what was wrong with this bloke, but one thing was certain. He was in trouble.

Enter the villain.

As we moved for the next shot, Fitch's hat-and-hair blew off, a harbinger of things to come. The wind had gotten stronger, and we could ill afford to wait it out (our cameraman needed to load the dryer). Moving her into position, I called for a rack focus, a shot that would highlight me in the foreground, then blur in favor of the dense thicket behind me. Having no idea what I was talking about, Mom opted for the now-familiar medium shot, Fitch, wearing a Lon Chaney mask and soon-to-be-soaring bowler, emerging from the weeds. Over the course of the eight-second scene, in which we introduce the villain with no explanation whatsoever, Fitch, as the ghoul, lost his hat 417 times.

And there were other problems.

The script called for a '*breathtaking chase*', where ghoul pursues football player '*like an animal*', then strangles him to death '*without mercy*'. It looked great on paper, but Fitch's lack of athleticism—remember, this was just his second trip outdoors, the first ending in blindness—posed a problem. No matter how slowly I ran, or limped, or stopped to nurse my wounds, my pursuer couldn't catch me. In his defense, Fitch couldn't see through the narrow eye-slits and was forced to run with one hand securing his hat.

Our dilemma led to a rewrite. The football player would have to trip—yet again—hitting his already-concussed head on a rock. The pratfall would not only steal his consciousness but give the unathletic ghoul time to catch up. Our new plot twist worked to perfection. As an out-of-breath Fitch dropped to one knee and began choking me, another gust of wind sent his hat spiraling, taking most of the drama with it.

With the emotionally-charged death scene behind us, we moved for the final shot. The one that would land us an Oscar. Enshrine our names between Kramer's and Kubrick's. Cement our footprints at Grauman's Chinese. Mom was to frame a close-up of my lifeless body, then pull to a dramatic low angle of the bloodthirsty killer. Once again, she opted for the lock-down medium, our villain, in blatant disregard of the 'fourth wall', trudging slowly toward camera.

"Cut!" I screamed from the dirt, feigning rigor mortis. As I leaped to my feet, Fitch's hat glanced off my forehead, cartwheeling into oblivion. Teeth filled with dust, I smiled at my costar. And he smiled back. "That's a wrap!"

We couldn't sleep that night, envisioning the blockbuster we'd captured and the accolades to follow. For the next two weeks, we called the photo lab every day—sometimes twice a day—getting the same annoyed clerk each time. "We'll call when it's ready."

When the film finally arrived (without a call, by the way), we couldn't wait to spool it on a projector. Fitch's house was closer, so we rushed there from Sav-On, killed the lights, and held our breaths. As the leader ran out, our homemade titles filled the screen, both producers cheering. Like proud parents, we watched our 'baby', praising every attribute, ignoring every flaw, including a twelve-second section with the lens cap still on. When the ghoul walked toward us (half his body off-screen), we cheered louder, rewinding the reel and watching it again and again.

"We need an audience!" Fitch proclaimed, grin wider than a CinemaScope production. I nodded in agreement, already imagining the reviews. We'd take it to school first. Then to The Meralta. Then to Venice or Cannes. We'd be the 'It Boys' in Hollywood, our names in lights, our stars on Sunset Boulevard.

"*One* showing," our exhausted teacher, Mrs. Moore, gave in. With half the class at recess, we turned off the lights and hit *PLAY*, the sound of churning sprockets filling the room. As our masterpiece flickered, our fellow third graders watched—even Marcy McTavish and her crew—riveted to the action on screen. Fitch and I glanced at each other. Who are the dorks *now*, Marcy?

When the last frame of film slipped onto the take-up reel, there was only silence.

Followed by the loudest burst of laughter in the history of cinema.

"Worst flick ever!" someone yelled, laughs multiplying to excruciating levels. When the lights came up, even Mrs. Moore was guffawing, our dreams of stardom lost in the fervor.

Years later, as our epic gathered dust in the back of my closet, I heard another quote from Spielberg, "Every time I go to a movie, it's *magic*, no matter what the movie's about."

Easy for you to say, 'Steve'.

You never saw *The Lost Football Player*.

17

KING OF THE ROAD

As a kid, I never visited Yellowstone, Mount Rushmore, or the Grand Canyon. There's a reason for this. Dad got two weeks of vacation every year. And we spent it in Oklahoma.

Like 'Old Faithful', the alarm would sound at four a.m., my parents already dressed, Dennis and I stumbling from bed in a drool-soaked malaise. That's how every trip began, Dad insisting on the early start, Mom backing him. Why we endured this painful ritual year after year is beyond me. It took twenty-one hours to drive from California to the 'Sooner State', the journey lasting two full days. Did it really matter *when* we left?

By the time we reached the freeway, a mere five minutes away, Dennis was always snoring. I, on the other hand, was too excited to sleep, despite having memorized the entire road ahead. We'd take the 5 to the 605 to the 10 to the 15, all under cloak of darkness, reaching I-40 in Barstow by sunrise. Long before *I* joined the clan, Dad took a labyrinth of surface streets to Route 66, where he, Mom, and Dennis '*got their kicks*' for the next 1,338 miles. The four-lane Interstate replaced the two-lane 'Mother Road' in '57, shaving hours off the trip—and killing dozens of small towns in the process. But economic hardship meant little to me.

I just wanted moccasins!

Ads for the Native American footwear began appearing the second we rolled into Arizona. Every hundred feet or so—at least it seemed that way—a giant billboard tantalized travelers with *DEERSKIN SLIPPERS*, *INDIAN HEADDRESSES*, and *TURQUOISE JEWELRY*. In addition, signs beckoned drivers to roadside attractions like *PETRIFIED FORESTS* and *METEOR CRATERS*. It all sounded fantastic to me! But Dad never stopped —"We need to make good time!" Mom made promises—"We'll do it on the way back." And Dennis slept like a corpse.

I don't know how *anyone* could sleep in that rolling oven! We vacationed in August, which meant triple-digit temps, hellish winds, and asphalt so hot my Keds would melt. In the early years, we did it without air-conditioning—every time my brother stopped snoring, I assumed he was dead—later with AC that died every time we climbed a hill. But unbearable as it was, heat wasn't the worst condition we endured.

Dad carried exactly two 8-track tapes in the car—Boots Randolph's *Yakety Sax* and Roger Miller's *Golden Hits*. They played, one after the other, in a torturous loop, song after song, mile after mile. Most people think of Benny Hill when they hear the title track of *Yakety Sax*. I think of barrel cacti. And though *King of the Road* was the perfect soundtrack, I favored *Dang Me* with its chorus, '*Dang me, dang me, they oughta take a rope and hang me,*' which is what we all longed for by the time we reached New Mexico.

From the moment I could speak to the last trip we ever took, I begged my father to stay at a Wigwam Motel. Is there anything cooler than sleeping in a concrete teepee? Even my brother (who decided he was too old for family trips in '74, and thus became the vacation equivalent of Chuck on *Happy Days*) would chime in between snores. But Dad had one criteria for lodging—price. And he'd drive fifty miles to the next town if he thought he could save two bucks on a room. For this reason, we were guaranteed a miserable night's sleep in a tumbledown motor lodge with buzzing neon and taco-shaped beds. "It's all the same when the lights are out," he'd argue.

It wasn't.

Day two featured the same call time as day one. As the motel alarm clock sounded, Dad would pack our bags while Mom folded towels. After Dennis began skipping our yearly trips, I'd roll out of bed alone, dazed and amazed that we hadn't been murdered! By the time I shook the cobwebs, there was no chance in hell (aka the New Mexico desert) that we'd be stopping for breakfast. "Not if we want to make Guthrie by dinner," Dad would point out. *I* should point out that 'dinner' in Oklahoma means lunch. And 'supper' means dinner. It's confusing as hell, but the food's so good, nobody cares!

As Boots played *Cacklin' Sax* for the eighty-fifth time, I watched signs for *ALBUQUERQUE*, *SANTA ROSA*, and *TUCUMCARI* fly by, half-asleep till we rolled into Texas. At nine a.m., the scorching 'panhandle' was already hotter than the 'pan', the back of my legs welded to our Naugahyde seats. But we were closing in on our goal, Amarillo a stone's throw from Oklahoma. It would've been nice, just once, to stop at The Big Texan, the iconic restaurant that offers a free seventy-two-ounce steak to anyone who can finish it in an hour. But like the moccasins, it would remain a dream. As a side note, I truly believe Dad could've done it. Having grown up poor, he learned to eat huge quantities of food (like a chipmunk packing nuts) when the opportunity presented itself. More than once, I saw him raze a T-bone down to the marrow, leaving the plate dishwasher clean.

But, alas, we'll never know.

Signs for *OKLAHOMA* were gratuitous, the soil turning

brick-red the second we crossed state lines. With *Do Wacka Do* playing, we couldn't help but smile, our destination just three hours away! Arriving at my aunt's house was a triumphant moment. There were hugs all around, queries about the trip, and references to my height. "He's grown a *foot* since last summer!" Uncle Otis would wager, Mom feigning shock as she headed off with Aunt Clara, a slightly-twangier version of herself. Ten minutes later, we'd be eating the best mid-day meal of our lives—chicken-fried steak, mashed potatoes and gravy, corn on the cob, and hot-out-of-the-oven biscuits. If that wasn't enough, there was sliced cantaloupe and watermelon, followed by peach cobbler, still warm in the middle and smothered in ice cream. We ate till our arteries clogged, then did it again four hours later.

God, it was beautiful!

But as great as the food was, and trust me, all six of Mom's sisters could cook, the best part of vacation was hanging with my cousins. Odell and Rowan, born two years and poles apart— Odell was dark-haired and favored Aunt Clara; Rowan was blonde and looked like his dad—were considerably older than their California counterpart. But they took me under their wings, probably by mandate. The second we finished dinner, we'd bolt to the yard for multiple games of Wiffle Ball. If you've never experienced August in Oklahoma (ninety degree temps with ninety percent humidity), imagine jogging through Hedes in a wool overcoat. Dripping with sweat, we'd head to the pasture for 'real' baseball next, my uncle having laid out bases between dollops of cow shit. The bovine mines made base running difficult, as did the occasional pissed-off bull, but stepping in dung was a small price to pay.

We were having the time of our lives!

In addition to 'America's pastime', we spent hours riding my cousins' minibike. With three speeds, all slow, we carved donuts in the drive, traversed jumps, and invented motorized games, our favorite 'Death Race '74', where one lucky rider—usually me —had to navigate the pasture while the others threw cow chips at him. *One* point was awarded for hitting the bike, *two* for the rider, *three* if the pie left a mark, and *four* if you downed the pilot altogether. By the time Aunt Clara rang the supper bell, we were covered—again, mostly me—in dirt, sweat, and shit.

After long, hot showers, we'd retire for the night. Because Odell had seniority, I shared a bed with Rowan who not only made fun of my name but threatened me with violence if I crossed the 'line of demarcation'. We always slept with the window open, thunder rumbling in the distance, breeze carrying the smell of sugar-sweet hay. For me, that smell *is* Oklahoma, and when I catch the scent today, I'm transported back there, to those carefree days and summer nights. And to the feeling of having your whole life in front of you.

Of course, it wasn't all fun and games. Part of the reason we visited in August was to help Uncle Otis on the farm. In addition to the pasture, he owned several acres in nearby Coyle, where he ran more cattle and harvested hay. The annual crop had to be baled, picked up, and hauled to the barn for storage, an all-hands-on-deck endeavor. Early on, I was too young to lift the bales, so my uncle let me drive, a huge thrill for a ten-year-old! With feet barely touching pedals, I snaked the old Chevy through an obstacle course of hay, the others loading the truck and watching for rattlers. We killed a *lot* of them on the farm, my uncle always cutting the rattle off for me.

If Arthur C. Fitch's house was 'another world', Oklahoma was another *universe*!

When the work was done, my cousins and I headed to the pond to fish. Or shot targets with our .22s. Or hiked down to the Cimarron for an afternoon swim. The muddy waters were a cool respite from the unflagging heat, but the snapping turtles and water moccasins made leisurely dips impossible. That said, our romps in the river are among my favorite summertime memories, one in particular.

I experienced my first 'girlie mag' on the Cimarron. Odell had swiped it from a buddy, he and Rowan deeming me old enough, at ten, to handle the images. And handle them, I did. Not since Emily Wexler's Uncle Wiggily routine had I felt so 'funny', my cousins barely able to pry the journal—if memory serves, it was called *Boobs*—from my hands. We stuffed it under a bush when Uncle Otis called, hoping for another gander the next day. But an overnight storm thwarted our plans, the thing saturated when we found it. Not the first time pages like *these* had been stuck together!

Over the course of our two-week furlough, we visited all Mom's siblings, from her oldest sister, Vinita, who let me gather eggs from the chicken coop, to her youngest brother, Dick, who hated me for calling him a "funny lookin' cowboy". We also stopped by the 'home place', the house where Mom grew up and her sister, Fran, still lived. Aunt Fran made the best cinnamon rolls on Earth, Cinnabon a sad imitation. After serving us a hot plate, she could get Dad to do just about anything—repair a fence, fix a pipe, even paint (a task he loathed).

For his hard work, Mom awarded him a quick visit to Missouri. Four of his five brothers still lived there, most around the little town of Moundville (population 147). My 'Show Me State' cousins were all female, but they could fish, ride motorcycles, and play ball with the best of them. And we did it all while our dads worked on cars, talked about people we didn't know, and drank Falstaff. The beer, along with everything else they consumed, came from Ashbaugh's, a little store in town straight out of *The Waltons*. Five or six times a day, we'd head there for Grape Nehis, Atomic Fireballs, or Mallo Cups, which explains why I ate so little dinner.

Ironically, Dad ate even less. Not because he was full of junk food, but because year after year, his own family forgot—or ignored—his aversion to chicken. Without fail, the hated poultry was the star of every meal, whether prepared by a sister-in-law or ordered at a restaurant. I can still see Dad's face as he dined on green beans, the rest of us wolfing down drumsticks at Chicken Annie's or Chicken Mary's.

But his 'fowl cause celebre' led to one of my favorite vacation moments. In a fit of hunger—and some say rage—Dad pulled into a Sonic Drive-In on our way out of town. "Three foot-long Coneys, three Pepsis," he ordered, voice muffled by a growling stomach. When the food arrived via roller-skate, he couldn't wait to dig in. But in his famine-fed haste, he failed to get a grip, the dog collapsing on his dubious first bite. "God-*dammit!*" Chili now blanketing his last clean shirt, he fired the Pepsi 'through' the window, forgetting it was closed. As cola and ice careened off the glass, joining the chili on his chest, arms, and lap, he turned to his wife and son. Mom snickered first...then me...then Dad, the three of us howling like halfwits for the next half-hour.

With time winding down, we'd stop at Aunt Clara's on the way home, Mom needing more hugs, Dad needing a chickenless meal. "Don't forget to write," the sisters would speak in unison, my cousins and I sharing no such intent. After one last helping of cobbler, we were off, first to the gas station, then to visit Mom's parents in the cemetery. Those visits, over time, grew to include not just Grandmother and Grandfather but Aunt Vinita, Uncle Verl, Aunt Fran, and Uncle LaRue, our flower bill growing exponentially. While we sat there, Mom would talk to her folks and every departed sibling, just like they were sitting next to us, Dad giving her as much time as she needed. Oddly enough, no matter how hot it was, a breeze always stirred the dogwoods, cooling our sweat and caressing our skin.

An hour later, we were back on I-40, Boots Randolph's *Lonely*

Street matching our mood. The ride home was never like the ride there. All the excitement was gone, replaced by thoughts of work, school, and stuff we had to do. As a result, Roger Miller's lyrics were a bit less peppy, the unfolding scenery a lot less interesting. Forgettable as these drives were, however, one stood out above all others.

I was thirteen at the time, a bored teenager on the cusp of entering high school. Five hours from home, Dad pulled off the Interstate, rolling to a stop at The Last Indian Trading Post. I glanced up from a magazine—which, for the record, was not *Boobs*—Mom and Dad grinning at me. "What?" I responded in typical teen timbre.

"Time to get those moccasins," my father announced. I looked from one to the other, then out the window. The store was on 'life support', a ramshackle reminder of far better days. I hadn't thought about moccasins in years, my fashion yens in '78 leaning more toward Brittania jeans. But how could I pass this up?

We made our way inside, past a wooden chief and a case of Thunderbird rings, the shoe section in back. On the way there, I found myself getting excited, no easy task for thirteen-year-old me, an apathetic, acne-ridden ass-bite who rarely appreciated anything. But let's face it, dreams are dreams, whether you've outgrown them or not. And *my* dream, for the better part of thirteen years, was to own a pair of *GENUINE HANDMADE INDIAN MOCCASINS*.

"Help ya?" a spiritless (white) clerk spoke up.

"Our son would like moccasins," Mom responded, she and Dad smiling at each other. I moved to the wall, scanning my options, eyes zeroing in on a pair of knee-high, buckskin beauties. They were the ones I'd pictured in my daydreams. Visualized in desert miasmas. Fantasized about from the age of two on.

"These," I uttered, stomach fluttering. As the man measured

my foot, memories abounded. My brother's snoring. The car breaking down near Gallup. Thunder rolling over a distant mesa. Through it all, I dreamed of *this* moment. Of *these* moccasins!

The clerk walked to the back room. And returned a minute later.

"We're out of your size."

18

FOR WHOM THE BELL TOLLS

Our doorbell rang often. In the days before Amazon Prime, neighbors dropped in for sugar, friends swung by to borrow tools, and salesmen pedaled the latest in vacuum technology. So when I heard the familiar *DING*, I barely looked up from my Hot Wheels.

I should've run for my life.

"Good evening, sir," I heard a voice from the porch. The man's tone was confident—*too* confident. He was selling something, that was for sure. But he'd already made a crucial error. He was introducing himself to my father, a man who'd worked a ten-hour day at the plant and who didn't suffer fools when all he wanted to do was sit in his chair and read the paper.

There was an awkward pause, the kind that came right before Dad got angry. I'd seen him threaten census takers, bark at Fuller Brush men, slam the door on Jehovah's Witnesses. I tossed my cars aside and waited.

This was going to be good.

"'Where words leave off, music begins'," the man quoted. My father stared, air thicker than creamed hamburger. "Heinrich Heine," he added, causing me to wince. The poor guy had no way of knowing Dad fought in World War II. Quoting a German guy was a terrible overture! "May I have ten minutes of your time?" I began to tremble, Dad's eyes moving from the man's face to the case he was carrying. I pictured both being tossed to the curb. But that's not what happened. My father eased the door back and motioned him in.

With a pronounced goosestep, 'Heinrich' strode into the room, smiling at me when he passed. As Dad told him to sit, Mom entered from the kitchen, everyone staring at his huge, leather case. It looked even bigger up close and far too heavy to tote from house to house.

"What *is* that?" Mom broke the ice, wiping her hands on a towel. The man smiled again, lowering himself to the sofa. He was thirty-something with stringy hair and specs that warped his eyeballs. His tweed coat looked like a thrift shop purchase. And his tie clipped at the neck.

"I'm glad you asked, madam." He lined up the case, then reached down to disengage the clasps. Mom sat in the rocking chair. Dad straddled the ottoman.

I, for reasons unknown, kept my distance.

He opened the lid, the smell of new car and musty closet filling the room, the vim palpable. With conviction, he reached inside, wrestling something from its confines, the thing groaning as he shoved both arms through the straps. When he pulled back, light struck the keys—forty-one of them arranged like a vertical piano, on the other side 120 buttons at the ready.

I'd seen an accordion before. Myron Floren played one on *The Lawrence Welk Show*. We watched every Saturday, Dad enjoying the Big Band numbers, Mom loving the dance routines. But I'd never seen one up close. The thing was beautiful, the keys, buttons, and knobs shining like polished marble.

"May I?" he asked, one eyebrow arched. When Dad nodded, he broke into a raucous (and surprisingly loud) version of *Beer*

Barrel Polka. How he tamed the savage beast was beyond me, but I was mesmerized! We all were.

After a crescendo that rattled Mom's china, he spoke again. "In six short months, your son..." *Uh-oh!* "...will be playing better than I am." They all turned to look at me, my collar constricting. I had to say something—*anything*—but I just sat there, tongue anesthetized.

"He's been asking for music lessons," my father responded.

Guitar lessons, Dad. *Guitar!*

"Well, this is his lucky day!" I didn't feel 'lucky'. The man continued to stare, patting the seat next to him. I looked to Mom in desperation—she smiled like a well-fed cat—then to Dad who cut his eyes to the couch.

Like a condemned man, I moved to the sofa, the 'executioner' transferring the instrument to my lap. After helping me with the straps, he forced my hands through the holds, placing my fingers on the buttons and keys. I looked to Mom and Dad, begging for mitigation. None came.

"Play!" Dad ordered, my face prickling with unseen needles. How had I gotten here? I was minding my own business, dammit! Just playing with cars and—

"Go ahead, son..." The man clapped me on the back. "...take her for a 'test drive'."

I looked at the thing, sweat pooling in every declivity. As I moved, it wheezed like a dying animal. Having received no instruction of any kind, I pressed the buttons and keys, widening my hands like Myron Floren. The result was a chorus of demons, Dad wincing, Mom looking to the carpet in shame.

"I knew it!" The salesman reached for a contract. "He's a natural."

Ten minutes later, I was signed up for lessons, my own accordion delivered the next day. When the thing arrived, we all gathered round. It wasn't as large as the salesman's, nor as shiny, and there were far fewer buttons and keys. But that didn't stop Mom from snapping an entire roll of pictures and requesting a concert. As I pulled, pushed, prodded—and butchered every note—she puffed with pride. "I'm going to watch you on TV someday. I just *know* it!"

Not if I could help it.

I'd told no one about this. The kids at school would crucify me! Hell, even the teachers would make me the butt of jokes. My plan was simple—report to my weekly lesson, say nothing to the instructor, and perform my Lawrence Welkian duties as quickly and painlessly as possible. Dad was on the hook for six months of lessons. I prayed that would be enough.

Two days later, we arrived at a blank storefront on Paramount Boulevard, doctor's office to the left, butcher shop on the right. I couldn't believe my eyes. There were at least ten other 'victims' waiting outside, each with a case identical to mine. "This is going to be lovely," Mom purred.

'Lovely', my ass! I was walking into hell.

After wrangling my accordion from the back seat, I moved up the sidewalk, taking my place in line. No one was smiling, not even the kid in front. It felt like Vaccine Day at school. When the door opened, a stream of older kids filtered out, each carrying the now-familiar case, all lifeless.

This was bad.

We moved inside, sheep on the way to mutton, our glazed eyes adjusting to the lights. Twelve chairs waited in the middle of the room, a frowning semicircle, more than twice that lining the walls. I'd assumed these were *private* lessons, held in a soundproof room, with no one to hear but the guy Dad was paying. As we took our seats, parents filing in behind us, a new reality struck me. I was learning the accordion with an audience!

"Velcome, students." A humpbacked man with a Prussian accent entered from the rear, looking like a constipated Albert

Einstein. I felt my bowels stir. "Open ze cases," he ordered. We did, hinges squeaking, parents murmuring. "Mount ze instruments." I half-expected a smartass comment, but the room fell silent, each of us grappling with our newfound burdens.

The man grabbed his own, a black Crucianelli with mother-of-pearl accents. "Middle C." He placed his finger on one of the keys, the rest of us following suit. "Unclip ze bellows." We followed instructions, moans rising from our laps like expulsions of gas. "And play." He widened his hands, the rest of us trying to mimic him. The chorus of middle Cs (and Ds) that followed was deafening. I wanted to weep.

Over the next sixty minutes, Mr. Fratzke—his name was scrawled on the chalkboard—demonstrated methods and reviewed techniques, our accordions braying like mules. I glanced at my mother. She was beaming! And so were the other parents. Apparently, Mom wasn't the only one envisioning her child on Welk's payroll.

When the man lowered his instrument at five o'clock sharp, I was sweaty and spent. The accordion had proven every bit as difficult as it looked. And I knew, even then, with one lesson down and twenty-five to go, that I'd never master it.

Over the next few weeks, I did my best to practice but quickly lost interest. Spring had arrived, and with it baseball. When I had to choose between playing scales and playing ball, the choice was obvious. As a result, my baseball skills improved considerably, my 'bass and treble' skills not so much. Over time, I ignored the thing more and more, finding every excuse possible to avoid it between lessons and eventually shoving it in the closet.

I would soon pay the price.

Calling Mr. Fratzke 'patient' was a stretch, 'understanding' an even bigger one. He'd taught the accordion for twenty-eight years and appeared to hate every minute of it. But who could blame him? We were *all* terrible. And I was the worst of the worst. By week seven, we'd learned a few basic tunes, nothing to be proud of, but at least we could match notes with chords. At the end of class, 'Herr Fratzke' assigned a new number (*Donkey Train* the ironic title), then made several announcements, all of which I ignored. Just glad to have survived another lesson, I stuffed the music in my case and bolted for the door.

When I returned the following week, the place was packed. Parents and grandparents filled every seat, surrounded by siblings, neighbors, and friends, another row of chairs added to accommodate the crowd. Mom had dropped me off on her way to the market, having apparently lost interest herself. "Sank you for attending ze recital," Mr. Fratzke augured.

Did someone say 'recital'?

"Ve vill now play de assigned piece..." He glared at me. "Vun by vun."

Oh, God!

The concert started—mercifully—at the other end of the arc, a pie-faced girl with fresh-cut bangs offering a flawless rendition. Applause followed, accompanied by flashbulbs. The next kid was possessed by Myron Floren himself, his version of *Donkey Train* a pitch-perfect polka. More applause. Someone yelled, "Bravo!"

As each little protégé performed like a maestro, my organs shut down 'vun by vun'. I hadn't practiced. Hadn't studied the music. Hadn't even—

"Ve've saved de best for last..." Fratzke glared at me again. Apparently, he'd noticed how seldom I practiced, how shitty I played, and how little I cared about the fucking accordion. "Mr. Capps..." Hearing my name was like sitting on an icepick. "Begin ven ready."

He and I both knew I'd *never* be.

I cleared my throat. Adjusted the music. Cleared my throat

again. How long could I stall? The overhead lights buzzed like dental drills. The clock ticked unmercifully. I glanced at the door—no Mom to save me—then back at Fratzke.

The bastard was *smiling*!

Determination suddenly replaced fear. I wanted nothing more than to beat this man at his own game. To embarrass *him*! As I leaned forward, my accordion wheezed, someone in the gallery chuckling. I found middle C, fingering the corresponding chord button. I could do this, I told myself. I *would* do it! After a deep breath, I began. C. D. *F-sharp.*

Dammit!

I looked up, Fratzke's smile widening.

I started again. C. D. *F-sharp.*

It was A-flat, goddammit! *A-flat!* The crowd began to stir, the kid next to me sighing. I tried again...and again...and again, the audience growing restless. My brain said A-flat, but my fingers ignored it. Another attempt, another *F-sharp.* I glanced at the clock, its hands past five, the next class pressed to the window and ogling. *Focus*, I begged myself, starting again. C. D. *F-sharp.* A man in a vest shook his head in disgust. A woman in a poncho scowled.

What I wouldn't give to be on a ballfield somewhere! To be *anywhere* but here!

"Dat vill do!" Fratzke stopped me. "Zese people have lives to get back to."

I hung my head in shame, *my* life seemingly-over.

Minutes later, after parting a 'Red Sea' of stares, I met Mom at the curb, the case heavier than ever. "What's wrong?" she questioned, feeling my forehead. "Do you have a fever?"

I shook my head, tears welling as we drove off. With great effort, I recounted the story, hyperventilating as I described Fratzke's smile, blubbering as I recalled the angry mob. In my mind, they had torches and pitchforks. When we made it home,

Dad was halfway through *The Signal*. I dropped the case and fell to my knees. "I'll do my chores for free...double them if you want...*triple* them!" He continued to read, face hidden behind a Red Devil fireworks ad. "Hell, I'll even go to church with no complaints!"

"Don't say 'hell'," Mom interjected.

"Please..." I begged, all shreds of dignity left at Fratzke's feet. "...*please* let me quit the accordion!"

Dad offered one of his famous pauses. I was sure I was going to puke. After what felt like hours, he curled the newspaper down and looked at me—"Sure thing, bud"—then went back to the funnies.

A smile sliced through my tomato-like face. It widened to a grin, then morphed to a laugh, my parents soon joining me. It was over. *Over!*

When the letter arrived, no one was laughing. We'd failed to read the contract in its entirety, page eight delivering the 'death knell'! Though one could cancel lessons at any time, the signee was liable for the entire cost of the instrument. And that little squeezebox cost 750 bucks! Translation? At three-and-a-half percent interest, my dad would be making ten-dollar payments for the next eighty-four months.

I kept my distance for a while, performing household duties without prompting, even picking up dog shit in the back yard. Over the next year, my allowance went missing, but I didn't dare ask for it. And my accordion case became an overpriced night-stand, Mom draping it with a doily to insure anonymity.

Things slowly and steadily returned to normal at the Capps house. But we never watched *Lawrence Welk* again. My dad had lost his taste for polka music.

We all had.

19

ABOUT THE BENJAMINS

By 1975, the Vietnam War had ended. Nixon had resigned. And I needed money.

I wasn't in debt or anything. But as kids get older, they want more stuff. Like records from Licorice Pizza, trips to Disneyland with delinquent friends, my own bowling ball, dammit! After the accordion debacle, I couldn't exactly ask my parents for cash.

I needed a job.

It took all of a day to learn that no one was hiring eleven-year-olds. Neighbors wouldn't even let me cut their lawns— "Why do you think *we* had kids!" I needed a shift in strategy. Since no one would hire me, why not start my own business? A lemonade stand failed miserably (not a great idea in January, even in soCal) as did my dog-walking service (three of the damn things bit me). I even tried selling my Irving Kumquat stories door to door, the first of many times I'd be rejected as a writer. Battered and beaten, I was ready to throw in the towel.

Then I met Guy (pronounced 'Gee') LeBlanc.

The young Canadian who not only looked like but dressed like Jack LaLanne (down to the polyester jumpsuit) had just transferred to Price from a school in Montreal. He spoke with a French accent, had no friends, and owned the biggest collection of Wacky Packs I'd ever seen. For those too young to remember, Wacky Packages were collectible stickers satirizing all kinds of everyday products, from 'Crust' toothpaste and 'Choke Wagon' dogfood to 'Yicks' cough drops and 'Cap'n Crud' cereal. At the height of their popularity—about the time I met 'Gee'—they outsold baseball cards. And every kid I knew, boys and girls alike, simply had to have them!

Two things became instantly-clear. 'Gee' needed friends. And I needed those stickers!

"Welcome to California, Guy!" I introduced myself.

"It's pronounced—"

"Are those *first* series?" I interrupted, envisioning the partnership we'd form, followed by its immediate dissolution. Not only did 'Gee' have the coveted first series but the second, third, and fourth. No kid in Downey, myself included, had *any* card prior to the fifth.

I was staring at the 'Lost Dutchman'...in polyester, of course.

"I'm not—"

I yanked him from the crowd, the naïve Canadian, in a bid to win friends, already giving cards away. "Ever watch *Let's Make a Deal*?" He shook his head. "This Monty Hall guy, see? He offers people cash for stuff they've won." 'Gee' looked more confused than ever. Time to go for the kill. "Put those cards away, and I'll come by after school with a five-dollar bill. You give me the stickers. I'll give you the money. We can even hang out for a bit." Before he could think, I shook his hand, the deal done.

On the way to 'Gee's', I calculated a Business Plan, from an Executive Summary (*'I'll sell Wacky Packs to make money'*) to a Competitive Analysis (*'With 'Gee' gone, there'll be no competition'*) to a Sales Strategy (*'I'll sell to addicted collectors at inflated prices'*).

Based on market research—as 'Gee' handed out cards, our class-mates foamed at the mouth—I'd turn five dollars into hundreds!

"Thanks, Guy!" I called over my shoulder, having spent exactly two minutes with him.

"But I thought—"

"No time to play," I cut him off. "I've got a business to run!"

In stores, the stickers sold for five-cents-a-pack, each pack containing two cards and a stick of gum. But *my* cards were out-of-print and available nowhere else, so setting the price was up to me. I knew most kids brought fifty cents to school for lunch. If I charged a quarter for two, half-a-dollar for five, I could nab most, if not all, of their lunch money. What did I care if they went hungry? This was capitalism!

I set up shop near the Gingko tree at recess, luring my first customer in with a flash of 'Cover Ghoul' mascara. In seconds, I had a run on the bank to rival George Bailey's Building & Loan, my classmates showering me with cash. By lunch, I was already out of product, my take more than twenty bucks!

In two hours, I'd quadrupled my investment. But with no more inventory—and no more 'Gees'—I had nothing left to sell. I thought about mining the complete sets I'd put aside, but the collector in me said no. Someday they'd be worth a fortune!

"How was your day, bud?" I looked up from the cash on my bed, Dad standing in the doorway. "Helluva lot better than mine, I see!" He reached in his pocket, fumbling for something. "Picked you up one of those Wacky deals today." He tossed me a pack, turning to leave.

"Dad, *wait*..." I stared at the yellow wrapper—the current packages were blue—ripping it open to reveal two never-before-seen stickers. "...this is *eleventh* series!" I might as well have been speaking Russian. "Where did you get these?"

"Trigg's Market in Commerce. I stopped—"

"We need to go there *now*!" I leaped to my feet, shoving coins in my pockets. With the increased demand, Topps had stepped up production, introducing new sets every month or so. I'd checked Don's Market on my way home from school, but the shelves were empty.

"Mom's got a roast—"

"You don't understand," I screeched, waving the new stickers at him. "It's a matter of life and death!" Yes, I was exaggerating, but if I could get there before anyone else...

I was back in business!

The new cards, as projected, generated more fervor than ever. After building my own set, I sold the doubles for huge profits, my bottom line fatter than the guy on 'Bigtumi' spaghetti sauce. Not only could I afford my own bowling ball now, I could rent the entire alley!

A month later, Topps introduced the twelfth series, the cards arriving at Trigg's two weeks before Don's. Plenty of time to exploit my clients. Those clients, after all, had become mindless junkies, hooked on Wacky Packs and willing to spend every nickel for another fix.

It wasn't hard to figure out who the neighborhood 'dealer' was. He was the guy with new Nikes, a sweet puka-shell necklace, and bell-bottoms wider than basketball hoops. I walked the halls with confidence now. And bulging pockets. But I was only *one* man! And the demands of running a business, in conjunction with doing my chores, perfecting the hook shot, and finishing my homework before midnight, were taking a toll.

The solution was obvious. I needed help.

With the extra capital, I hired longtime pals, Benny Sherman and Norbert Barker (who went by 'Bert now), at base salary plus commission. They'd service my existing customers, freeing me up to streamline the supply chain and explore new markets. The plan worked to perfection, 'Cappy's Wackys' soon providing cards to the entire school!

By the time the thirteenth series arrived, I was 'shitting in high clover', to borrow a phrase from Dad. Not only had I purchased every gag item at House of Humor, but my album collection had doubled, and I was a regular at 'The Happiest Place on Earth', at least till my friends and I were banned for having the names *EATME*, *SUCKME*, and *FUCKME* embroidered on our Mouse hats.

In school, I bought everything on the Scholastic Book Order Form, even the Judy Blume offerings, and signed up for another Summer Movie Series at The Meralta, featuring such awful titles as *Benji*, *Herbie Rides Again*, and *Digby, The Biggest Dog in the World*. My friends and I had no interest in the films, but the events—God knows who hatched this brilliant idea?—were epic. When the lights dimmed, the ensuing free-for-alls featured flying Jujubes, farting contests, and fistfights, the theater a freakin' war zone! It was dangerous, yes, but incredibly entertaining, along with a nice break from the heat.

As was bowling.

With profits from the fourteenth series, I bought a shiny, blue bowling ball with my name etched in gold. My salesmen were doing well enough to buy balls of their own, so every day after 'work', we'd head to Del Rio Lanes, bags bungeed to bike racks. At thirty-five-cents a game, another thirty-five for shoes, we'd blow off steam from a long day of sales, guzzling Cokes and inhaling enough smoke to land us in the Schick Center. Life was good! And we laughed like imbeciles every time Benny hit the *RESET* button, and 'Bert's ball slammed into the pin-sweeper.

But my kingdom, unbeknownst to me, was about to crumble.

As the fifteenth series landed at Trigg's and demand for Wackys reached an all-time high, I planned an unabashed blitzkrieg. Pooling my hard-earned profits, I cleaned out their inventory, hired more salespeople, and raised prices to unseen levels.

After *this* haul, I told myself, 'Cappy's Wackys' could go public!

But trouble was brewing. Not only were Benny and 'Bert threatening to unionize, but our teachers began a united assault on free enterprise, holding secret meetings to discuss my pursuits—"He's turned this school into a Turkish marketplace!" —and demanding action from the principal.

At the same time, I grew careless. I'd always managed to find trouble, but the 'golden calf' I'd raised led me to more. With salesmen shouldering the load, I found time at recess to tape *KICK ME* signs on Glen Torkle's back, organize games of dodge-ball, where crotch shots were legal, and force Henry Hashimoto to "go long" on every pass, never once tossing him the football. These acts and more—my sales force was accused of strong-arming first graders for tips—landed me in Phelps' office, where in the midst of the blitzkrieg, he sliced me at the knees.

"No more selling Wacky Packs, Shannon."

"What?" The room spun like a Battling Top. "But you can't do this!" He reached for his budget reports. "I've got a corpora-tion to run! Payroll to meet!" I slammed my fist against the desk. "My employees have *families*, dammit!"

Phelps shot me a threatening look. "If I were in your shoes..." He glanced at my Nikes, the now-famous 'swoosh' logo still a curiosity. "...I'd get back to class."

And just like that, it was over. No Chapter II reorganization. No controlled liquidation of assets. No restructuring of business affairs. 'Cappy's Wackys' was dead.

Over the next two weeks, I auctioned off puka-shells, fenced Disneyland tickets, and sold doubles for pennies to kids on my street. When the sixteenth and final series came out, I didn't even go to Trigg's. I waited, like everyone else, for Don's Market to stock them, buying only enough to build my own set, then retiring from the game forever.

Mr. Phelps' actions, as much as I hate to admit it, were warranted. I'd gotten 'too big for my damn britches', to borrow another Dad phrase. School was a place for learning, not for making my first million. That being said, I still managed, even with a hostile shutdown, to walk away with a new bowling ball and sixteen sets of Wacky Packages, organized in binders and waiting for the day their values would peak.

That day came in 1989. I'd just finished a two-year stint at the CBS affiliate in Ardmore, Oklahoma, where as a news reporter, I'd grossed a cool $5.75 an hour. Needless to say, with my income stream dammed and future uncertain, I found myself needing money again. After selling most of my worldly goods, I remembered the Wacky Packs. Their values, like every other collectible at the time, had skyrocketed, single stickers selling for ten bucks a piece, sets for hundreds! I just had to find them.

Hopping in the car, I made the drive to Guthrie, my parents having moved there two years earlier. Dad and I scoured the house, looking for the box I'd seen in the moving van, the one with *WACKYS* scrawled on the side. Never one to give up, he grabbed a ladder, remembering some items he'd placed in the attic. When I poked my head through the scuttle hole, it nearly combusted, the air hotter than a convection oven's. Eyes bulging, I searched the crawl space, shoving a bag aside to reveal the box. The ink had bled, forming a massive 'bloodstain', but there was no mistaking it...I'd found what I was looking for.

Covered in sweat, I struggled down the ladder, placing the box on the kitchen table. As I peeled back the flaps, my heart raced. Not only had I located a tremendous source of income— the sets would net me at least two-grand—but I was about to revisit a wistful chapter of youth.

As Dad wandered off, I grabbed the first notebook and peeled back the cover. To my horror, the plastic sheets had melted, turning my once-valuable first series into a warped slab of gunk. I grabbed the next one—*more* gunk—the plastic hot and sticky, the artwork unrecognizable. Slowly and painfully, I checked all sixteen binders. But the results were the same. My entire collection was ruined.

Staring into the abyss, I had but one thought.

Somewhere out there, 'Gee' was smiling.

20

FAMILY LIFE FILMS

I'd taken hundreds of letters home from school, most leading to spankings. But this one was different. It came not from my teacher or principal but from the District Chairman of Health Services. And I knew exactly what was inside.

The Downey Unified School District was teaching us about sex!

I'd been waiting for this letter—we *all* had—for as long as I could remember. For the kids at Price, fifth grade meant three things: 1) mandatory Glee Club tryouts; 2) promotion to middle school; and 3) Family Life films.

What I already knew about sex, like most fifth graders, would fit on an index card (with most of the paper blank). The older kids had told us everything *they* knew, which wasn't much, and taken time to review the films, their accounts ranging from "Total snooze-fest!" to "They let us watch porn!" Hoping for the latter, we braced ourselves for '*the study of human reproductive systems and their functions*'. But we had to get through singing tryouts first.

No eleven-year-old boy of sound mind wanted to be in Glee

Club. Just ask Peter Brady whose football teammates razzed him unmercifully for being "a canary". Unfortunately, like Pete on *The Brady Bunch*, I was cursed with the ability to carry a tune. And NFL star Deacon Jones (who'd shown up to defend Pete in his hour of need) was nowhere in sight.

Mr. Sealey, a fifty-year-old arts teacher who wore Coke-bottle glasses and jumpsuits like 'Gee's' was in charge of the tryouts. Every pupil in all three classes had to audition, the 'winners' to gather weekly for after-school singing practice. "I turn crows into songbirds!" he boasted. I didn't want him turning me into anything. As he called us, 'crow by crow,' to the back of the room, my stomach gurgled. Just sing badly, I told myself, like my pal, 'Bert Barker, who couldn't carry a tune if it came with a hand strap.

"Shannon Capps?" I'd never hated my name more! As I stood, I practiced singing off-key—it was harder than expected —then trudged to the table in back, passing Penny Wozniak along the way. A year ago, I'd barely noticed my pigtailed class-mate. Now, with all this Family Life talk, I couldn't stop staring. She glanced up and smiled. And my plan turned to shit.

"*My Country 'Tis of Thee*," I crooned, heart suddenly full. Mr. Sealey flushed red, making notes in his Steno pad. By the time I sang, "*Let freedom ring*," I'd sealed my fate.

Mom was ecstatic when I told her. A dreadful singer herself, she'd always wanted a child with pipes like Bing's, especially after Dennis who sang like a dying yak. My father who had a decent voice himself couldn't care less, which is why he took my side (as much as a husband not wanting to sleep on the couch can) at Parent Night. After a spirited rendition of *You're a Grand Old Flag*, Mr. Sealey introduced himself, reading the names on the Glee Club list, mine at the top.

"I'm *not* doing it," I dug in.

Mom yanked me aside, looking like someone had slapped

her. "Why can't you *ever* just go with the flow?" It was a valid question, one my wife would copyright two decades later. But there was no way in hell I was joining this club! As my father shrugged in mild support, Mom, in desperation, offered me five bucks to reconsider. I offered her ten to drop it.

On the way home, I stared at my empty wallet, Dad smiling, Mom frowning. Penniless again but happy to have the Glee Club fiasco behind me, I could now concentrate on the *real* matter at hand. Sex!

By the time I reached fifth grade, I was more than familiar with male anatomy. I'd studied my own privates for years, showered with Dad, even compared willies with every kid on the block, shocked when Sean O'Leary's sprouted hair. No one dared touch anyone else's, except for Jerry Flax who was known for using the 'penis pinch' in times of war. The controversial technique ended every fight he entered, but at what cost? We all thought the tactic should be outlawed but secretly wished we had the guts to use it ourselves. In all my years of research, which included zipper mishaps, failed cannonballs at the pool, and hundreds of bad hops on the baseball field, I'd found that *pain* was the most common sensation associated with the area.

But it wasn't the *only* sensation.

I'd learned that lying face down on the rug while Mom vacuumed, thanks to vibrating floorboards, made me feel 'weird', as did watching TV with a pillow in my lap. I also knew this odd tingle, if left unchecked, could lead to a full-blown stiffy, a condition I had no idea what to do with. Worse yet, the disorder could (and did) afflict me at inopportune times, like the day Mom took my friends and me to the Bob Baker Marionette Theater in Los Angeles. As the wooden can-can dancers twirled on strings in front of me, I got wood myself, hiding it with the paper crown they'd issued. It happened again in Billy Friedhoffer's room, Raquel Welch staring down from her iconic *One*

Million Years B.C. poster. And it was starting to happen in school, especially during Heads Up, Seven Up, a game where girls touched boys on their erect, little thumbs.

I began to note a cause-effect relationship. The 'weird' feeling typically followed a brush with the opposite sex, whether in person, on paper, or of the aforementioned wooden variety. And the less clothing involved (i.e. Raquel's deer-skin bikini), the stronger the reaction. I've spoken ad nauseam about the Emily Wexler incident, but there were more nude encounters. When I was six, I found a pack of playing cards in Dad's sock drawer, featuring drawings of topless women in various poses, the Joker's breasts hopelessly trapped in a clothes wringer. A year later, my family went camping, the site overrun with nudists. Before Mom could cover my eyes and make Dad repack the tent, I caught my first glimpse of actual, real-life boobs! It would be another three years before I saw more. While selling candy door to door for Little League, I passed an open window. Behind the screen, an unwitting high school girl disrobed under a ceiling fan, her hair blowing seductively in the wind. For eight straight days, I returned to the house next door, begging them to buy Helen Grace chocolates, my *real* mission to get another 'fan dance'. Fortunately for all of us, I never saw the girl again, but I did win 'Salesman of the Year' honors, securing a transistor radio for my efforts.

These innocent experiences were all I had to go on when Mr. Phelps, at long last, made the announcement in class. "Good morning, students." We sat on tenterhooks. "Today, we'll be separating the boys from the girls..." Given the subject matter, this seemed counterproductive. "...for the viewing of our highly-informative Family Life series."

He paused, waiting for the comment that would banish me from Sex Ed.

But for the first time in years, I kept my mouth shut.

"Gentlemen," he addressed us, tone all business. "Follow me to the cafeteria." We stood, fighting back smiles. This was the moment we'd been waiting for, a rite of passage, if you will, far more notable than the graduation ceremony we'd experience in two weeks. "Shall we?"

We moved outside, joining the other fifth-grade boys and proceeding up the hall, a long, fidgety snake. We'd be seeing one film, Mr. Phelps explained, the girls three. No one questioned the disparity. Female genitalia seemed infinitely more complicated than male. As we entered the cafeteria, it felt foreign, the smell of sloppy joe meat lost in the malaise. We'd gathered here for lunches, school assemblies, class pictures, etc. But today, we gathered for something *far* more important. Our 'transition to manhood'.

"Move down!" a booming voice cut through the tension. It was Mrs. Beales, our resident lunch lady, a 4'10" Tasmanian Devil with orange hair and a Cockney trill. "*Move down!*" she repeated, imploring us to maximize space. We had no idea why. At best, we took up three tables. Squeezing in like skittish sardines, we waited for Phelps to issue more warnings. He did, then cued the lights.

Not a single Meralta film garnered this much excitement. As the janitor swapped mop for projector, we held our breaths, the movie jittering to life. The opening scene was set in a city park, a young couple strolling hand in hand over the grounds. As they sat on a bench, smiling at each other, I glanced up the aisle. Benny Sherman and 'Bert Barker stared at the screen, mouths open. Arthur C. Fitch frowned at the crude cinematography. And Seamus O'Leary flashed a thumbs-up sign, his expression saying, 'It's go time!'

It wasn't.

Before the couple could even kiss, the picture cut to a bland illustration of male and female forms, the narrator beginning a diatribe that would put a Yuban tester to sleep. In numbing monotone, he used words like "meiosis", "fertilization", and "zygote", the drawings straight from a doctor's office. He went on to mention the "uterus" and "ovaries" before spending an inordinate amount of time on the "testes" and "vas deferens". In the entire presentation, only two lines got laughs, one referencing "gonads", the other "erections", Phelps clearing his throat for both. Much to our chagrin, there was no more live action till the end of the film, the young couple—still fully clothed—ordering snow cones from a street vendor.

Fade to black.

As the lights flickered on, reactions varied. Benny and 'Bert looked confused. Fitch chuffed in disgust. And Seamus gritted his teeth, his brother, Sean, having promised full-frontal nudity. My own thoughts were jumbled. First off, whoever hailed this as 'porn' had clearly never seen one. And second, I felt no closer to 'manhood' now than I had at breakfast that morning. That being said, I did feel *different*, the feeling not unlike the one I'd have four years later...after my first shot of whiskey.

In both cases, I wanted to vomit.

The next two weeks passed without incident, the Family Life experience, as these things tend to be, a major letdown. We played kickball at recess. Finished our SRA reading labs. And signed each other's autograph books, even though we'd all be moving to middle school together. On the last day of class, the faculty, which included Mr. Sealey belting a final rendition of *Dear Old Price*, honored us with an assembly, reading our names and handing out diplomas. As I took mine, my eyes scanned the crowd, catching a glimpse of Penny Wozniak. She wore a cute peasant blouse, her hair long and shiny, her pigtails a memory. Suddenly beautiful—and I mean *beautiful*—she smiled and winked at me. And I looked away.

If I'd learned one thing from Sex Ed, it was this. I wasn't ready.

There were still bike rides to go on. Prank calls to make. And middle school to endure—the most awkward, painful, self-conscious years of our lives. Having a girlfriend would only complicate things. It was best to go it alone.

After bidding our friends farewell for summer, Seamus and I headed home, weighed down by books, middle school information packets, and apprehension. As we turned up Coolgrove, Billy Friedhoffer rumbled to a stop, his motorcycle belching exhaust. He wore cut-off jeans, no helmet, and a Black Sabbath T-shirt, a pack of Camels rolled in the sleeve. Revving the engine, he stared at our paper mortarboards. In all the hubbub, we'd forgotten to remove them. "You pussies actually graduated?" I thought about correcting him—the proper term was 'vaginas'. "Middle school next?" We nodded, Billy puffing on his cig, then flicking the butt. It hit me in the chest. "Well, buckle up, bitches!"

Before we could respond, he roared away, engine drowning out laughter.

IV. NO ONE
WAS SAFE

21

ROCKET MAN

M iddle school began with a splash. Thirty seconds in, the girl next to me threw up.

She'd told Miss Begonia she was sick, but our teacher thought there was time for an office pass. There wasn't. When the chunks hit the floor, everyone shrieked, the poor girl standing there in shock. As I stared at the yellow-orange puddle, I was more curious than aghast. Turns out, you can learn a lot from a person's puke. This girl who none of us knew had eaten a quality breakfast—scrambled eggs, O'Brien potatoes, Jimmy Dean pork sausage, and a cinnamon roll. She must be, I reckoned, from the 'rich side of town', a place we'd heard of but never seen.

Maude Price was one of three elementary schools feeding Griffiths Middle, Gallatin and Rio Hondo the other two. All three schools shared the same demographics, but Gallatin featured a small pocket of wealth that separated its occupants from their middle-class neighbors, 'Puking Girl' an abashed representative. A few years later, fans of teen-angst movies would see this 'clash of class' storyline beaten like a murdered mare. But for us starry-eyed sixth graders, it just meant some kids ate better breakfasts than others.

As Joe the custodian sprinkled sawdust on the pond, we cowered in our seats, a few more of us ready to hurl. Middle school had slapped us in the face, letting us know in painfully-acrid terms that no one was safe. There'd be new classmates to meet, multiple teachers to pacify, and a vice principal who, legend had it, wielded his paddle like Thor's hammer.

According to students, Ernest T. Bathgaite had spanked more asses than the Norse god had slayed giants. And the worn scull hanging in his office, which held the focused beam of an overhead light, verified the stories. Surprisingly-fit for a man in his sixties, Mr. Bathgaite boasted coat-hanger shoulders, Popeye forearms, and two tufts of clown hair that framed his bald melon.

Despite the obvious resemblance, he warned, no one *dare* call him 'Bozo'.

As a result, every kid at Griffiths did.

"Welcome to sixth grade," Miss Begonia squeaked, still shaken from the flying chunder. She was five feet tall with long, black hair and a ninety-pound frame. "I'll be your Combined Studies teacher this year." Her smile exposed jagged teeth. "And that means you'll be spending three of six periods with me." The other three would be devoted to Math, Exploratory Courses, and for the first time ever...P.E.

I was both anxious and excited about the prospect. A week earlier, Mom and I stopped at Gene's Sporting Goods (per the middle school info packet) to pick up a pair of maroon shorts for Gym. Every male at Griffiths was forced to wear the unflattering garment, along with a white T-shirt, sneakers, and the piece de resistance...a jock strap. I had no idea what to do with this thing. It looked like unfinished underwear, with an elastic waistband, straps that cupped each bun, and a pouch that swallowed me whole. Putting it on was like solving the Rubik's Cube, especially with the sweat I'd amassed on my first day of middle school. But I somehow managed, reporting to the blacktop with all the other jock-wearing doinks.

"When I give you a number," Coach Fredrickson barked, "find it and stand on it!" For some reason, the middle-aged gym teacher who boasted swollen quads and a chrome whistle was already pissed. "Number one, Aaron Aamodt!" A kid with knobby knees skulked to the painted *1*, followed by Biff Bagwell to number 2, and so on. When every digit was filled, Coach Fredrickson lowered his clipboard. "You'll find this number every day! You'll stand on it with your feet twelve inches apart! And you'll listen to me!"

As we assumed the position, I surveyed the troops, having never seen a more pathetic crew of misfits in one evenly-spaced assembly. There were fat kids, gaunt kids, kids with severe acne, even some with hairy legs, the disparity in size and maturity alarming. It was my first class with seventh and eighth graders, and I felt like a boy among men. Fortunately, I wasn't alone. Vernon Nessler and Jerry Flax were shaking. Saul Tannenbaum's shorts were on backwards. And Willie Haskins looked like the lovechild of two horny eighth graders. Of all my friends, only Keith Budro looked confident, having sprouted pubes the summer before.

"If you're late, I'll send you to Bathgaite's office!" The coach angrily uncapped a Sharpie. "Out of uniform, Bathgaite's office!" He walked up each aisle and down the next, scrawling names on our chests. "Refuse to participate, Bathgaite's office!" As he dotted the *i* on Zack Zrelli's shirt, the first of two bells sounded. "Fifty pushups, girls. Then hit the showers!"

We were already nervous. Now we were petrified!

Moving with the urgency of a school fire drill, we made our way to the locker room, the moment we'd been dreading now here. Budro was the first to disrobe, the rest of us dropping our trousers like fifty-year-olds at a prostate exam. As steam billowed, we grabbed our towels and slunk into the cloud. There was a small sitting area outside the shower room with wooden benches and puddled concrete, the smell a combination of mildew and fear. Up ahead, ten spray nozzles clung to the wall, an army of naked boys, some pubescent, others (like me) severely *pre*-pubescent, jockeying for position beneath them. As a rule, eighth graders got dibs on showerheads, followed by seventh graders, larger sixth graders, and finally us fledglings.

We had five minutes to shower. It felt like eternity.

As I claimed a spigot, I saw most of my pals do the same. The older kids were gone now, unleashing a chorus of sighs. Benny Sherman soaped up to my right, 'Bert Barker to my left. The last kid to trudge into the room was Danny Delgado. He was small for his age with spindly arms and a comically-large head. We'd known Danny for years, but the friendship was casual at best. As he moved to an open stream, nervous chatter built to a crescendo, then stopped cold. All eyes had moved to Delgado's crotch. He was hard as a granite countertop!

Caught by surprise, no one said a thing, having never seen a classmate in this 'condition'. But the unsettling *first* would be one of many that year. For the first time ever, we were assigned lockers, mine broken into immediately. I blamed Billy Friedhoffer, of course, he being the only hoodlum I knew. But he was in high school now, the chances of him wanting my Social Studies notes incredibly slim.

We'd attend our first dance as well. When the lights dimmed, no one dared ask a member of the opposite sex to dance, except for Timmy Hofbrau who led Darla Klapp to the dancefloor as Otis Redding sang *Sittin' on the Dock of the Bay*. We were impressed, till learning he'd flunked four grades, already had his Learner's Permit, and would eventually spend time in prison.

Exploratory Courses were another big first, designed to prepare us for all walks of life. In six-week increments, we'd study subjects like Sewing, Cooking, Typing, and Wood Shop, learning just enough in each to be dangerous. In Sewing, Budro stabbed 'Pip' Pipchinsky with a needle, the sore-assed youngster claiming, "I now have tetanus!" In Cooking, Lynn Grafton baked a two-layer cake that doubled as a doorstop. And in Wood Shop, Mr. Fawkes fired a screwdriver across the room, hitting Ann Phillips in the forehead, her scar forever bearing the tool of her namesake.

Outside class, Seamus O'Leary smoked our first cigarette, swiping a Kool from his mom. Kevin Briar sparked our first joint, the first of many, as it turned out. And there were rumors, though unconfirmed, of Russ Banaway and Carrie Bartman having our first sex. I personally doubted this, however, Russ having also claimed he saw Bigfoot at Shakey's. On a tamer note, we watched the first episode of *Saturday Night Live*, heard Freddie Mercury sing *Bohemian Rhapsody* for the first time, and saw our first R-rated movie at The Avenue, the theater six doors down from The Meralta. We'd snuck in, of course, catching the end of Woody Allen's *Everything You Always Wanted to Know About Sex*—to this day, I still can't eat rye bread.

Meanwhile, back in gym class, Danny Delgado entered the showers on day two, with the same diamond-cutter he'd brandished on day one. Again, we said nothing, but we'd all taken note, our walk to Music filled with lewd lyrics and laughter. Mr. Bellows (who'd been teaching since Mozart was our age) told us to "pipe down", putting on a Wagner album and falling asleep. He did this every day, hoping the classics would tame us while he caught some extra Zs. The plan worked to perfection till Bart Kinsey tied his shoelaces together, his accomplice, Eddie Spatch, banging the kettle drum. At the sound, 'Old Man' Bellows stiffened like Delgado's penis, tripping over his laces and tumbling to the floor. When 'Bozo' arrived, Eddie (who'd failed to ditch the drumstick) was dragged to the office for a date with 'The Hammer'.

In P.E. the next day, Coach Fredrickson outlined the 'Road to Gold Trunks', the "highest honor a human being could ever hope to achieve!" It required the performance of infinite physical feats (i.e. five thousand pull-ups, a million sit-ups, running the mile in two minutes, etc.). As I surveyed the oafs and twits around me, I knew without question...we'd be in *maroon* forever. Entering the showers, we were all on high alert. Could Delgado render wood three days in a row? Like a massive curtain, steam parted to reveal the answer, Danny's dagger sharper than a Ginsu.

"I'm *nervous!*" he defended himself. Looking back, I'm sure he was, getting no sympathy from his moronic classmates. Instead, we did what sixth graders do best—pointed and jeered, just glad it wasn't *us*.

At the same time, our Math teacher, Mr. Hicks, introduced the concept of ratios and rates, which helped us calculate the possible length of Delgado's erection run. As we plotted pairs on coordinate graphs, we came to the conclusion that 'ten straight days' was the most likely scenario. Never before had we shown such enthusiasm for Mathematics, our interest in Music peaking as well. While listening to Bach's *Concerto for Two Harpsichords in C-Minor*, I was inspired to write the equally-impressive *Pop a Boner in the Shower Room*. Benny and 'Bert came over that night to help record it. As I crooned in Dad's bathroom—it had great acoustics—Benny played bongos while 'Bert flicked the doorstop, creating the perfect 'boner-popping' sound.

Our efforts were rewarded on day four, Danny sporting another boinger.

On day five, Delgado launched a fifth rocket.

And on day six, after a weekend break, 'Rocket Man' fired a Cuban missile.

The atmosphere in P.E. had morphed from one of shock and disgust to exhilaration and suspense. Everyone was talking about 'The Streak', from eighth-grade boys in Metal Shop to sixth-grade girls in Typing, my sophomoric song the official anthem. Even 'Puking Girl' asked for a copy, making her own predictions and booking bets on the side.

Day seven, another husky.

Day eight, a hoisted tent pole.

Day nine, a peering meerkat.

On the morning of day ten, we were coming out of our skin. All pie charts and Venn diagrams pointed to this moment, a tenth chubby virtually insured. As we circled the track, Coach Fredrickson's whistle sliced through the tension. "Move out!" he hollered, everyone bolting for the showers.

With steam wafting, the eighth graders didn't leave, nor did the seventh and sixth graders, the space filled to capacity. As the clock ticked down on the locker room wall, we waited...and waited...and waited. But Delgado didn't show. Unbeknownst to us, he'd gotten a note from his mother, excusing him from all future athletic endeavors *'due to an undisclosed health condition'*. As we filed out, one disappointed voyeur after another, I couldn't help but feel guilty. Not only had I ignored Danny's feelings, but I'd laughed and pointed more than anyone. I'd even written a theme song (with three verses, a chorus, and bridge)!

Despite my recent promotion to middle school, I had a lot to learn.

And my first lesson was pending.

As I left the showers, I came face to chest with Ozzie Pagnozzi, the hairiest eighth grader in the history of Griffiths. The towel he was using looked uncannily like mine, right down to the name patch Mom had sewn on. Naked and wet, I stood there shivering, waiting for the galoot to finish, my once-clean drying cloth swabbing his fur. After a final wipe of his ass-crack and junk, Ozzie tossed me the towel, noticing my scared, little wiener. With a Neanderthal grunt, he alerted his friends, the four of them enjoying a good laugh at my expense.

Now running late, I leaped into my clothes and rushed out of Gym, hoping to make Music on time. But a fleshy wall in the form of Mr. Bathgaite stopped me. "Glad I ran into you, *Capps*." He paused to sniff, clearly wondering why I smelled of eighth-grade ball sweat. "First off, you're late." He paused again, the bell ringing on cue. "And second, there's a 'hit song' making its way around campus. Have you heard it?" I cut my eyes to the pavement, confirming my guilt. "What say we go find a tape player?"

When I looked up, a smile not unlike 'Bozo's' brightened his face.

"Check it out, bros!" The vice principal and I turned, Ozzie and company loitering behind us. "'Skin Muff's' in trouble!"

Everyone cracked up—the 'cavemen', Joe the custodian, a guy refilling the Coke machine, even Mr. Bathgaite—laughter echoing down the halls.

Although I'd longed for a nickname in life...

'Skin Muff' wasn't my first choice.

22

TERROR HAS A NEW NAME

It was the biggest interview of my life. In fact, at twelve, it was the *only* interview. Mom saw the ad in *The Penny Saver*, and Dad agreed to give up his Saturday, though he was none too pleased.

A family in nearby La Mirada had placed the ad, seeking a '*family for adoption*'. Not of a child—my parents had adopted one too many—but of a dachshund. The authors loved their dog, the memo asserted, but their apartment had recently changed hands, the new landlords cat people. If interested, '*potential parents*' were to call and '*schedule an in-person interview*', a decision to be made '*by the end of the month*'.

I was beyond excited, having pestered Mom and Dad for a new dog for more than a year. When Saturday arrived, I leaped out of bed, threw on my church clothes, and begged my parents to do the same. Mom assembled her Sunday best. Dad wore wrinkled pants and a frown.

The twenty-minute drive, as I recall, took seven hours, Dad missing every light. If I didn't know better, I'd swear he was trying. But when we finally reached the apartments on La

Mirada Boulevard, we were all nervous. Okay, Mom and I were. Dad didn't give a shit.

A fiftyish man in nipple-high shorts answered the door, looking us up and down before letting us in. Mom went first, performing a mock-curtsey, followed by me doing my best to look charming, then Dad trying without success to appear friendly. We were told to sit on the couch, then interrogated one by one on everything from religious affiliation to personal hygiene. Dad, patience all but spent, cracked his knuckles, the place smelling of bratwurst.

There was no dog in sight.

After sixty minutes of *60 Minutes*-style grilling, Otto Heimlich—he'd introduced himself between questions—looked to the nearby hall. "Lena," he shouted. A shoulderless woman with red-rimmed eyes appeared, trying to smile and carrying a dachshund. "This is Schnucki," he announced, voice cracking. The couple stared at one another, Lena lowering Schnucki to the rug. As the dog surveyed his potential new roommates, my pulse quickened. Schnucki was the cutest thing I'd ever seen, his black-and-tan fur shining, his coppery eyes conveying innocence and hope.

After a pregnant pause, he walked to my father and sniffed his ankles, Dad giving the pup an obligatory pat. From there, Schnucki moved to Mom, receiving a quick scratch and an "Aren't *you* lovely?" As Lena slipped a trembling hand in her husband's, all eyes moved to me. Schnucki sauntered over and nuzzled against my leg, the adults in the room offering a collective "Aaaaww!"

For the next ten minutes, I played with Schnucki, learning his tricks, testing the limits of his short 'wheel base', and wrestling with his favorite chew toys. This dog loved me! And I loved him, save for the name, of course, but that could be changed. When Otto and Lena showed us the door, I felt an overwhelming urge to take Schnucki with me, but there were three more families to interview, they explained. And Schnucki himself would make the final decision. "I *will* say this," Otto acknowledged, looking directly at Dad. "Schnucki likes you."

I was on cloud nine all the way home, chatting excitedly about "my new dog". Fred would be his name. And he would sit next to me on the couch when we watched TV, sleep at my feet when I did homework, follow me down Guatemala like a squat, baby brother. Fred would be my best friend! And I pictured the little fella shagging balls at baseball practice. Sneaking into the car on my first date. Staring from my bedroom window as I drove off to college.

I'm not sure why I allowed myself to get so excited. The Capps family had terrible luck with pets. Tim, my brother's rat terrier, died young. Crackers, a mutt from the local pound, threw herself under the first speeding Pontiac she could find. And Horace, a bullfrog I caught at Legg Lake, went on a hunger strike till we released him into the wild. After Crackers became a throw rug and Horace hopped away, we gave up all hope of another pet. But three years later, I convinced Mom and Dad to try again. And Trixie, an Australian silky with the worst case of ADHD in canine history, set up camp in the back yard.

Things started off well enough. Dad converted an old TV console into a dog house. I cleaned up Tim's rusty bowl for food. And we cut a hole in the gate so Trixie could relieve herself in the riverbed. But she refused to sleep in the one-time television set. Turned up her nose at the bowl. And pissed and shit every-where *except* the riverbed. True, she was fun to play with on occasion—she could chase balls faster than ex-Angel outfielder Mickey Rivers—but I soon lost interest, my promises of feeding her, playing with her, and picking up poop as hollow as the console.

When I hadn't crossed paths with Trixie in months, I had the audacity to approach Mom (the dog's primary caregiver now) with a proposition. "What if Trixie had puppies?" At nine, I had no idea how the process worked, but I was certain a cute batch of pups would re-spark our connection. After weeks of debate, my parents agreed, Mom making scores of phone calls, Dad driving to Torrance to 'rent' a male silky. When two of my friends and I watched the thing mount Trixie from behind— after *zero* foreplay, by the way—we were sure he was trying to kill her. "Dad!" I screamed, the three of us finding him in the garage. "What in the world's happening?"

Face covered in metal shavings, he peered over the fence, about to rescue three fathers, himself included, from the 'birds and the bees' speech. "Hell, they're screwing!" Sure he'd answered every query we had, he fired up the drill press, Trixie spitting out pups two months later.

She had six of them, three males and three females. I named the smallest and cutest Speed after my favorite television character, *Speed Racer*. The name went nicely, I thought, with Trixie, the cartoon racecar driver's girlfriend on the show. It was a huge mistake. Less than a year later, after giving five of the pups away, I watched Speed corner his mom in the yard, forgetting every mother-son moment they'd spent together. Freud would've enjoyed this four-legged version of *Oedipus*, but I, for one, was disgusted. And so was Trixie. After having another litter of pups with her own son as the father, she used the hole in the gate to bolt for freedom, a far better fate than Queen Jocasta of Thebes'.

It was impossible to blame her.

But I *did* blame Speed, finding it harder and harder to play with him, take him on walks, even look at the flea-bitten male-factor. Eventually, the scorned cur got bored and utilized the same hole his mother had, putting the Capps family in his furry rearview mirror.

After Speed sped off, we vowed *never* to get a dog again.

Then came Fred.

I don't know why I wanted him so badly. Nor do I know why my parents acquiesced. But two weeks after the interview, Mom got a call from the Heimlichs. Schnucki had selected us, they announced, and we were to come get him immediately. I was ecstatic, Mom apprehensive, Dad disgruntled. But we piled into the car and took out for La Mirada, a pillow for the new adoptee in the back seat. Before handing Schnucki over, Otto read a six-page manifesto that included what to feed him, when to walk him, how to bathe him, etc. We listened dutifully, Lena holding the poker-faced pup to her chest. When there was nothing left to say, Otto looked to his wife...and she let Schnucki go.

"One more thing," he added as we turned for the car. "If it doesn't work out, *please* give us the opportunity to take Schnucki back." It was an odd request—why *wouldn't* it work out?—but we nodded anyway and headed off.

"Your new name is Fred," I announced, placing him on the pillow. The 'artist formerly known as Schnucki' glanced at me, then hopped over the elbow rests and crawled into my father's lap. We all laughed, even Dad, and I can remember the feeling of warmth I had, the sense that we were already a family.

When we got home, Mom handed me the leash. "I'm sure he needs to tinkle." We'd never had an indoor dog before, Otto having explained the 'call of nature' regimen in scrupulous detail. When the pooch stood at the door, you had one minute to let him out. When he walked in a circle, you had thirty seconds. And if he hadn't been out in an hour, you better walk him soon! This all sounded great to me. The more time we spent together, the better.

I clipped the leash to Fred's collar, Mom smiling, Dad grabbing *The Signal* and heading for his chair. As I led my new pal up the walk, my face beamed with pride, but there was no one there to see it. It was early evening, streetlamps ablaze, houses quiet. I walked Fred to the freeway and back, passing eighteen yards, twenty-four trees, and 236 bushes. Fred sniffed them all but refused to hoist his stubby leg. After what seemed like hours, I returned home, convinced he didn't have to go.

As we walked in, Fred ran straight for my mother's newly-upholstered chair and pissed all over it. "Fred, *no!*" I screamed, the dog ignoring me. After shaking a few last drops on the carpet, he hopped on the ottoman, burrowing between Dad's ankles. Had I not spent the last half-hour on a worthless wee-wee walk, only to have Fred thumb his wiener at me when we got home, I might've found this endearing. But Fred was *my* dog. And if there was any burrowing to be done, it would be between *my* ankles!

Sensing my dismay, Dad nudged Fred off the footrest. As he landed, I lured him over with a toy, Mom already scrubbing her chair with Borax and vinegar. We played for two hours, forgoing primetime TV for the first time I could remember and staying up well past my bedtime. Fred was having as much fun as I was. And my parents chuckled as they watched us.

When Dad finally headed to bed, we were all exhausted. But I was excited, too. Fred, as Schnucki, had slept in the same bed with his masters, so my parents (after hearing items sixty-one through sixty-four on the instruction list) promised he could do the same with me. After walking the neighborhood again, only to have Fred piss on the drapes, I crawled into bed, placed him between my legs (item sixty-three), and turned out the lights. He felt warm against my thighs, his breath coming in little pants. I could even feel his rapid heartbeat. This was our first night together and—

Without warning, Fred tunneled through the covers and slipped out of bed, heading for my parents' room. When I found him, he was sitting on Dad's slippers. Mom got out of bed, picked Fred up, and took him back to my room, placing him under the covers. When I joined him, I heard a muffled growl, followed by silence. A minute later, Fred mined his way free, returning to Dad's bedside. Undeterred, Mom retrieved the dog, shut the door behind her, and brought him back to me. But when she turned to leave, he bounded again, scurrying back to the now-closed door.

"Why, you little booger!" Mom chuffed, walking back to repeat the exercise. I heard Fred growl again, followed by a stereophonic yelp—his and my mother's. The little bastard had bitten her! And she clutched her left wrist, blood trickling through her fingers. There were two things you didn't do in Dad's presence. Hurt his wife. Or hurt his kids. A notoriously-light sleeper—he'd learned to nap with one eye open in New Guinea—he was at the door immediately, glaring down at the perp. When Dad picked him up, there was no argument, Fred a lot smarter than he looked. Tucked under a flexing arm, the wiener dog hung limp, ready to go wherever Dad wanted, which in this case was back to my room. Without a word, he dropped him in bed and secured the covers, daring Fred to escape. He didn't. But for the next two hours, I lay there frozen, listening to the sound of growling at my crotch.

The next day, Fred repeated every transgression, adding nonstop barking, destroying the magazine rack, and pinching a loaf in the kitchen to his repertoire. Over the next six weeks, things got even worse. Fred never once peed on our walks, opting for chairs, drapes, laundry piles, shoes, and carpet again and again. Nor did he spend a full night in bed with me, choosing the dark, sterile hallway instead. And he bit Mom, Dennis, me, several friends, neighbors, a meter reader, the Avon lady, and a guy who stopped for directions. But never Dad. I'm not sure if he was mad about his midlife adoption or the name change—maybe both—but he was mad, all right. Till the day we loaded him in the car and drove him back home.

It was like a scene from *Lassie*, the collie returning to her beloved family after a harrowing escape from kidnappers. As Schnucki licked happy tears from their cheeks, the Heimlichs thanked us again and again, scarcely noticing our bandaged hands and urine-soaked clothing. Dad handed them Schnucki's things. Mom wished them well. And I stared at my ex-best friend, wondering if he'd even look back. He didn't.

Five years later, Stephen King wrote *Cujo*, the story of a crazed dog that attacks a family. Two years after that, the film hit theaters, and I was convinced it was about Schnucki.

No, King didn't live in southern California.

But 'Mainers' read *The Penny Saver*, too, don't they?

23

SILENT POETRY

I don't blame my parents for what they did. They were raising a child who ate dirt on occasion, bathed only when forced, and thought The Three Stooges were comic geniuses—still do, by the way. In addition, I was known to nap in the dog house and (after discovering alcohol a few years later) pee on the VCR, mistaking it for a urinal.

Something had to be done, Mom convinced Dad, lest their son grow into an adult version of the boorish boy they were raising. She found the solution at a PTA meeting, a place where like-minded moms gathered once a month to discuss child labor and cruel disciplinary techniques. The answer, which came after several motions and a unanimous vote, was ballroom dance lessons.

What better way, they insisted, to reform their ill-mannered sons! We'd learn to dress like gentlemen, bow to young ladies, and move with the grace of Fred Astaire. Refinement was what we needed. A little dose of civility.

"You'll get a suit," my mother ordered. "And *like* it!"

I doddered behind, wanting to melt into a clothing rack—The Broadway had 8 million of them! It was summer, for God's sake! My friends were off playing football, throwing rocks at road signs, or dog piling on one another. This was worse than the wooden spoon, which Mom had thankfully retired (and bronzed) when I entered middle school.

"How about this one?" she asked, attacking a sales rack. We didn't have a lot of money. After thirty-one years at the same plant, Dad had been laid off, Mom stretching our savings like taffy. We couldn't afford a new suit, or fancy shoes, or *dance lessons*, for that matter, but Mom refused to fold in front of the PTA ladies. "I think it's lovely."

I stared at the lime-green leisure suit in her hand. It featured brushed-denim fabric, huge pockets, and embossed stitching. It was the single ugliest garment ever to 'grace' a hanger. "Jeez," I groused, Mom shoving me into a dressing room.

When we got home, she forced me to model again. And not just the suit this time—the entire hideous ensemble, from rayon shirt (so scratchy it made my neck bleed) to ghastly tie (it looked like a dead squirrel) to white, patent leather shoes (they'd make a *pimp* self-conscious). While Mom killed yet another roll of film, Dad fought laughter with everything he had.

After the 'fashion shoot', I was told in no uncertain terms that life was changing. From this point on, I'd comb my hair, brush my teeth between meals, and shower more than once a week. Furthermore, there'd be no more belching at dinner *or* depositing boogers under the sofa. "'Cotillion'," Mom quoted from the pamphlet, would teach me "'manners, etiquette, and a myriad of social skills'"—I stared at the wax I'd just picked from my ear—the "'fun to begin in two weeks'".

Despite my suddenly-improved hearing, it all sounded terrible. But what choice did I have? If I wanted free lodging, I had to comply. Fourteen days later, I reported to the Women's Club of Downey, feet aching in new shoes, skin stinging from a hot shower. Fortunately, most of my friends were there, too, each wearing a horrible suit of his own, a rainbow of polyester and scowls.

Instinctively, boys flocked to one side of the room, girls to the other. On our side, the conversations ranged from "You look like a boob!" to "Where's the fire exit?" In the midst of it all, a sudden clacking sound usurped the clamor. We turned, an elderly woman in full-length gown sashaying onto the dancefloor. Like a well-dressed barnacle, she clung to the arm of a doddering man in beige, her free hand clicking castanets.

For reasons unknown, we stood at attention.

"Good evening, ladies and gentlemen." That was a stretch! "I'm Mrs. Delight, and this is my husband, Mr. Delight." The man bowed wordlessly. "As in 'trip *delight* fantastic'." A few parents chuckled as they moved to the benches behind us, the place smelling of Johnson's Wax. "These are my assistants, Gilbert and Darrell." She gestured to a pair of doughy twenty-year-olds, each wearing a suit worse than mine. "Welcome to your *first* Cotillion!" I glanced at 'Bert Barker. Normally pink, he was whiter than my shoes. "Let us begin."

Over the course of the next hour, we learned to properly introduce ourselves, to sit and stand—*I'm serious!*—and to advance through a receiving line, a skill we'd no doubt need for the *many* receiving lines of our future. We also learned (and this is when I started sweating) the proper decorum for 'asking a lady to dance'.

As we faced off like little gunslingers, my knees began to rattle. I'd never asked anyone to dance before. Never called a girl on the phone. Never even admitted I *liked* one. It was all happening too fast. Couldn't we review the whole sit/stand thing again? How about another receiving line?

"Gentlemen, place your hand on your partner's waist." With an impish grin, Mr. Delight demonstrated on his wife. We all followed suit, avoiding eye contact as our jitters turned to fear.

"Ladies, place your hand on your partner's shoulder." The girls did so, every boy feeling nauseous. "Now lock hands." There was a collective gulp, along with some tittering in the gallery, our palms slippery on contact.

Mrs. Delight nodded to Darryl, her employee dropping a needle on the record player. As music coughed through the speakers (some sort of waltz, I guess), we stiffened in unison. One quick note on Gilbert and Darryl. In all my years, I'd never seen two workers less interested in their jobs. These guys had zero enthusiasm, zero personality, and zero charisma. It was oddly comforting, however, to know there were two people in the room who hated this more than I did.

"Gentlemen, you will lead." Toes pointed, the Delights glided left, then left again, music carrying them in lockstep. We tried to copy their moves, staring at our feet as we stepped on our partners'. "Now back." They floated right, then right again, smiling at each other like dust-covered newlyweds.

This simple back-and-forth routine went on for days, the song on the turntable refusing to end. Two steps left, two steps right, two steps left, two steps right. This was *torture*, I wanted to shout. If only I'd sprained an ankle earlier. Or ruptured my damn spleen!

"Eyes up." I looked, at last, to the girl in front of me. She had straight, brown hair, bobbed neatly at the neck, and Cleopatra eyes, her mouth a budding rose. Had I still been breathing, I'd have smelled perfume. But I wasn't breathing. I was staring at the most beautiful creature—

"Switch partners," Mrs. Delight ordered, the music grinding to a halt. As Darryl flipped the record, I continued to gawk—stupefied—at the girl I'd just danced with.

She offered a smile.

And I turned to goo.

Without warning, a behemoth stepped between us, coaxing

my hand to her muscular hip. In the process, she blocked my view of the 'goo-rendering goddess', blocked my view of just about everything. "Take my hand," she snorted, breath horrendous—I was sure she ate dirt, too. In an instant, her oversized mitt devoured mine, her mountainous shadow swallowing me whole. The next three minutes passed like detention, shoulder sagging under the weight of her paw, feet taking the brunt of her oft-wayward steps.

If 'dancing', as the saying goes, is 'silent poetry'...

This was ear-piercing prose.

"Gentlemen." Castanets clacked, Mrs. Delight taking her husband's arm. "Escort your partners to the snack line." Still void of expression, Gilbert stood near the kitchen, balancing a tray of donut holes. I glanced at the Amazon next to me—she'd never looked happier—extending my arm as we hurried off to food. Along the way, I tugged at my collar, craning my neck in search of the 'goddess'. With *At Last* playing on the turntable—not the Etta James version but a cheap knockoff—I found her, six couples ahead, on the arm of Arthur C. Fitch.

He was my best friend. We'd played together, wrote stories together, even taken vacations together. I'd do *anything* for Fitch.

Yet now all I wanted to do...was murder him!

As *my* partner grabbed twelve donut holes, Fitch escorted *his* to the nearest bench. They talked, laughed, whispered in each other's ears. I'd never felt jealousy before. As I sat next to 'Andrea the Giant', it raged like *The Towering Inferno*.

And it was about to burn hotter.

Over the next half-hour, I watched six of my friends take turns with the 'goddess' while I danced with a convoy of retainer-wearing lumps. It was more than one man (even a man of twelve) could take! And I had no idea what to do about it.

When the Delights excused us that evening, a grim realization struck me.

I didn't even know her name!

The next month passed like a walk to Mr. Bathgaite's office. I couldn't stop thinking about her. Nor could I shed the urge to assassinate my friends. We'd all fallen in love with the same splendid sylph and as a result, were each serving time in our own private hells. Football games held no meaning. Dog piling led to blows. Even the Stooges seemed less riotous—and not just the ones with 'Joe' as the third Stooge.

Life, as my mother warned, was changing. I showered more. Clipped my nails once in a while. Even asked Mom to iron a shirt. And when Cotillion arrived thirty days later, my friends and I were ready, hair coiffed, suits pressed to perfection.

Fitch was the first to dance with the 'goddess' again, followed by Nils Svensson, Benny Sherman, Bart Kinsey, and me. As I took her hand, my body trembled. I'd never felt like this before —nervous, excited, timid, hopeful—emotions bombarding me from all sides. As I did my best to remember the steps, I mustered the courage to ask her name. "Jenny Mayne," she told me, voice sweet as a cherry Zotz. "I go to East..." East Middle School, I calculated, was only a few miles away. Maybe I could get a boundary exception, negotiate a transfer, talk my parents into— "...but we're moving to Idaho."

The needle scratched on the *Blue Danube* record, Darryl barely noticing. "Did...you say..." I stammered, an unseen weight crashing down on me—I was sure the ceiling had collapsed. "'Idaho'?" She nodded, my heart pounding. "But..." I smelled peach shampoo, stared into her deep-green eyes. "... *when*?"

"Next week," she issued the final blow. Everything swirled into fog, in the center of it all, her perfect face, my gut feeling like everyone in the room—boys, girls, mothers, fathers, Mr. and Mrs. Delight, even Gilbert and Darryl—had punched it.

Why was this happening? *Why?* I'd showered *twice* today!

As the music stopped, she walked away, dragging my heart with her. When my new partner arrived, the turntable malfunctioned, forcing us to dance without song. Fitting. To make matters worse, the thermostat failed, rendering the donut holes stale. It was the longest hour of my life. Of *our* lives. Like zombies, we finished the session, each feeling the same crushing heartbreak as the next, twenty well-scrubbed boys slashed by the same savage sword.

The next few months were agonizing. We went to school without energy. Played games without fervor. Did homework without quarrel. Cotillion came and went—sans 'goddess'—the Delights doing their best to teach us the Box Step and Cha Cha. Sensing a dip in morale, they introduced modern dances like the Hustle, even swapped donut holes for brownies.

None of it worked. We were dead inside.

But time, the great healer, did what it always does. Things steadfastly returned to normal, or at least a *new* normal. We'd survived our first real threat from the outside world, in the form of a beautiful maiden. And though we'd been willing to 'kill' for her, no one had, our friendships stronger because of it.

When it came time to re-up for Cotillion that summer, I shocked myself by saying, "Yes," most of my friends doing the same. We showed up in new synthetic-polymer suits, veterans of dance *and* love, ready to take on all challenges. As a result, the Delights were...*delighted*. Together, we'd Waltz and Merengue our way through the next two years, showering more often, learning which forks to use with salad, and actually enjoying it.

Hard as it was to fathom, Mom's plan had worked.

Sadly, we'd never see Jenny Mayne again, but as we'd come to realize, there'd be dozens of Jenny Maynes in life, starting with the new crop of partners in Cotillion 2.0. In actuality, most were returnees from the year before, but twelve months does wonders for girls at that age. They began to look better, smell better, even say things worth listening to. And every one of them, from the ballroom crushes to the high school flames to the college steadies, would add a crucial layer of growth to the men we'd one day be.

Our last Cotillion was bittersweet. Mrs. Delight teared up. Mr. Delight said nothing. And Darryl almost smiled (Gilbert had disappeared a year earlier, taking the assistant manager's job at Tastee Freez). As much as we hated the archaic dance routines and force-fed formalities, I knew, even then, they'd be part of us forever.

No, I never danced the Cha Cha again. I'm pretty sure none of us did. But I did open doors for dates, slide chairs out for dinner partners, even offer my arm to ladies on occasion. And ten years later, when I attended a friend's wedding...

I knew *exactly* what to do in a receiving line!

24

WRESTLEMANIA ½

Of all the activities forced on us in middle school, Wrestling was the worst.

First off, it was nothing like the sport on TV. There were no colorful outfits or feathery boas. No ropes to leap from or chairs to hit our opponents with. And no stars like Killer Kowalski, Tito Santana, or Haystacks Calhoun. Let's be honest, without all *that* stuff, Wrestling is just two dudes rolling around on a mat.

At Griffiths, the Wrestling room was attached to the Girls' gym, a place of mystery and intrigue for every middle school male. Setting foot inside was a class-A felony, punishable by swats, expulsion, and in rare cases death. We all wondered what the secretive digs looked like, how the showers were configured, and what sorts of lurid things went on inside. It was rumored that Ms. Hafner, a middle-aged spinster whose mustache rivaled Ozzie Pagnozzi's, not only forced girls to shower but supervised the activity, citing "safety concerns". We didn't know if the rumors were true, but that never stopped us from spreading them.

A dim, stale cube, the Wrestling room housed all kinds of

ancient equipment, from leather vaults and balance beams to dangling rings and pommel horses, the entire collection smelling like 1959. In the corner, two bulky ropes ran from floor to ceiling, 'Gold Trunk' applicants expected not only to climb them but to gnaw their way through the asbestos and plant a flag on the roof. With zero upper-body strength (or *any* strength, really), I couldn't get my feet off the floor, Coach Fredrickson on Rope Day looking like he'd eaten a cockroach, of which the room harbored many.

"Eyes front, girls!" he hollered. 'Gender fluidity' didn't exist in '76, so it was perfectly legal to call boys "boys", girls "girls", and in this case, boys "girls" to challenge their manhood. "Today, we start Wrestling!" There was a mass groan, Saul Tannenbaum's lip quivering. "You'll learn to shoot your opponent, lift him, and take him down!" The larger kids nodded, appearing to salivate, the rest of us searching for cover. "You'll master the 'hip toss', the 'arm throw', and the 'sprawl defense'!" The only moves I knew, thanks to *Championship Wrestling* on Channel 52, were the 'pile-driver' and 'figure-four leglock', both banned on the middle school mat. "And the *best* of the best of you..." He paused for effect, adjusting his cap. "...will earn a spot on the Wrestling team!" I glanced at Arthur C. Fitch, his eyes glazed. Apparently, he'd gone to his 'safe place'.

Seventh grade, thus far, had been better than sixth. But not much. Although we weren't the youngest and most vulnerable anymore, we still served as prey for the newly-anointed eighth graders, many of whom had 'matured' over the summer. I, like most of my friends, checked for pubic hair daily but remained balder than Telly Savalas. To make matters worse, my brief stint in Girls' Chorus had served as riotous fodder for students and teachers alike. And my failure at Math Field Day—I answered just two of ten questions correctly—'helped' us to a third-place finish in a four-school field. As a result, Mrs. McPheely who, though frail in appearance, once clocked a student with a slide rule, loathed the sight of me.

"Line up by size!" Coach Fredrickson yelled. "Smallest to largest!" This didn't sound good. As we surveyed the room, more than one stomach gurgled. Without even looking, Willie Haskins walked to the back of the line, followed by 'Pip' Pipchinsky and two other kids who'd yet to qualify for Disneyland rides. Keith Budro and Timmy Hofbrau (who could now legally vote) headed up front, joining the biggest of the upperclassmen. And I, flanked by faithful pals Benny Sherman and 'Bert Barker, found my place near the middle. "Time to see what you're made of!"

Although fighting was strictly prohibited at Griffiths, at least on paper, we were constantly being pitted against one another. From spelling bees and art contests to science fairs and footraces, everything was a competition. On rainy days, coaches handed out Bataka Bats, staging elaborate 'main events' in the gym. More than one combatant was beaten senseless with one of these foam-filled billy clubs, my neighbors, Sean and Seamus O'Leary, fan favorites. With every coach watching, they'd swap Batakas for fists, fighting like gamecocks till someone drew blood. As much as I enjoyed the spectacle, I feared being called next, my plan (should it happen) to sprain both ankles climbing into the ring.

Coach Fredrickson blew his whistle, the room going silent. We sat in ascending order at the edge of the mat, a lopsided serpent, thin at the tail, thick at the mouth. "Haskins! Pipchinsky!" The frightened flyweights stood. "Face off!" With matching sighs, they entered the circle, hands at the ready. "Wrestle!" Like rabid Chihuahuas, they clashed in the middle, roars from the crowd supplanting the silence. As Willie downed 'Pip', pinning him in *short* order—sorry, I couldn't resist—we screamed like bloodthirsty Romans.

"Next wrestler!" Coach Fredrickson ordered, Glen Torkle replacing a deflated Pipchinski. As Willie, now winded, faced his next challenge, I glanced down the line. There were twelve spots before mine, all featuring sixth and seventh graders scrawnier than me. If Benny, to my immediate right, proved successful, I was sure I could take him. But on my left, a fresh 'Bert who outweighed me by three pounds at our last Pop Warner weigh-in would be tough. If I did score a victory, the next two matches —Eddie Spatch and a bespectacled eighth grader—could go either way. After that...*oh, God*...was Tom Pinklin!

The Pinklins—there were at least six of them—were *not* from the 'rich side of town'. Not only did they dress like hobos, but their teeth were gray or missing, and they smelled of bad cheese. Of all the Pinklins we'd encountered, Tom was the grossest. He wore the same undies (not the same brand but the same *pair*) for the entire sixth grade. He ate anything he could get his hands on (from ant-covered burritos to a bag of Cheetos Bart Kinsey had sneezed in). And he never once entered the showers at P.E. (not even when Danny Delgado was chasing the record)!

The whistle blew again, Torkle pinning Willie in less than a minute. I glanced at the clock, urging the hands to move forward. I wanted no part of this. And time was the only thing that could save me. But there were thirty-six minutes left in the period, with twenty-six 'swordsmen' preparing to duel. At number thirteen, I couldn't possibly avoid 'the blade', but I didn't have to take it in the heart! As Jerry Flax tossed Torkle to the mat, I formulated a plan. I'd try my best to beat Benny and 'Bert—bragging rights, after all, were on the line—maybe even give my all against Spatch. But there was no way in hell I was pinning the bifocaled eighth grader!

Not with Tom Pinklin on deck.

"Pinklin!" Coach Fredrickson screamed. All eyes turned to the pungent pugilist, sweat oozing from every orifice. "You're out of your weight class! Move down five spots!" *Sweet Jesus, NO!* Tom stood, galumphing to his right, a miasma of Munster trailing behind him. Fortunately for me, Pinklin was no Math whiz either, miscounting badly and walking too far. "Just sit, for Christ's sake!" Coach Fredrickson roared. With a throaty giggle, Tom dropped to one knee, squeezing between two crestfallen sixth graders.

Pinklin was four spots behind me now. No longer a concern.

With a sigh of relief, I watched the next match, Flax escaping a headlock to pin Nils Svensson. Exhausted from the move, he lost to Kyle Blount who swept the next three contests before facing Tom. As the sweat-soaked seventh grader rose to his feet, the tension mounted. No one wanted to spend five minutes with Pinklin, let alone touch him! We had no idea when Tom last bathed or brushed his teeth or ran a comb through his hair.

And he was glistening from head to toe!

"Wrestle!" Kyle bum-rushed Pinklin, capturing him in a 'half-nelson'. But he lost his grip on the way down, Tom's sweat the perfect lubricant. As the four-time champ struggled to recover, Pinklin pounced, an armpit blanketing Kyle's face. With the crowd clamoring, Blount flailed and kicked, then went limp, asphyxiated by the acrid appendage. Coach Fredrickson used smelling salts to revive him, ammonia a *huge* upgrade over what he'd been breathing, then helped him back in line. "Next wrestler!"

The waiting sixth grader leaped to his feet, cracking his knuckles and jogging in place. But Tom proved too much for him, too, the pair ending up in a fortuitous '69' before the poor bastard tapped out. Pinklin was 2-0, with Vernon Nessler on deck and Benny in the hole. "Vern'll take him," I whispered, no one within earshot believing it.

The two squared off, Pinklin drenched, Vernon dry as kindling. In no time at all, Nessler gained the upper hand, throwing a leg over Tom's torso and pinning a shoulder against the mat. But the other shoulder refused to cooperate, Pinklin fighting as the bellicose crowd bayed. In a *real* Wrestling match, the 'near fall' would've garnered points, but here it just served to tire Vernon out. Ten seconds later, he lost his grip, Tom rolling on top of him for the win.

As Nessler staggered off, bearing his opponent's musk, I looked to the clock again. Only ten minutes had passed! *How was that possible?* When I lowered my gaze, Benny was staring at me, eyes begging for solace. "Sherman..." He winced. "...get out there!" Benny rose to his feet, goosebumps stretching skin. I offered a quick thumbs-up, but it fooled no one.

In Benny's defense, his match lasted longer than anyone else's, mostly because he ran for his life. For more than two minutes, the harried halfback of our Downey Razorbacks football team juked and jived before submitting to his sweaty shadow. I was praying the entire time but to no avail. Benny landed awkwardly, Pinklin's stomach, then crotch, smothering his face. He struggled for a while—I thought he might actually escape—then calmly let go.

The crowd went nuts, a grease-soaked Benny slithering off like a slug. All eyes turned to me. I'd hoped to avoid this fate, hoped someone—*anyone*—would grant me a reprieve. They didn't. I stood, glancing at the clock one last time. Its hands seemed to mock me now, as did the voices in my head.

At times like these, my mind often strayed to the terrible things I'd done. Like Ding-Dong-Ditching Mrs. Noid's house at two in the morning. Or making Scotty, my four-year-old neighbor, eat dog shit. Or herding kids into the bathroom to laugh at Sicole, a Laotian boy who, having just moved here, still 'squatted' over the toilet. I knew deep down these things were wrong. And that I deserved to pay for them.

But did it have to be *today*?

I stared at my opponent, the din unbearable. As Tom crouched in readiness, I noticed his teeth—a brown picket fence under ruby-red gums. I shuddered, perusing the rest of him. His hair was matted wool, his skin pale and filthy, his once-white T-shirt a gamut of grays. When he looked at me, he was wild-eyed and giggling, an unnerving combination. And every square inch of him shimmered like glass, the smell...*indescribable.* "Wrestle!"

My brain spun as if caught in a blender, one thought—like a chunk of unscathed banana—rising to the top. *I needed to end this!* As Tom attacked, I clutched his waist and pulled him on top of me, the sensation not unlike hugging a salmon. At just under two seconds, it was the quickest pin of the day—of the entire year, actually—but it was *over!*

Coach Fredrickson blew his whistle, his stare one of repugnance. As Pinklin let go, I turned to the crowd, every head shaking in disgust. *Who cares what they think?* I'd survived. And with a mere trace of 'fish oil' on my chest. To my right, Benny looked (and smelled) like he'd swum the Rio Hondo. And Vernon resembled an ad for Wesson Oil.

As I climbed to my feet, I glanced back at Tom. Although he still giggled, his wild-eyed expression was gone, replaced by one I'd never seen before. He was...*proud.*

That's when it hit me. The Pinklins didn't 'win' in life. From being born into poverty to wearing hand-me-down clothes to being laughed at in school when they scrounged for extra food. My own father had grown up in much the same way. And if not for blind fortune, I might've, too. As I passed a stricken Spatch —'Bert had somehow scored a bathroom pass—I looked back again, pondering what I was seeing. This was the best day of Tom Pinklin's life! For the first time ever, something *good* was happening. Something to make him feel good about *himself.*

The thought humbled me.

Pinklin went on to defeat Eddie and the bookish eighth

grader before succumbing to Trig Bechtler and exhaustion. By the time he left the mat—to thundering applause, by the way—he'd won seven straight matches. The longest streak of the day!

Over the years, I lost track of Tom. He may've found new friends in high school or simply moved away. Truth is, I rarely thought of the boy. But in 1986, while attending a WWF event at the L.A. Sports Arena, Tom Pinklin was *all* I could think about. Six matches in, a wrestler named Mr. X entered the ring, wearing a mask and dripping with sweat. Thanks to his disguise, I had no idea if it was Tom or not, but it *could've* been. And I *wanted* it to be! Perhaps that magic day at Griffiths, I thought to myself, launched Pinklin on an equally-magic career, one that landed him on Wrestling's biggest stage.

There was no way of knowing, but as the match wore on, I found myself rooting for him.

Of course, I still had to sympathize with Billy Jack Haines, the wrestler now *covered* in Mr. X's sweat.

25

SKATE-O-RAMA

Like most of us, I remember exactly where I was when Elvis died. Mom was driving me to football practice when a guy on KFWB reported, "'The King of Rock and Roll' is dead." At the time, it didn't mean much. Having older parents—Mom and Dad were pushing sixty now—I'd grown up listening to Artie Shaw and The Andrews Sisters. But one thing resonated.

If 'The King' was dead, no one was safe.

Two weeks later, the point was hammered home. "We regret to inform you," the school secretary announced, "that one of your classmates, Laird Willits, has died." The matter-of-fact dispatch, which came on the first day of eighth grade, caught everyone by surprise. Laird was a friend of ours, a better-than-average student, and a 'Gold Trunk' athlete. We played football together, and Little League baseball, his jokes in the dugout better than most. He was a good kid, a *nice* kid, his only crime... going on vacation. He died in a single-engine plane crash, his pilot father perishing with his son.

The news, of course, was devastating, but no grievance counseling was offered. Tragedy, our teachers explained, was part of life. And the sooner we learned that, the better. Laird's death was a painful reminder that as we grow older, *change* is the one thing we can count on. And in 1977, everything was changing.

Jimmy Carter took over the White House, the first Democrat to do so in nearly a decade. NASA tested the first space shuttle. And Commodore introduced the first personal computer, equipped with a monitor, keyboard, and audio-cassette drive. In theaters, *Star Wars* and *Rocky* broke box office records while TV's *Roots* captured 100 million viewers. More folks than that caught *Saturday Night Fever*. And the Yankees, Raiders, and Blazers all brought home titles.

Things at the Capps house were changing, too. In June, Dad brought home our first VCR. Impressive as it was, our new, cutting-edge toy proved a double-edge sword. Yes, it provided new forms of entertainment—combined with ON TV, the precursor of Showtime and Netflix, we could record first-run movies with no interruptions—but the new technology, in effect, killed the old. No longer was I willing to spool up a Chaplin film. And 'home movie nights', which included burgers, memories, and root beer floats, went the way of the rotary phone.

The biggest change of all, however, came from within.

I suddenly, inexplicably, and overwhelmingly couldn't stop thinking of girls!

It started with Jenny Mayne and escalated from there. Everywhere I looked, a beautiful girl loomed. From homeroom English class, where they showed up in Dittos and Dorothy Hamill haircuts, to church on Sundays, where miniskirts and makeup turned my virtuous thoughts to vile. I couldn't even watch TV anymore, shows like *Charlie's Angels* and *Three's Company* suggesting sex with every scene. It was more than a thirteen-year-old boy could take, especially one who couldn't quite grasp (no pun intended) the concept of masturbation.

Worse than that, in the cruelest of cruel twists...

As every girl got prettier, I got uglier!

It wasn't my imagination. Thanks to my football chinstrap, I sported a rocky beach of acne under my crooked smile, my skin a glimmering beacon. The zits went well with my bowl haircut, however. And the fact that I'd stopped growing (but not eating) added twenty pounds of fat to my off-putting arsenal. Sucking in my gut didn't help. Nor did borrowing Dad's cologne. I was a 'dog', to use the slur of the day. And no girl with clear vision could dispute it.

As a result, I went to school dances and stood in the shadows, watched Keith Budro and Tanya Lawrence hold hands at lunch, and played Around-the-World alone after school. I wasn't sad exactly, just sort of adrift, wondering why longtime friends had become 'men' while I stayed a 'boy'. Don't get me wrong, I wasn't the only one. Old pals Benny Sherman and 'Bert Barker still joined me for mischief—tossing poop on porches, pinching Playboys from their dads, etc. And with matching VCRs, Arthur C. Fitch and I watched more episodes of *Monty Python* than good health dictated. But for the first time ever, I felt left out. Not a single classmate, male or female, invited me to a party that year. In the eighth grade, those functions were reserved for 'cool' kids, a club I couldn't join.

Having no idea what to do, I put my head down, listened more in class, and focused on schoolwork. But it wasn't easy. There were distractions everywhere. ON TV began showing soft porn at midnight. Every kid but Fitch had a Farrah Fawcett poster in his room. And in school, more and more friends found suitable mates—even Nils Svensson, for Christ's sake! Along the way, my old friend, baseball, even let me down...when my Pony team went to a Dodger game, Budro brought his girlfriend, kissing her between innings till, in frustration, I fired a wiener at them. The last straw came on the blacktop at lunch. With the entire school watching, Wendell Biggs and Brenda Pine consummated their relationship under the bleachers, Bathgaite arriving a minute too late (more than enough time for two eighth graders to seal the deal).

Though intrigued, I stormed away in disgust, a tempest of thoughts raging. Wendell was *way* uglier than me! How the hell did *he* land a girl? Not that Brenda was anything to brag about. And not that I was ready for sex anyway. But was it too much to ask for a female—*any* female—to sit with me at lunch? Call me on the phone? Hold my damn hand once in a while? *Jesus*, I couldn't even get one to *look* at me!

That's when I read the handbill.

EIGHTH GRADE SKATING PARTY!!! THE END OF MIDDLE SCHOOL IS NEAR; COME TO SKATE-O-RAMA AND CELEBRATE HERE!!! There were more details—date, time, etc.—but I'd seen enough. The shindig was set for the final week of classes, a 'last waltz', if you will, before heading off to high school. My experience at school dances, as previously noted, had been as 'spectator' only. But *this* might be different. Thanks to Roller Derby, I could skate, and skate well. A stubborn smile pulled at my lips, the first in a long time.

"What in the world are you looking for?" Mom called from the kitchen. I was rummaging through my closet, tossing everything—socks, Odd Rods stickers, copies of *Cracked* magazine—onto the just-vacuumed floor.

"Skates!" I hollered back.

"You grew out of them," she countered, suddenly right behind me. Mom was a master at surreptitious movement. Her ninja-like stealth would make whacking off (when I finally figured it out) near impossible. "I gave them to Goodwill *ages* ago!"

"Dammit!" Before she could scold me, I was halfway to

Skate-O-Rama, weaving through traffic on the seat of my ten-speed. The mammoth building was on the opposite end of town, a thirty-minute ride, even on Saturday. I paid the entry fee and rushed to the counter, grabbing a pair of skates. When it wasn't hosting events, the place was a ghost town, floor silent, snack shack empty. Ideal conditions if you'd come here to *practice*! As I circled the track, music pumped through the speakers, signs cycling from *ALL SKATE* (with the fluorescents on) to *COUPLES* and *TRIOS* (where light danced off a disco ball). I was one of three skaters in the rink that morning, the other two a couple, gyrating to the Bee Gees.

I made four trips to Skate-O-Rama, all in preparation for the big event, my skills on wheels improving with each visit. At the same time, I started listening to FM radio. *Stormy Weather* and *Chattanooga Choo Choo* were of no use to me now. I needed *Hotel California* and *Stayin' Alive*! I also needed clothes. So I scraped some cash together and pedaled to Stonewood, spending hours at Miller's Outpost before I found the perfect shirt—open collar, faux-ivory snaps, snakeskin print.

As I stared in the mirror, I actually felt good about myself.

It wouldn't last.

A day before the big skate, Griffiths hosted Eighth Grade Honors Day. The annual event featured music, speeches, and student awards, the mid-day gala a sort of graduation bash. Book readers were handed certificates. Laird Willits was honored posthumously. And Mr. Bathgaite announced academic standouts, ranging in subjects from History to Home Economics. With two minutes to go, I'd won absolutely nothing...which was just fine with me! I'd sprouted a fresh pimple that morning, and the last thing I wanted was attention.

"It gives me great pleasure," Mr. Bathgaite leaned into the microphone, "to announce this year's 'Outstanding Scholar' awards." I slumped in my chair, staring at Nigel Binks. He wore wire-rimmed glasses and carried a protractor, his friend, Maggie Chin, ever-armed with a compass. They were shoo-ins for the honor! "For the girls, the winner is Laura Leigh, and for the boys..." Bathgaite checked (and rechecked) his notes. "Shannon Capps?"

What the— Feedback pierced the silence, followed by laughter and applause. As I stood, praying I'd misheard, I saw my parents, clapping and gushing. *Jesus, Dad missed work for this?* Stumbling to the podium, I heard everything from "What a geek!" to "We want a recount!" As I covered my chin, I thought of all the studying I'd done.

It had *ruined* me!

The next twenty-four hours were difficult, Mom and Dad bragging about me, kids in the neighborhood shunning me. But as tough as it was, I stuck to the game plan, ironing my new shirt, dabbing Clearasil on my chin, and heading to Skate-O-Rama. As I laced up, my heart beat to the music. Every girl in class was here, as was every boy, Foreigner's *Hot Blooded* pulsing through the sound system. The sign flashed *ALL SKATE*, the rink overflowing with skaters. After a deep breath —it smelled of nachos and Lysol—I rolled up my sleeves and merged into traffic. "Nerds can't skate!" someone sniped. *Watch this, asshole!* I pumped both legs and gained momentum, passing 'nerds' and 'cools' alike. My snakeskin shirt made me look like a cobra, soaring over the track in steely mid-strike. With every lap, my confidence grew. This is what I'd trained for, what I'd—

"All right, gents!" the DJ trumpeted. "Time to find your ladies!" With *How Deep Is Your Love?* playing, the fluorescents dimmed, the disco ball spraying pellets of light. As one hit my zit, the *COUPLES* sign flashed, lone skaters morphing into duos. Gotta take a whiz, I lied to myself, skating briskly to the bathroom. When I returned, Jimmy Buffett sang *Margaritaville*—I could've used one—*ALL SKATE* flashing again.

This happened five times—three *COUPLES*, two *TRIOS*— my bladder dry as a snack shack pretzel. Why was asking someone to skate so difficult? Other guys did it. Some didn't even ask. They just grabbed a female and pulled her into the rink. I tried everything, from standing near the Ladies' room to making silent deals with myself—"If you ask the girl in the blue dress, I promise to (fill in the blank)..."

It didn't matter what I vowed. I never came through.

And I hated myself for it.

"Last skate, guys and gals," the DJ announced, already packing up albums. "And this one's for 'The King'." A doleful guitar solo filled the room, the perfect score for my mood. All around me, classmates paired up, the same classmates who once mocked or ignored one another. Those things made sense. The world I lived in *now* did not. I leaned on the rail and stared, Nigel Binks skating by with a partner. *Are you kidding me?*

As Elvis crooned *Are You Lonesome Tonight?* my answer was yes.

"Dude!" two voices screeched behind me. I turned, assuming I was the only 'bachelor' left. "Svensson's in the bathroom!" 'Bert squealed, hair sweaty and matted. "Taking a dump!" Benny added, a smear of cheese on his shirt.

I stared at my friends, 'boys' in every way. I wheeled to see Budro skate by with a girl. As I glanced at the clock, Elvis sang with newfound urgency, '*Is your heart filled with pain? Shall I come back again?*' That's when I saw her. A girl in a blue dress standing to my left. Was it fate? A gift from the gods? As she looked at me, I cleared my throat.

"I...uh..." She smiled, my mouth turning to sand. "How about..." *You can do this! You HAVE to do this!* "How about we..." *PLEASE*, I begged myself, digging deeper than ever before. But I choked on my words, turning back to my friends. "...go kill the lights on him?"

"Hell, yeah!" they screamed, yipping like puppies and racing for the restroom.

As 'The King' sang his last mournful note, I skated off to join them.

26

LOCKER NIGHT

I don't know who came up with it, but Locker Night was the single worst idea in the history of education. Instead of assigning lockers, Warren High officials scheduled cable removal for five a.m. on the last day of summer, creating an unsupervised brannigan of overnight partying and turf warfare.

The hair-raising event was my introduction to high school.

And it took years, possibly decades, off my life!

Seeking strength in numbers, we decided to go as a team— from Benny Sherman and 'Bert Barker (my stalwart sidekicks and Pop Warner pals) to Keith Budro and Raymond 'Stretch' Wurtz (my longtime friends and Little League teammates)— plotting our way to Warren for the first time. On ten-speeds. In the middle of the night.

What could possibly go wrong?

My alarm clock buzzed at three. At 3:05, I was pedaling up Guatemala, shirt backwards, zipper down. I didn't even have the strength to Ding-Dong-Ditch Mrs. Noid at this hour! Our plan was simple. I was to meet 'Stretch' on the Island, then ride to 'Bert's house to rendezvous with him, Benny, and Budro. From there, we'd roll to Warren, like a benign biker gang, to claim our bank of lockers.

Things went south immediately.

When I got to 'Stretch's', the place was dark, his dad answering the door in boxers. "I...is...Raymond here?" I asked timidly. He waved me in, scratching and muttering, his son still fast asleep. By the time I got him up and walked him to his bike, we were twenty minutes behind schedule.

When we made it to 'Bert's, everyone was gone. Budro had grabbed a ride with a junior he knew, the guy's '68 Camaro far more comfortable than a Schwinn. And Benny forgot his lock, heading back home to grab it before he and 'Bert took out together. That left 'Stretch' and me to navigate the ink-black Downey streets alone. No easy task with one of us drooling.

Getting through the neighborhood was simple enough— hell, I could do that blindfolded—but everything after that was a crapshoot. 'Stretch' suggested Rives Avenue, apparently dreaming about the Little League fields there, but I overruled him, pedaling up Suva (where Bart Kinsey and I had recently egged a house) to Paramount Boulevard. It's amazing how different things look at night, but I slowly got my bearings, 'Stretch' snoring the entire way.

We passed the Women's Club (of ballroom dance lesson fame), the Bank of America (that Dennis broke into), and Don's Market (where I nabbed my first Wacky Packs). Every building held a memory, every corner a yarn. I once bought Near Beer at the liquor store on Florence, pouring it out after two repellent sips. And at Sal's across the street, I'd purchased more macaroni wheels (for school art projects) than all the Italians in Downey combined. My first dentist had an office on the left (till he died in a helicopter crash). My pediatrician ran a practice on the right (his hairy nostrils forever haunting me). Even in the dark, I could see the A-frame peak of Foxy's up ahead, a diner we'd passed but never entered. Next was Pina Pizza (formerly *Pina's*). They served the best pie in town but had dropped the *apostrophe s* for...obvious reasons.

As we crossed Firestone, 'Stretch' yawned, *stretched*, and turned left, disappearing up Phlox. "Wurtz!" I called after him, skidding to a stop. We were three blocks from the high school—*three damn blocks!*—my lanky riding partner turning to vapor. "'*STRETCH*'!" I yelled again, peering into the abyss. "Dammit!" I thought about spelunking after him but talked myself out of it. The 'big man' was on his own now.

And so was I.

Head down, I logged the last leg of the journey 'totius solus'. As I slowed to a stop at the bike racks, I smelled smoke. There were fires everywhere, yellow-orange smears on an otherwise-black canvas. Chaining up my ten-speed, I headed toward them, having no idea where to go from here. "Your fly's down, dumbass!" someone yelled from the shadows. I reached down to zip it, a plume of laughter billowing.

There were people everywhere, their bodies misshapen in vague silhouette, their faces revealed in flashes of flame. I counted twelve trashcan fires—a scene from *The Omega Man*. But I wasn't 'the last man on Earth'. I had friends here. Somewhere.

I just had to find them.

Feeling my way up the hall, I smelled more smoke. But it was pot this time, and plenty of it. Joints were ablaze everywhere, a galaxy of stars on a deep-velvet sky. "Hey, freshman!" someone carped, his cohorts cackling. "You want a hit?" No, I did not. Though, in retrospect, it might've been a good idea.

Despite the cool morning temperatures, I was sweating, my heart thumping to the beat of Cheap Trick's *Surrender*, which was blasting on a boom box twenty feet away. A band of boozers joined in on the chorus (most off-key), one firing an empty bottle at the wall behind me. I winced, making a hard left and nearly walking through the piss stream of a teetering drunk.

"Watch it, dude!" I was watching it, all right. The guy's schlong was bigger than my arm! As he shook the thing and stuffed it back in his jeans, he glanced up, eyes racking into focus. "'Skin Muff'?" *Oh, God!* I hadn't seen Ozzie Pagnozzi in years. He'd actually gotten hairier! "Hey, guys..." He lit a cigarette and dropped the match, dragging me off to a pack of troglodytes. Sitting around a fire, they looked like the 'man-apes' in *2001: A Space Odyssey.* I half-expected one to attack me with a bone. "...you 'member 'Skin Muff'?" One of them grunted, the others ignoring me. "Hey, Shirley..." He turned to a blonde, her lips at the business end of a Boone's Farm bottle. "...you gotta see this guy's—"

"*Shannon!*" I jerked to the voice, seeing Benny and 'Bert up the hall. In my 5,368 days on Earth, I was never happier to see two people! I yanked my arm from Ozzie's mitt and ran, the three of us reuniting near the cafeteria. "Where the hell's 'Stretch'?" they clamored. I shrugged, wanting desperately to hug them both but knowing it was a bad idea. "We can't find Budro either. This place is nuts!" It was more than 'nuts'. It was dangerous, at least for a naïve trio of undersized freshmen. We needed to increase our numbers. *Immediately!*

I looked around, music and laughter echoing in every direction. "This way," I took charge, gesturing down an ominous corridor. We inched forward in 'wedge' formation, me at the point, Benny (strong side) and 'Bert (weak side) flanking. At times, we forgot to breathe. At others, we panted heavily, scoring a serious 'contact high' in the process. It made us even *more* paranoid—and suddenly hungry.

Most of the cable was missing by now, hoodlums and thugs

swiping tools from their dads. The remaining sections were heavily guarded. "Don't even think about it!" someone rasped from the shadows. "These are *ours*, dickheads!" someone else croaked. Every bank was spoken for—"Keep walkin', douche-bags!"—every locker claimed—"You tools want your asses kicked?" As we trekked deeper and deeper into the labyrinth, hope slipped away in the darkness.

Would we *ever* find our friends?

"*Oh, Merci!*" We wheeled in unison, 'Gee' LeBlanc running up behind us. He was joined by Vinnie Bonetti and the Gunderson twins, all gasping for breath. "Tannenbaum's dead!" he announced, pausing to collect himself. "Dead as a door-knob!" Vinnie confirmed, butchering the bromide. The Gunder-sons could only nod, their glazed eyes playing the scene on 'continuous loop'.

"What happened?" I questioned, Benny and 'Bert closing ranks.

"We were in the quad!" 'Gee' began, glancing over his shoul-der. "Looking for lockers!" Vinnie clarified. "That's when Saul and Nils asked if they could join us." He paused to wipe sweat, 'Gee' jumping back in, "Before we could say no, a bunch of Varsity football players tackled Tannenbaum..." The Gunder-sons were twitching. "...and stuffed him in a locker!"

"But how's that even—?"

"They *folded* him up!" 'Gee' insisted. "Like a human sweat-shirt!" Three years later, the world would watch a six-foot monk named the 'Yogi Coudoux' fold himself into a two-foot box on *That's Incredible!*, proving the feat *was* possible. "When they slammed the door, we ran for our lives!" 'Gee' swallowed hard, Vinnie taking over, "We think Svensson's dead, too!"

"Hold on," Benny spoke up, all of us turning. "You found *empty* lockers?" He'd missed the point, but it was a valid ques-tion. As 'Gee' started to answer, an explosion lit the night. We recoiled, blinded by the flash, a wave of laughter replacing the ringing. "What the—?" Another explosion. Someone was throwing M-8os at us. *"Run!"* 'Bert screamed, seven freshmen scattering in seven directions.

By the time I could see again, I was lost and alone. To my left, a crowd of long-haired 'wows' (the term we used to describe pot-heads in those days) formed a weed-laced circle. To my right, a pack of melancholy misfits strummed guitars. Both guarded banks of lockers. Neither looked friendly. As a girl with an ear-bruising voice sang, *"Turn! Turn! Turn!"* I took her advice and backtracked up the hall. But as I rounded the corner, I came face to face with the gridiron grizzlies—*one, two, three, four,* I counted—all salivating, all enormous.

One stepped forward. "Looks like you took a wrong turn... *Capps!"* I squinted to see, the man's Cro-Magnon features bulging from a blue jersey. It was Dale Lingenfelder, the guy I mentioned in the opening sentences of this book. A few years earlier, he'd sat the bench on my Pee-Wee football team, and I, as the 'Pigskin Don Rickles', had taken it upon myself to make fun of him, teammates loving it more than halftime orange slices. Since then, however, Dale had added fifty pounds, eight inches, and six shoe sizes, and in the process, remembered every insult. "Been waitin' a long time for this!"

"Easy, Dale." I backed away, searching for an exit, but the goons had me surrounded. My father had raised me to be fearless—like *he* was—from tossing me up in the air as a baby to sending me into a crawlspace years later to hunt for rats. Along the way, he set a valiant example himself, never backing down from a fight, surviving a bullet to the skull, and barely flinching when a baseball (thrown by a kid he was hitting flies to) struck him in the head. He was the toughest man I knew, his son anything but. "Can't we discuss—?"

Lingenfelder pounced, grabbing me by the throat and slamming me against the wall. "Beat his ass, Dale!" someone hollered, my back bearing brick prints. As my spine popped, Dale's big, red face, complete with ovoid forehead and soul-less eyes, moved closer, his breath a mix of Budweiser and Copenhagen. I had two options: 1) fight the giant and suffer acute bodily harm; or 2) reason with him, the tack I'd always preferred. Given the fact the Warren Bear was *growling*, option two seemed fanciful.

I'd been in just two fights. In third grade, I punched Maynard Peeks in the arm, the boy crying all the way to the office to report me. In fourth grade, Lisa White's older sister, Mickey, tracked me down after school and shoved me into a yucca bush. I'd been making fun of Lisa for years, and Mickey (who, if memory serves, was 6'4", 250) had seen enough. My career record, therefore, was 1-1. But it was about to be 1-2.

"Fuck 'im up, Ling!" a guy in a festive Hawaiian shirt urged. Dale complied, digging his thumbs into my trachea. Unable to escape, I knew this was it...

The end. *Death at fourteen!*

In desperation, I scanned the horizon, searching for friends...teachers...campus security, for God's sake! I'd come here to get a locker, a *metal* box to secure my books! Was doing it without being fitted for a *wooden* box too much to ask? Still growling, Ling cocked his fist. At least it would be over soon.

But as I braced for impact, I heard a commotion, Dale's grip weakening. Flexing my lids, I saw a muscular 'wow' with a wad of blue jersey. "Choose off, bitch!" he sniggered, stepping into the light. As blood rushed back to my brain, I squinted. *Billy Friedhoffer?* I had no idea why Billy was at Locker Night. He was at least twenty years old, worked at Bobo's Arcade, and had dropped out of high school at sixteen. But in all our years of living on the same street, I'd never known the 'Fried-Dog' to miss a party.

Dale sized him up, his teammates closing in. "Think you can take four of us?" 'Hawaiian guy' snorted. Before he could answer, fifty 'wows' stepped from the shadows, armed with beer bottles and bongs.

"Pretty sure," Billy answered, sparking a jay. Turns out, not all football players are dumb, these guys bolting immediately. As the 'wows' gave chase, I turned to my left, Benny, 'Bert, and Budro jogging up to meet me.

"What happened?" Before I could explain, 'Gee' and the Gundersons showed up, Vinnie waving us up the hall.

"Tannenbaum's *alive!*" he proclaimed. I glanced at 'Bert who looked disappointed. "He and Svensson found lockers." He paused, 'Gee' taking over, "Right next to the library." We were far from excited. The library was nowhere near the action-packed quad and was, in fact, a total 'dork magnet', but after everything we'd been through, we just wanted to go home. On the way there, we ran into Kyle Blount and Arthur C. Fitch. The ten of us, without a word, shambled to our Siberian digs, Nils and a still-creased Saul greeting us there.

As the sun bloomed on the horizon, bathing the campus in amber light, we walked to the bike racks, stepping over beer cans, bottles, and puddles of puke. I think we knew, even then, that our lives would never be the same. Grade school and middle school were behind us now, our days of bedroom forts and Nerf football games gone the way of the night. Some of our childhood friendships would endure. Others would not. Either way, a 'brave new world' lay ahead, the map filled with shifting topography and uncharted waters.

Navigating it wouldn't be easy. Nor would the voyage itself.

But what choice did we have?

In silence, we unchained our bikes, each (like the 'Yogi Coudoux') seeking refuge in his own private box. In twenty-four hours, high school would begin. If it was anything like Locker Night, we were nowhere near ready. But ready or not—

"Hey, guys!" We looked up to see 'Stretch' duck through the gate, a bag of Bugles in one hand, a Cactus Cooler in the other. "Did I miss anything?"

V. EYES WIDE,
MOUTHS
AGAPE

27

STAG REELS

He called it an "opportunity" but refused to elaborate. "Meet me at snack," the voice came again, filtered by the books between us. Three weeks into ninth grade, my English class had been 'sentenced' to the library, Miss Traeger needing a break from her minions. We'd fallen well short of both her and Dickens' *Great Expectations*. "In the bungalows," the voice added. "And come alone."

Snack fell between second and third periods, a ten-minute break allowing us just enough time to copy a friend's homework and buy a Hostess pie. The bungalows—four standalone units added to ease crowding—were located as far away from the quad as possible. Why I opted to hike there with nothing but a cryptic message to go on is beyond me. But even then, my reporter's instincts were strong, leading me to trouble more often than not, the 'bungalow conclave' another example.

When I arrived, the place was deserted. Sighing, I dug out my Algebra homework and sat. As I stared at a binomial (which made less sense than a map of the Balkans), I heard stirring behind me. "Eyes front," a voice came. Before I could identify its source, a kid in an OP shirt ducked behind a bush. "If you say no," he chided, the branch in his face quivering, "this meeting never happened!"

I sighed again, recognizing the voice. I'd known it since Tee Ball! "No to *what*, Willie?"

After a beat, Willie Haskins stepped from the foliage, keeping his back to me. As he picked leaves from his hair, he scanned the terrain, avoiding eye contact. "Word has it," he continued, voice an octave lower, "you have a film projector." It was like a bad 1950s spy movie, minus the trench coats and fog.

"You *know* I do, Willie." He'd watched 8mms at my house dozens of times. I shoved my homework back in the bag, done with all this. I had an Algebra quiz, a Drama scene, and two Art projects due, neither of which—

"Stag reels!" he whispered, peering over one shoulder.

I froze, then circled to face him, wondering if I'd heard right. There was no Internet in those days. No video stores. The only place to see an adult movie was in an X-rated theater. And you had to be eighteen to get in. "Did you say—?"

"My dad scored 'em. From a guy in his Pinochle group." He finally looked at me, leaf dangling from one sideburn. "They're hidden in the closet, but he's out of town all week."

"And you want me to bring—?"

"No..." He shoved his hands in his pockets and began whistling. I turned to see Mr. Titus pass, the Health teacher having just grabbed a smoke in the parking lot. Convinced he was out of earshot, Willie finished his thought. "...we have to do it at *your* house. My mother never leaves."

That changed everything. With *my* mom's cloak-and-dagger movements, we didn't stand a chance. When she caught us, Willie would be sent home in disgrace, and I'd spend the next four years in military school. Dad would be pissed, too, or at least *act* pissed, having no idea I'd unearthed the nudie cards in his sock drawer. It was settled then. This was not happening. It was *never* happening.

"Okay," I heard myself say.

As the bell rang, I shook his hand, the two of us leaving in different directions. My mind began to cycle. Dad worked six days a week now, gone from five in the morning till five at night, his movements easy to track. But Mom was more difficult. She didn't have a job, at least not a *paying* job, and came and went on a whim. She'd go to the market, visit the church office, swing by the yardage store...God knows what else! And when she wasn't doing all that, she was cleaning the house or cooking, eyes in the back of her head. This was hopeless. Why did I—?

"Love the new 'do', Ms. Eliot," Tanya Lawrence spoke up. Lost in nefarious thought, I hadn't realized I'd walked into Drama class, my young teacher blushing at the compliment. She'd cut and restyled her hair, boasting a new, 'more sophisticated' look. I, as an uncultured ninth grader, couldn't care less. Spending hours in a hair salon was the stupidest—

I nearly dropped my books, deep in thought again. *I'd* spent hours in a hair salon, at Alma's on Paramount. As a kid, I'd gone there once a week with my mother, jailed in a half-circle of hairdryers, stifled by the scent of roasting hair and dye. It was a miserable experience, from listening to endless gossip to reading about it in one of the 6 million dog-eared magazines there. Mom went every Friday. At ten a.m. And didn't come home till noon.

I smiled as I took my seat, having just solved a 'linear equation'. My house would be empty on Friday. For two full hours. All I had to do was get out of class.

Over the course of the day, I forgot half my lines in Drama, failed the Algebra quiz, and turned in one halfhearted Art project, a scribbled attempt at Cubism I'd hammered out at lunch. Not my best day, to be sure, but I had bigger fish to fry. I couldn't feign illness. Mom might cancel her appointment and stay home with me. I had to go to school, get a class or two under my belt, and find a way to evaporate. Snack might work, but there were hordes of people around then, teachers and narcs included. A thought bloomed. Miss Traeger sent us to the library on Fridays. With *no* chaperone. The perfect chance for a 'jail break'.

I nodded and grinned. This just might work.

Over the next few days, I affected normalcy. I did my chores, checked for pubes (still none), even rode my bike to Middle Earth Records for the new DEVO album. But I couldn't stop thinking of Willie's words. I'd never seen a 'stag reel' before. Oh sure, I'd watched my share of 'porn-light' on ON TV, but *Emmanuelle* featured frustrating edits and *Last Tango in Paris* put me to sleep. As time wore on, two things became apparent. First, watching hardcore porn with *one* other dude seemed...well, a little creepy. And second, I couldn't trust Mom to be gone for the full two hours.

I needed an insurance policy.

On Thursday, we invited two more guys to the viewing— Barry Tiller, a quiet boy I'd met on the basketball court that summer, and Jim Crandall, a scrawny kid in my English class who said yes ("Fuck, yes!" if I'm quoting) before I could finish my pitch. Both were members of the West Middle contingent, a group that, combined with Griffiths students, made up Warren's freshman class. Mom had encouraged me to make new friends. This was the perfect opportunity.

We agreed to 'ditch' on our way to the library, Willie and me on bikes, Barry and Crandall on roller skates, using two different exits to bolster success. On the morning of the 'Great Escape' while toasting a Pop-Tart, I mentioned to Mom in passing, "How about that Hal Linden, huh?"

"What do you mean?" she queried, a big fan of ABC's *Barney Miller*.

"He's *gay*, is what I hear." I grabbed the pastry and walked to the table, careful not to look at her. "Said so in *People* magazine. There's an article, pictures, the whole nine yards." I took a bite, burning my tongue.

"I can't believe it!"

Neither could I. Mainly because I made it up. *This* was my insurance policy. Mom and her friends would search every magazine at Alma's for the feature, and that would give us the extra time we needed. Stuffing the half-eaten Pop-Tart in my pocket, I headed for the door. "Have a good day, Mom."

First period Health class moved slower than a sports physical, Mr. Titus using the overhead projector to detail every function of the gallbladder. By the time we made it to English, I was done with the human body...well, the *inside* at least. As Miss Traeger called roll, Willie lifted a paper sack, grinning at me. When I looked away, I saw Crandall nodding, a massive smile on his conspicuous face.

What had I gotten myself into?

"Today's library assignment," Miss Traeger droned on, "is to define the term 'virtue' as it pertains to Dickens' themes." Twenty-six of thirty students scribbled notes, the other four looking extremely *un*virtuous. When she released us, we bolted for the exits, Barry and Crandall fumbling with skates, Willie and I sprinting for the bike racks. It was the first time I'd cut class in high school, heart thrumming as I unlocked my ten-speed. Normally, there was a guard on duty, but advance scouting revealed he often took a dump before snack, today no exception.

Willie and I traversed Paramount Boulevard in record time, arriving at my house at ten on the nose. Mom's car was gone, as was Dad's, the place emptier than Ozzie Pagnozzi's cranium. As we headed for the door, I turned to my co-conspirator, "You gave them directions, right?" His vacant stare spoke volumes. "Are you kidding me?" I couldn't be mad at Willie. Directions were *my* responsibility and the first detail to slip through the cracks.

"I...think I said...Guatemala."

"Great." I shoved my key in the lock. "Guatemala's a *mile* long!"

We headed inside, the air smelling of fresh zucchini bread—Mom had found time to bake, do laundry, and reshuffle the spice rack before heading to Alma's. As I grabbed the projector, Willie reached in his bag, hands shaking so badly he dropped the first reel. The thing rolled down the hall—"*Shit!*"—and disappeared around the corner, unspooling the entire way.

"Go find it!" I ordered, lugging the Eumig into my room. "I'll get the projector going." As I moved the chair, it toppled over, taking me down with it. "*Jesus!*" We were a Stooges comedy come to life, 'Moe' chasing celluloid down the hall, 'Shemp' trapped under the weight of his own furniture. Struggling to my knees, I glanced at the clock. It was already 10:15!

"*Shannon!*" I flinched at the reference, praying it wasn't Mom. It came again, louder and more frantic...from outside. Willie dashed to the window, pulling back the curtain. Eyes wide, we watched our fellow fugitives skate by, yelling my name.

"They're gonna roust the entire neighborhood!" I snatched the reel from his hand. "Go get them. I'll have everything ready when you get back." As he darted off, I set up the screen, fired up the projector, and loaded the film, the first of three twenty-minute offerings. I glanced at the clock again. If we wanted to watch them all—and we damn sure did!—we wouldn't finish till 11:30. That gave me half-an-hour to clean up, cover my tracks, and vacate the premises before Mom came home. Not easy. But doable.

When 'Larry' and 'Curly' skated into the room, I signaled Willie to kill the lights. A white square filled the screen, followed by numbers, each flashing like scenes from a nightmare. It was the longest leader in cinematic history. When the title finally emerged—*VEGETABLE GIRL*—I dialed in the focus, the placard giving way to a weathered front door. A guy in a windbreaker walked up, carrying groceries. There was no sound when he knocked, no sound on any of these films. We stared like bass as a woman—an *unattractive* woman, if I'm being honest—invited him in. The man who was fat and fifty-something appeared to be selling vegetables door to door, a questionable premise at best. When he produced a cucumber, the woman, without pause, went down on it—also questionable—eventually swapping gourd for 'real thing'. The room went quiet but for the sound of churning gears and Crandall's occasional titter, the scene ending as one would expect.

"Gross," someone commented. "And terrible acting," someone else added, eliciting more giggles. We were 'whistling in the graveyard', each of us beyond uncomfortable. But the critiques were accurate. The production value of *Vegetable Girl* was worse than *The Lost Football Player*'s. And as we were about to learn, it was the best of the three.

The second film—*IT'S A PISSER!*—featured a near-identical set up. Another guy knocked on another door (no groceries this time) to be invited in by another unattractive female, this one dressed like a stewardess. After ten seconds of silent conversation, they agreed to have sex, using the kitchen table as a landing strip. With no audio, it was like watching a dance routine without music, the various moves and thrusts almost comical. But the worst was yet to come. For nineteen minutes, we questioned the film's title. The final sixty seconds made us wish we hadn't.

As I loaded the last reel, the air was thicker than paste. Willie stared at the empty screen, Barry and Crandall looking like they smelled a dead rat. After a deep breath, I hit play. The film jittered, then locked into place, the title—*ANIMAL LOVERS*

—scrawled on a board. *Oh, no!* I won't burden you with details. I don't want to relive them myself. But I *can* tell you this. The cast featured two women, a bewildered St. Bernard, and a very reluctant horse.

When the last strand of film unfurled, it slapped the projector ten times before I found the *OFF* switch. Barry stood up first, followed by Crandall a millisecond later. "Thanks," Crandall offered, Barry unable to speak. As they skated for the door, I passed the movies back to Willie, wanting them out of my possession. He looked right through me, having new questions, I'm sure, about his old man—and Pinochle. Stare more vacant than ever, he took them and left.

I wish I could say we all paid the price for our misgivings. That Barry and Crandall got caught on their way back to campus. That Willie's dad placed him on endless restriction. Or that Mom came home and made me confess. But none of that happened. Perhaps our punishment, if one can call it that, lay in the experience itself. These films were the 8mm equivalent of saltpeter, an *anti*-Viagra pill that produced less excitement than a Bea Arthur centerfold. If there *was* a silver lining, however, it was this. The event expunged, at least for a time, our interest in adult films, which allowed us to be *non*-adults a little while longer.

Dazed and disturbed, we all went back to school, Willie ceding all hope of a CIA career, Barry and Crandall now added (despite an unsettling genesis) to my growing list of friends. Were we changed? Yes. Damaged? Perhaps. But not destroyed.

It would take more than a few 'stag reels' to accomplish that.

I rode back home at 2:45, parked my bike, and walked in the house. "How was your day?" Mom asked, hair dyed and sculpted.

"Same as every other," I lied, grabbing a cookie.

She poured me a glass of milk. "Tell me about the *People* you saw."

My heart stopped, as did my ability to chew. "I...uh..."

"The *People* magazine, the one where Hal Linden..." She blushed, putting the milk away. "We scoured every magazine at Alma's today and couldn't find a thing!"

"Oh...that..." I swallowed hard, remembering our conversation. "...I made it up."

As I turned to go, I saw her expression, one of profound disappointment. *Again.*

'*Vy do you do eet?*' I heard her ask in my head, her thick (albeit fake) Hungarian accent pronounced. Truth is, I didn't know. I *never* knew. But I deserved the look she gave me. And so many more. Not just for lying about Hal Linden, or for ditching school that day, or for the unsanctioned 'bachelor party' in my room but for everything I'd done to embarrass or sadden her over the years, of which there were too many episodes to count.

"I'm sorry, Mom." And I was. *Again.*

But I also knew—and so did she—there'd be *many* more episodes to come.

28

COOL CITY

I learned early on that there were two types of people in high school. Those who drank. And those who didn't. Having no discernible backbone at fourteen, and not wanting to spend the next four years in Agape Club, I signed up with the first group.

I made the decision on Locker Night, somewhere between Ozzie Pagnozzi's schlong reveal and Dale Lingenfelder's assault. Scary as these people were, they seemed to be having fun—sharing beers, hanging out with friends, even attracting females. If I wanted that (and I did), it was time to make a change, one that would lead me away from 'Dork Town'—I'd yet to attend a real party—and straight to 'Cool City', where I hoped to be the life of one.

All I had to do...was learn to like liquor.

My father had a drink every night but never two. Mom sometimes joined him, depending on the level of 'assdom' I'd reached that day, but never drank to excess either, a miracle as I look back on it. From the age of two, I'd been sipping Grandpa's Falstaffs, tasting Mom's margaritas, or sharing the occasional Brown Derby with Dad.

I didn't love the taste of alcohol. But I didn't hate it either.

What I *did* hate was Careers class.

Every freshman at Warren was forced to take the course, its ancient curriculum exposing us to vocations like farmer, secretary, bus driver, and farrier. Over the course of the year, future jobholders learned how to fill out applications, construct resumes, and undergo interviews—"Yes, I'd *love* to shoe horses at your fine establishment!" It was a pointless exercise. How many ninth graders know (or care) what they'll be doing in ten minutes, let alone ten years? But there *was* an upside. We had unlimited access to a Xerox machine, which is where I found the flyer that changed everything.

I was making copies of my resume, which included no diploma, no internship, and no work experience—employers would be lining up!—when I raised the lid and found it. Assuming it was a better resume than mine, I grabbed the thing, hoping to plagiarize. But it wasn't a resume at all. It was a handwritten bulletin, inviting *ANYONE & EVERONE* to a *KICK-BUT TOGA PARTY* on *SATURDY THE 18TH*. Below the assault on spelling was a horribly-drawn beer can and the words *PARDOO* and *BYOB*.

As the bell rang, I shoved it in my pocket, gathering friends in the hallway. "This is huge, guys!" I announced, already devising a plan to steal one of Mom's sheets. "And we're *going!*"

Everyone nodded—Benny Sherman, 'Bert Barker, Vinnie Bonetti, the Gunderson twins—everyone but Kyle Blount who had two older sisters. "It says 'BYOB'," he pointed out. "You know what that means, right?" *Of course, we did!* We had no idea. "It means, Bring Your Own Beer." We looked at each other, blood draining from our faces. "And last I checked, no one here's twenty-one!"

I opened my mouth, but someone cut me off. "Big deal!" Jim Crandall sidled up, hands in pockets, shoulders back. He had tousled hair, the beginnings of a mustache, and eyes filled with mischief. "There's a place in Hermosa. Best fake I.D.s on the planet." We turned, riveted to his every word. "My brother, Vic, got one last week. And trust me, it's legit!" As color returned to our faces, so did hope, at least till Kyle spoke again.

"How are we supposed to get to Hermosa? It's twenty miles away!"

He was right, none of us having considered logistics. "My brother can drive us," Crandall responded. The plan was risky but a hundred percent worth it. Fake I.D.s, as we'd come to realize in the last five minutes, were a must. And if we wanted to enter 'Cool City', we *had* to have them!

"One question," I posed, the tardy bell ringing behind me. "How much?"

"Thirty bucks," Crandall answered, the rest of us wobbling as if punched. As we fought to regain balance, he laid out a plan —gather at El Taco after school, pile into Vic's Karmann Ghia, and cruise like clowns in a Volkswagen to Hermosa Beach.

Everyone agreed to meet there.

Crandall and I were the only ones who showed.

Vic drove in silence, gut full of the quesadillas he forced us to buy him, his brother and I hatching a strategy. We'd walk in together, act casual, maybe even drop some humor on the guy. My name would be 'Henry Forbes', born July 8, 1957. Crandall's would be 'Earl Graham', his birthday August 6, 1956. Per Vic's directives (which couldn't be argued since he was a senior), we were to use fake names and bogus addresses, preferably from different states. He'd selected a Hawaii I.D., calling Molokai home and using Kalani Kalikimaka as a moniker.

As we rolled to a stop, my skin tightened. Could I really do this? I looked at 'Kalani' who was already thumbing through a surf magazine, then at Crandall who now looked more nervous than I did. After a beat, we stepped out of the car.

The storefront featured soaped windows, scattered trash, and no signage. It was anything but welcoming, but we hadn't traveled an hour (*and* bought Vic lunch) to turn back now. Crandall and I nodded to one another, then stepped inside, a bell tolling. The place was little more than a cramped waiting room and counter. No posters. No products. No personnel. After what seemed like forever, a man stepped through the curtain, wiping his mouth with a napkin. "What can I do to you?" he asked in a thick Indian accent. Neither of us answered, the air filled with hing and hesitation.

"We...lost our licenses," I finally spoke up.

"On the same day!" Crandall felt the need to add.

We glanced at each other, then back at the clerk. He wore a tattered sweater and crotch-stained sweats. "And, trust me, the wives are none too happy," I chuckled.

"Women!" Crandall chimed in, hoping for a reaction. None came.

"Cash?" We dug in our pockets and produced the bills, showing them off like straight-A report cards. He snatched mine first, reaching for a notepad. "Name?"

My mind went blank. We'd memorized our profiles in the car, recited them to each other, even developed comprehensive backstories. But for the life of me, I couldn't remember a single detail. "Shannon Capps," I answered, adding my real address a few seconds later. When he asked for date of birth, the fake one surfaced—"July 8th"—but the year remained elusive. "19..." Sweat dotted my upper lip. "...49." *Perfect.* That made me—a kid with acne and the voice of Julia Child—twenty-nine years old!

Ten minutes later, I walked out with the worst fake I.D. ever laminated, followed by 'Earl' from 'Arizona' with the second worst. It would've been nice to let them cure in our wallets for a while, but time was of the essence. The toga party was thirty hours away!

We met at Ed's Liquor the following night—Benny, one of the Gunderson twins, and me. Crandall had a basketball game. He'd buy his own beer, he said, and meet us at the party. The others (Vinnie, Kyle, et al) had either wised up, lost their nerve, or forgotten, proving they were infinitely-smarter than we were.

"Six-pack of Bud," Gunderson whispered, handing me a five.

"Quart of Miller," Benny ordered, counting out three ones.

I now realized why no one showed up at El Taco. We didn't *all* need fake I.D.s. Only *one* of us did—one schmuck, cretin, or palooka. And it was *me*.

I took the money and shoved it in my pocket, sweating bullets. Word on the street was that Ed sold to minors, as long as they had I.D. Seems there was always a liquor store like Ed's, with a cashier willing to roll the dice and look the other way. Over the years, we'd shift our loyalties to Phil's, Hi-Ho's, Omar's, and Jim-Bob's, depending on who was still waiting to be busted.

After a deep breath, I moved inside, an ear-splitting tone announcing my arrival. The man at the register barely looked up, adding pine tree air-fresheners to a hook. Acting blasé, or at least trying to, I grabbed a pack of SnoBalls on my way to the cooler. Halfway there, I bumped into Floyd the midget from Warren. The word 'midget' was used commonly in those days, but Floyd hated the term, preferring the far-less-popular 'dwarf' and fighting anyone who dared call him a 'little person'. He wore a twin sheet, possibly a pillow case, pulled up at the shoulder and knotted. Ignoring the Bud *talls* he was carrying, I kept walking.

As I opened the fridge, a burst of cold air enveloped me, cooling my roasting skin. Tossing the SnoBalls inside, I grabbed the sixer, the quart, and a twelve-pack for me, having no idea how much I could drink. When Floyd toddled off in his toga, I stacked everything on the counter. "I.D.?" Intestines kinking, I pulled it out. The clerk stared, then glanced up.

"Twenty-nine, huh?" I nodded, multiple gas bubbles popping. "Baby face."

"That's what they called me in 'Nam." I passed him the sweaty bills.

"Did you get it? Did you get it?"

I hurried down the steps—"What do *you* think?"—lifting the bag in triumph. Benny grabbed the quart, the Gunderson twin (I never knew which was which) seizing the six-pack. Wrapping our ill-gotten gains in sheets, we bungeed them down and pedaled off, the cool winter air smelling sweet. I couldn't believe it! I'd walked into a liquor store and bought beer. And now I was about to walk into my first real party.

God, I loved high school!

It was a three-mile ride, my heart soaring the entire way. We checked the map on the flyer, then followed the music, parking our bikes and changing into our togas. Benny was ready first, ripping some ivy from a bush to create a headpiece. Gunderson and I did the same, grabbing our beer and making our way to the door. After a quick look around, we stepped inside.

The living room was sparse, posters of the Coliseum, Pantheon, and John Belushi hanging over worn furniture. A door, presumably to the garage, had SEX ROOM painted on it, the *Animal House* album blasting from speakers. We reached in our bags and cracked our first beers, trying without success to look confident. On the right, six juniors sat at the kitchen table —five actually; Floyd was standing—bouncing quarters into a glass. On the left, a dozen sophomores huddled in clumps, shouting over the music. We moved with caution, sipping our way to the den, where a pool table was pushed aside to make room for dancing. Keith Budro was there, moving to the beat of Sam Cooke's *Twistin' the Night Away*, his new woman a slight upgrade from his old. He and Tanya had broken up shortly after the Dodger Dog incident.

We found space next to a potted plant, Benny nursing his quart, Gunderson and I moving from beer one to beer two. The place was absolutely packed, with every species and subspecies —football players, 'wows', cheerleaders, punkers—represented. In addition to Budro, I noted a few more familiar faces. There was Rick Marinetti from Health, Mark Thompson and Gary Gardiner from P.E., and the prematurely-bald Randy Cummings from English who, having missed the toga memo, wore cords and a Kennington. There were girls, too—Heidi Pierce, Shelly Bertrum, Susie Quantrill, Cindy Taft—more girls than I'd ever seen in a gathering outside school. And unlike Cummings, they were all dressed in skin-tight sheets. Smiling, I killed my second beer and opened my third...feeling pretty good.

"This is awesome!" I shouted over the din, Benny and Gunderson nodding. As *Shama Lama Ding Dong* played on the stereo, more people arrived—Trig Bechtler from baseball, Andy Zolig from Art class, and Dottie Deveraux, the hottest senior at Warren. Rumor had it, she'd already posed for *Playboy*. This wasn't just awesome...

It was the greatest night of my life!

Gunderson and I clinked our cans together, my third beer turning to my fourth, fifth, and sixth. Having no idea how to pace myself, I moved past tipsy to tanked, barely noticing. "Nice toga, Randy!" I slurred from the shadows, several people laughing (Cummings excluded). With liquid confidence, I stepped into the light. "Not sure if the Romans had terrycloth, though." More people laughed, even a few girls. "But at least you've got Caesar's haircut!" The whole room was laughing now, a far bigger high than the booze I was guzzling. I moved to the dancefloor, aiming 'clever' insults at three other guys. More laughter, a crowd gathering now. *I was on fire!* I busted out my Nixon impression. Quoted lines from *Young Frankenstein*.

Pretended to be Tattoo—"De plane, de plane!"—from *Fantasy Island*. "Sorry, Floyd!" I offered, hoisting another beer.

The crowd roared.

'*You know you make me wanna*—'

"*SHOUT!*" everyone yelled, joining me on the dancefloor. As Otis Day and the Knights played their signature song, the house shook.

'*Throw my head back and*—'

"*SHOUT!*" we yelled again, a senior with a Mohawk passing me a bottle of Jack Daniels. I chugged it like Belushi, the crowd going nuts! Gunderson, wanting to bask in my newfound fame, tossed me another beer, the crowd cheering again. Everyone was looking at me—pumping their fists, flashing thumbs-up signs, or both. This is what I'd dreamed of in eighth grade. What I hoped for when I found the flyer. What I pictured when I bought the I.D.

This was 'Cool City'. And I had arrived!

'*A little bit softer now*,' Otis sang, everyone lowering themselves to the dancefloor. As I followed suit, I felt my stomach gurgle. '*A little bit louder now*,' he changed the command, all of us rising. I felt it gurgle again. '*Jump up and shout it now!*' he cried, the entire horde bouncing as one. '*Hey, hey, hey, hey!*'

"HEY, HEY—" It happened somewhere between the third and fourth "HEYs", my esophagus no longer able to cap the lava within. As I shouted, vomit silenced my larynx, spraying everyone in a six-foot radius. Laughter and singing turned to horrified screams, Otis judging me with a well-timed '*Come on, now!*' Before I could apologize, 'Vesuvius' erupted again, scattering partiers and vacating the den. Someone grabbed me—a football player, I think—wrestling me into the kitchen. Along the way, I passed the blurred and sickened faces of Heidi, Shelly, Susie, and Cindy, all drawing back as if exposed to radiation. I spewed near the sink, breaking up the Quarters game, then *in* the sink, banging my chin on the faucet. As girls cowered in fear, boys laughed and high-fived, grateful it wasn't them.

Coughing and spitting, I felt more hands—Benny's and Gunderson's this time—my friends dragging me out the door. The world outside spun like the drain I'd just soiled, the air doing little to quell my nausea. I threw up again, first on the lawn, then in a rosebush. As Bobby Lewis sang *Tossin' & Turnin'*, Benny helped me into my pants while Gunderson lifted me onto my bike. How I found my way home without becoming a puke-soaked hood ornament is beyond me, but after two more stops to ralph, I rolled up to my house and parked...well, hit the curb and nosedived onto the grass anyway.

Stumbling to the door, I fumbled for keys, aiming one at the lock. But the damn knob kept moving! After a third attempt, the door flung open, Mom standing there like a miniature sentry. I couldn't believe she was still up. Till I looked at the clock and saw it was 9:30! "Dear *God!*" she shrieked. "You're *drunk* as a *skunk!*" I had no idea how she knew. Maybe it was the stupid look on my face. Or the toga tucked halfway down my pants. Or the smell of barf-tinged liquor wafting from my pie hole. But she grabbed my arm and dragged me to my room, peeling my clothes off—"Is that one of my good sheets?"—and ushering me into bed.

I lost consciousness when I hit the pillow, dreaming about my big, albeit brief, moment in the spotlight. In the dream, I wasn't entertaining high school party guests but huge crowds on a cruise ship, the floor rising and falling, then turning upside down like the SS Poseidon. As water flooded the stage, I gasped and choked, wiping fluid from my eyes. "Je-*sus* Christ!" I heard the captain shout, his voice sounding a lot like Dad's.

More hands were on me now—big, powerful hands—my eyes blinking through a wall of saltwater. No, not saltwater... *vomit!* I'd puked all over myself, all over my sheets, blankets, and pillow, Dad manhandling me down the hall and into the shower. I stood under the spigot for ten minutes, the ice-cold water doing more to sober me up than the four cups of coffee Mom made.

When I awoke the next morning, head pounding to the beat of Dad's favorite swing record, I glanced at my bed. It featured new sheets, blankets, and a pillow case. Thanks, Mom. Holding my breath, I floundered up the hall, careful not to make any sudden movements. When I reached the kitchen, breakfast was waiting—runny eggs, fatty bacon, and toast slathered with butter. The sight made me retch but not as much as the glass sitting next to it. Dad had filled it with Cold Duck, the smell alone sending me back to the bathroom. After hurling again, I stared at the mirror. My skin was sallow. My hair was matted. And a stubborn chunk held fast to my lip.

I shook my head in disgust.

"To *hell* with 'Cool City'!" I whispered, vowing never to visit again.

And I kept my promise. Till the next Saturday when I drank a bottle of Schnapps, stumbled out of bed to pee, and ruined the VCR.

29

NO VISITING

F ifteen-year-old boys have one thing on their minds... well, two things, actually.

Fifteen-year-old girls. And cars.

The car of my dreams was a '77 Pontiac Trans Am, the one Burt Reynolds drove in *Smokey and the Bandit*, midnight black with a big, gold eagle on the hood.

There was just one problem. I had no money.

"I'll put in a good word for you," Keith Budro promised, heading off to his job at the local nursery. As the oldest kid in our class, by two full months, he was the first to achieve gainful employment. His brother, Kit, had scored him the gig, one that seemed simple enough. Budro's task was to listen for orders over the loudspeaker, then help customers load stuff in their vehicles. Hell, any idiot could do that, *this one* included.

"How much does it pay?" My first question always involved money.

"Almost three bucks an hour!" he answered, climbing into Kit's 260Z.

I thought for a moment. If my calculations were right, that

translated to almost fifty bucks a weekend, which meant I could get the Trans Am in...*carry the one*...four years.

Great. I'd be in *college!*

"Well, let me know," I called after him. Four years was better than never.

As Kit peeled rubber, I set out for the garage. Dad, like every other Saturday, was sawing and sanding, the place teeming with dust. Waving a tunnel, I moved inside, telling him about my conversation with Budro. At fifteen-and-a-half, I needed permission for a Work Permit.

I also needed a sizable loan.

"I can't wait four years, Pop." I pictured myself on the seat of my ten-speed, rolling up to parties, football games, school dances, or worse, sitting in the back of Dad's Lincoln while Mom chatted up my date—*'He was such a fussy baby, and the skin rashes he used to...'* "Can you help me, please?"

He lowered the jigsaw, wiping away sweat. "We could probably loan you a little. Maybe the goddamn bank can do the rest!" I wanted to leap over the sawhorse and hug him. But he had strict rules against showing affection around power tools.

Budro called that night. The job was mine if I wanted it. Dad patted me on the back. Mom warned me about schoolwork. And Dennis tried to smile. If only things had come that easy for him. The next afternoon, I begged Dad to take me car shopping. After a sigh, he agreed, foregoing his Sunday nap to drive me up Firestone Boulevard. He warned me about making snap decisions, but I didn't listen. *Why start now?* At the first dealership, I found a '76 Celica GT—white paint, worn tires, and 20,000 miles on the odometer. No, it wasn't the Trans Am of my dreams, but it did get better mileage, a huge asset with gas approaching ninety cents a gallon. "I'll take it!"

My parents believed in letting us make our own decisions and thus our own mistakes. The Celica was a fine car and all, but I paid *way* too much for it, despite all the 'Fuck you!' looks Dad gave the salesman. "That's how you learn," he told me afterwards. And he was right. Every time I wrote those checks—one to my folks, one to the bank—leaving me with twelve bucks in my account at the end of the month, I kicked myself. But not *too* hard.

I did, after all, have my own wheels. Six months before I had a license!

When I arrived on Saturday, Budro was nowhere to be found. With more angst than ever, I stepped through the gate, a Japanese man in his mid-fifties greeting me. He wore a collared shirt and Dickies, his smile putting me at ease. "New guy?" I nodded, introducing myself. "Okay, I'm Kaen. You're 'Cappy'." I followed him past a pallet of chicken fertilizer—the smell was *so* much worse than the name implies—through the store, and to a staircase in back. "Go up and see Sad." It was pronounced 'Sod', like the grass we sold, the equivalent of a guy named 'Meat' running a butcher shop. "He'll give you the 'what's what'." Kaen smiled again, slipping through the back door.

I made my way up the stairs. Six months later, I'd defy death here, painting the ceiling on a rickety ladder. When I reached the top, I saw a man in a green jacket bent over a desk. Sadaharu Miyagi turned to look at me. He had salt-and-pepper hair, smoked a pipe, and was *not* smiling. After an awkward silence, he went over the requirements of the job, more or less what Budro had told me, then handed me a name badge. As I turned to go, he stopped me. "One more thing..." He puffed on his pipe. "No visiting." I nodded and left, having no idea what that meant but realizing five minutes into my first shift...I *hated* the man!

When I got to my post, Budro and his brother had arrived, both hungover. Kit had started as a carryout boy but thanks to my arrival, had moved up to delivery driver, a covetable position that placed another dime an hour in his pocket. "Have fun, pansies!" he sniped, heading off to the florist. The place was divided into three sections: the nursery, which sold plants, fertilizer, etc.; the florist, where every kid in town bought corsages for prom; and the pet store, home to countless (and foul-smelling) hamsters, parakeets, and fish. Budro and I worked for the nursery, but as I'd soon come to find out, we were at the mercy of all three.

"Carryout front desk, please!" a voice boomed over the speaker. Budro sat on the electric cart, eyes shut. When they stayed shut, I walked inside. Sheila, a forty-year-old ex-cocktail waitress, pointed to an old man with a cane. "He needs twenty-five bags of steer." I nodded, again having no idea what that meant but figuring Budro could tell me. When I shook him from slumber, he helped me load half-a-pallet of steer manure—by now, my nostrils were numb—into a Datsun B210. As the man drove off, bumper scraping asphalt, there was no tip and no word of thanks, a trend that would continue throughout my tenure.

"Carryout front desk, please!" This time it was forty bags of planting mix, the next time twenty bags of potting soil, Sheila's 'Pavlovian bell' peeling every few seconds. I would (and sometimes still do) hear it in my sleep, not salivating but tensing with trepidation. By 9:30, I was covered in sweat and smelled like multiple species of feces.

Over the course of the day, Budro introduced me to more coworkers. There was Tommy, another Japanese man who watered plants and ignored customers. Mun, Sad's younger brother, who knew everything about everything but hated when you asked him anything. And Tobias, a thirty-five-year-old 'wow' who used his employee discount to buy pot supplies. Two women and a man worked in the florist: Sakura, Sad's niece and the nicest member of the Miyagi family; Mindy who not only had the largest breasts I'd ever seen but according to Tobias, "loved to party with them" (whatever that meant); and Reginald, the first openly-gay male I'd ever come in contact with. I was admittedly nervous till I realized he was no more attracted to me than he was to Mindy. On the pet store side, Asahi, which means 'morning sunshine' in Japanese, was anything but.

There were others as well: Chick, a retired police officer who smoked like a condemned man; Herm, an emaciated Vietnam vet who, by working here, hoped to land an Asian girlfriend (he was still waiting); and 'Pete the Mexican'—he gave himself that name—who spoke perfect English but pretended he didn't.

These were the people I'd come to know as a second family, spending every weekend and multiple summers with them. We knew very little about each other, really, but had one common bond. We all worked at the same place, at the same time, for the same penny-pinching asshole. And that was enough to make us, if not friends, something beyond mere acquaintances.

"What do we have here..." A few days in (while I was talking to Herm about his favorite cathouse in Saigon), Sad approached from behind. "...a little visiting?" Herm who already knew the drill turned and began watering. I stood there like a manikin. "Come with me, young man." Sad walked me out back to a giant mound of manure, fifteen feet high and thirty feet across. "I need this pile..." He packed his pipe and lit it, puffing till he tasted smoke. "...moved six feet to the right." With that, he handed me a shovel and walked away.

It was the first of thousands of projects Sad gave me, most as punishment. Of all the things that pissed him off—and trust me, there were many—nothing irked him more than catching one of his carryout boys in conversation. Those innocent chats led me and/or one of my cohorts to hosing down the parking lot, dusting every pot in our 10 million-pot collection, restacking the unstackable pallets in back, or as I mentioned earlier, painting every inch of the fifty-thousand-square-foot building. And that wasn't the worst of it. More often than not, Sad would stand there for the first twenty minutes or so, criticizing our technique —"That's *not* how we coil a hose!" or "I need *longer* strokes, up-down, up-down!" Despite the Miyagi surname, this was no 'wax-on, wax-off' routine. We were convinced Sad hated us as much, if not more, than we hated him.

And his 'henchmen' did, too, the nastiest being Asahi the pet store manager. She'd make us scrub algae from fish tanks, move cages with finger-eating parrots inside, and sift rodent shit from piles of endless sawdust. But all that paled in comparison to the worst 'bullet in her gun'. Three or four times a month, she'd hand us a paper bag with something flittering inside. "This animal sick," she'd caw in broken English. "Go kill."

And just like that, we went from employee to executioner. I'll never forget those agonizing walks, bag in hand, mind spinning at Mach 3. "Dead man walking?" one of us would probe, the other nodding in shame. We had no idea how to do this humanely, receiving no instructions after the kill order. Was drowning the thing merciful? Smothering it somehow? In the end, we placed it on the ground and smashed it with a two-by-four, hands shaking as we dropped it in the dumpster.

Amazing what a kid with a car payment will do for $2.95 an hour!

Of course, not everyone put up with it. Budro left after six months, his brother a few weeks later. With Kit's departure, 'Pete the Mexican' took over delivery duties, happy to be driving an air-conditioned Toyota instead of a propane-belching forklift. My buddy, 'Stretch' Wurtz, replaced Budro, then 'Gee' LeBlanc replaced 'Stretch'. I'd learned a thing or two by then, the most important being Sad's schedule. At 12:30, he'd disappear upstairs, devoting the next hour-and-a-half to bookkeeping. It was the best ninety minutes of the day. 'Gee' and I spent it playing paper football, racing the electric carts, or feeding bugs to the Venus Fly Traps. When we grew bored with that, we'd have Sheila make fake announcements on the PA—"Paging Mr. Meoff, Mr. Jack Meoff"—or rearrange letters on the company sign to spell *FUCK*. We were kids after all, and God knows we'd pay for our sins the second Sad came down.

That being said, and for reasons unknown, I remained loyal to the man for four years, outlasting Budro, Kit, 'Stretch', 'Gee', two more friends, and 'Pete the Mexican'. Along the way, I killed dozens of innocent animals, moved a mountain of shit, and paid off my car. I only thought of quitting once, when Sad forced me to trim the Bougainvillea bush devouring our chain-link fence. After taking my shirt off in the ninety-degree heat, I fell from the ladder, careening down through thorns like a tortured Pachinko ball. Landing in a bloody heap, I stormed to the stairwell, Sad greeting me with the Toyota keys. "You're the new 'Pete'." He blew smoke, looking me up and down. "Clean yourself up and report to Sakura." I wanted to tell him off, to let him know once and for all just how I felt. But the words wouldn't come. As I turned to go, skin stinging, he added, "And no visiting!"

As it turned out, delivering flowers was better than wrangling bags of manure. But not much. I didn't realize how many funerals I'd be attending, coming face to lifeless face with the 'stiff of the day'. In one case, the poor bastard was laid out on a table, plants, flowers, and food items surrounding the carcass. As the family broke bread, I actually saw a lady pass fruitcake over his nose, her young daughter calmly taking a slice. "What a way to go out!" I said to myself, adding on the way back to the truck, "Too bad it wasn't Sad!"

"Ah, he's not so bad, 'Cappy'," Kaen argued one hot summer day. We'd just delivered five thousand shrubs to a house in north Downey, Sad failing to mention that we'd be planting them, too. As we slaved in the heat, digging hole after hole, I bitched about the man who'd sent us there, no longer worried my words would get back to him. I'd accepted a job at Gene's Sporting Goods, and after two hundred weeks of taking Sad's crap, was about to walk up those stairs and hand in my notice.

"If he was my age..." I pitched a shovel of dirt. "...I'd kick his damn—"

"He was *never* your age, 'Cappy'."

I wiped sweat from my neck. "What's that supposed—?"

"He spent his teens in Manzanar," Kaen interrupted, packing earth around a poppy. "His brother, too." As he spoke, my breath escaped me. I knew what Manzanar was. My History teacher had described it in detail. More than a hundred thousand Japanese men and women, including sixty-six thousand U.S. citizens, spent World War II in internment camps, sleeping on cots, confined to cement barracks, surrounded by barbed-wire. "I didn't know him then," Kaen added, shoving a fern in a hole. "But I do now."

I stood there frozen, not knowing what to say. I'd decided a long time ago that Sad was a bad guy, every encounter with the man wretched. My assessment had been simple, black-and-white. Now it was anything but. After an interminable pause, I managed an "I'm sorry", all further comments stuck in my throat.

The next few days were a blur. When I gave Sad my notice, he glanced at the letter and tossed it on the pile. "Okay," he uttered, making another entry in his ledger. I waited, hoping for a "Thanks"...a "Good luck"...even a "You're making a big mistake". But there was only silence, save for the faint puffing of lips against pipe.

And that's how it ended. No fanfare. No gold watch. Not even a "Goodbye".

But I didn't walk away emptyhanded. Not only had I learned to paint, to landscape, and to coil a damn hose, but I'd grasped the concepts of hard work and frugality. And I could drive a stick with the best of them! These gifts would pay dividends in the years to come, resurfacing in one form or another as I moved from job to job. Yes, I'd grow to dislike other bosses, but the lessons I learned at the nursery were forever in my mind. No one is black-and-white, each of us—man, woman, adult, child, boss, employee—living somewhere in the gray.

As I 'packed the last bit of soil' around this story, a thought blossomed. If Sad was alive today, he'd be pushing a hundred. The nursery itself was long gone, gobbled up by corporate giants in the 1990s, leveled to make room for an AutoZone a few years later. I grabbed the mouse and Googled Sad's name, an obituary filling the screen. There was no photo, just the image of a single white rose and the year of his death—2009. He was survived by *'his beloved wife, Yui, his daughter, Sara, and his brother, Mun'* with no mention of the company he ran for thirty years.

As I stared at his name, something strange happened. A tear slipped down my cheek, something I never could've imagined four decades earlier. I wiped it with the back of my hand, emotions swirling. "If you made it to heaven," I whispered, "I hope they allow pipe smoke."

I leaned back in my chair and smiled.

"But no visiting."

30

FOR I HAVE SINNED

The 'oil painting' of me, as a kid anyway, is one of many colors. I was a wise guy. A miscreant. A dork. And a troublemaker. Not a great resume but nonetheless mine.

The trouble I'd make, I told myself, was of the innocent variety—prank phone calls, Ding-Dong-Ditch, the occasional loaf on someone's doorstep—all documented in previous text. But when I got my driver's license, things escalated. As much as I'd love to skip this chapter of my life, I must, for the sake of 'naked honesty', confess my sins. Not all of them, of course, but a reasonable list. My apologies to both victims and partners in crime.

As I waited for the big day, the day I'd finally take control of the Celica, everything was in flux. The 1970s had Discoed to a close, taking polyester, perms, and most of my youth with them. I had no way of knowing what the next ten years would hold, terms like 'yuppy', Pac-Man, and MTV meaningless at that point. But in the final analysis, the '80s would be *my* decade, the one in which I'd finally, unabashedly, and indisputably grow up.

Of course, that wasn't happening anytime soon.

As luck would have it, 1980 was a leap year, delaying my driver's test even further. While I waited, I watched President Carter bail out Chrysler, Egypt and Israel establish diplomatic relations, and the U.S. hockey team defeat the Russians in Lake Placid. "Do you believe in miracles?" Later that same year, John Lennon was killed, Mount St. Helens erupted, and the country elected Ronald Reagan as its fortieth president.

While these events unfolded, I continued to check for pubes (still zero), my focus on larger matters. *I wanted to drive!* And wheeling my bike past the shiny, white car in my driveway was getting harder and harder. But '*Time*,' as Steve Miller once sang, '*keeps on slippin*',' so when my sixteenth birthday finally arrived, I convinced Mom to let me cut class for a trip to the DMV. At 5'7", 130, I looked more like a kid in a car seat than a man behind the wheel, but I somehow passed the exam, the expressionless clerk handing me a crisp, temporary license.

Yes, Al Michaels, I do 'believe in miracles'!

My first solo drive came less than an hour later. "Use your blinkers," Mom begged as I pulled away from the curb. "And don't play the radio!" she hollered, shrinking in my rearview mirror. As I turned up Suva, forgetting to signal, I reached down and cranked the stereo, Blondie's *Call Me* jarring the speakers. I'd never felt so grown up in my life. And in retrospect, so alone.

But that would change five days later.

In high school, weekends meant freedom, independence, and a chance to blow off steam. Most boys, once they can legally drive, can't wait to take a girl on a date. I, with not a single female in the Western Hemisphere remotely interested in my company, couldn't wait to hang with the fellas. I rolled up to 'Stretch' Wurtz's house at six, a half-hour after another long shift at the nursery—I think Sad made us sweep the roof that day! Showered, dressed, and ready to burn gas, we picked up Benny Sherman and 'Bert Barker on the way out of town, the first time we'd all been in a vehicle together since Dad drove us to the batting cages in Little League. I'm not sure which was more dangerous...twelve kids in the back of a pickup on the 91 or four teens cruising the 605 for the first time. Somehow we survived both.

On a whim, we stopped at the Alondra 6 in Norwalk. We'd snuck in before—many times—and did so again, sitting through ten minutes of *Death Ship* before 'Bert pulled a bag of water bombs from his pocket. Nodding, we got up and left, driving to the nearest gas station. With balloons filled and ready, we drove back to the theater, 'Stretch' bracing himself as he leaned out the window. To give our targets a fighting chance, we'd yell things like *"HEY, FOUR-EYES!"* or *"HEY, BIG-HAIR!"* bombing them when they looked our way. 'Stretch', the starting shortstop on our JV baseball team, rarely missed, the rest of us feeding him ammo like a spring-loaded clip. It was the greatest night of our lives, which says a lot more about our lives than the night itself.

A week later, we did it again, bombing four diners at The Regency, three shoppers at Pick 'n Save, and two workers—*"HEY, PIZZA BOY!"*—at Frantone's. The next weekend, more friends joined in the idiocy—Jim Crandall, Barry Tiller, Bart Kinsey— each of us honing our skills from 'pilot' to 'navigator' to 'tail gunner'. This was so much better than Over-the-Line or Pickle, better than anything we did as kids.

And *driving* was the key!

When we grew bored with water bombs, we added flour bombs (paper towels with Gold Medal inside) to our arsenal. The result, if done in proper sequence, water first, flour second, was the creation of 'human dough boys'. More than once, we left some poor, unsuspecting bastard—*"HEY, BRIEFCASE GUY!"*— with biscuits for eyes and a dry-cleaning bill. I know now...okay, I knew it *then*, too...that our actions were deplorable. But they were also addicting.

Before long, we were conducting 'bombing raids' every day. When we couldn't afford balloons (or Mom mysteriously ran out of flour), we'd resort to fruit—limes, lemons, anything we could throw. And since Downey was once an orange grove, trees were abundant, as was the 'free fruit' they produced.

When we lacked *all* weaponry, we resorted to what God gave us. It started with drive-by BAs, the public unveiling of one's derriere, but escalated to nude 'Chinese fire drills', streaking through neighborhoods, and on one occasion sending a naked provocateur (the guy who drew the short straw) to a random house for directions. "Can you point me toward Wiley Burke Avenue?"

I doubt the shaken homeowner has answered the door since.

When I think back on this chicanery, I offer two postulates: 1) we *really* needed girlfriends; and 2) the minimum driving age should be eighteen. Not that all our shenanigans required wheels. One could argue, and many a teacher did, that our behavior in school was worse. In one two-week period, my friends and I slipped dissected frog parts into Maggie Chin's purse, ran Glen Torkle's bike up the flagpole, and covered Bob Cobb's locker with mud. While he chiseled away crust, we tossed banana peels into the crowd, watching one heedless student after another slip from view. It was quality entertainment, believe me, till Ms. Trachsel, our sixty-year-old vice principal, fell prey to the trap, spraining her ankle and spurring a manhunt for the perps.

Time to get back on the road.

"Check it out, dudes!" Crandall held up a paper license, the rest of us having no idea how he passed the test. "*I'm* driving Saturday. And I know exactly where we're going!" His statement flew in the face of conventional wisdom. Rarely, if ever, did we have a game plan, most nights beginning with, "What are we gonna do?" He shoved the license in his pocket, offering a devious grin. "We're going to 'Munchkin Land'!"

I suddenly smelled fear, and not just my own. We'd all heard of 'Munchkin Land', a legend passed down, in Native American oral tradition, from one generation of Downey kids to the next. According to seniors, it was located on the Island, its entrance featuring no markers or signs. The little, dirt road, if one could find it, appeared to dead-end but actually jogged left, snaking into a hidden neighborhood. Creation stories vary, but my favorite involved P.T. Barnum, the man who said, "There's a sucker born every minute!" The circus magnate, as claimed by the likes of Ozzie Pagnozzi, bought the land in 1890, erecting miniature houses for the dwarfs he exploited in his 'traveling menagerie'. His plan was to care for them in retirement, but he died in 1891, leaving them stranded, penniless, and downright pissed-off. The tale, of course, had more holes than a Wiffle Ball. For one thing, even the youngest dwarf would've 'kicked the little bucket' years ago. But we chose, like Ozzie and all the 'Ozzies' before him, to believe it verbatim.

"Meet me at Ed's," Crandall insisted. And we did, at midnight on Saturday, grabbing a twelve-pack, killing it in the parking lot, then driving to the Island. Buzzed but *not* relaxed, we rolled to a stop, Crandall, 'Stretch', Barry, and I shaking like the San Andreas. Headlights revealed what looked to be an over-grown driveway. But it wasn't a driveway at all. There was no house, no garage, no—

"This is it," 'Stretch' wheezed from the back seat, the rest of us silent. Crandall took his foot off the brake, his anxious Capri hiccupping forward. We were headed straight for a fence, but the road suddenly zagged, narrowing as it plunged into a crushing shadow. "God help us," he added, the rest of us nodding in unison.

"You know what we have to do," Crandall whispered. We

nodded again, each knowing what was expected. We were to drive through the shrunken development, stop at the turn-around, and scream, "Fuck you, munchkins!" at the top of our lungs. Then, and only then, were we allowed to leave. And it better be in haste since there were credible reports of tire-popping spike-strips, knee-high roadblocks, and angry dwarfs with hatchets and rocks.

"Look at the houses!" 'Stretch' gulped as we crunched through gravel. There were dozens of them, one after another, like boxcars on a toy train. Other than being built to half-scale, there were no other quirks to buttress the legend. No tiny bicy-cles. No Shetland ponies. And the cars on the street were the same size as ours.

Still, the place gave us the heebie-jeebies!

"This is the end," I spoke up, unconsciously quoting Morri-son. Crandall braked, executing a clumsy three-point turn, the rest of us rolling our windows down. I smelled Evening Prim-rose, heard four pounding hearts. "Ready?" No one responded, the air thicker than a Big Boy milkshake. "In three...two..." I swallowed hard. "...*one*."

"*FUCK YOU, MUNCHKINS!*" we screamed in concert, Cran-dall hitting the gas. As we strangled the door handles, porch-lights flashed like tracers, a wake of gravel fanning behind us. It took five minutes to crawl our way in, thirty seconds to speed our way out, no one seeing a spike-strip, roadblock, or rock-wielding little person. As we dashed from the Island, hearts still in our throats, we couldn't help but laugh. Nothing had happened. Absolutely nothing. But *we* were the 'yarn spinners' now, responsible for conserving the legend and passing it on, much to the ire of the hard-working (full-size) people of 'Munchkin Land'.

"Pomegranates!" 'Stretch' yelled, Crandall skidding to a stop. We leaped from the car and attacked the tree, grabbing eight of the ripest orbs. Pomegranates, according to Jewish tradition, are the symbol of righteousness, but our intent was anything but. Speeding up Suva, we targeted an innocent jogger, 'Stretch' offering a rare miss. Still confident, we turned up Tweedy, a giant motorhome blocking our path. Grinning, we moved into position, sending a salvo of Sweet-Tart-Wonderfuls at the can't-miss target. *BAM-BAM-BAM-BAM*, we heard from the darkness, the aging driver squinting into our headlights. At the last possible moment, Crandall swerved, turning right on Dinsdale with plans for a second strike. But as we paused to reload, lights filled the rearview—*red* and *blue* lights. *Oh, shit!*

"Out of the car!" a megaphone crackled, the four of us soiling our boxers. "Hands where I can see them!" We followed instructions, Barry still holding a pomegranate. "You *bozos* have a seat on the curb!" We did, the cop snatching Crandall's license on his way to the RV.

"We're *fucked!*" someone muttered, thoughts of the impending charges (from 'assault with a deadly pomegranate' to 'attempted fruit cocktail') swirling but unspoken. We were in no mood for levity. And neither was Officer Graves.

"I'm not sure why," he snarled when he returned, "but the old man's *not* pressing charges." We looked at each other, shocked but relieved. "So if you're eighteen..." No one moved. "You *are* eighteen, aren't you?" Still no movement, Barry offering a pained whimper. "In that case..." He smiled, putting no one at ease. "...you'll need to follow me downtown."

We were '*fucked*', all right.

The drive of ten minutes felt more like ten hours, all of us mulling our futures. What we'd done deserved punishment, I knew that. But as I stared at the swirling lights, feeling sick to my stomach, I wondered *why* I did such things. My parents had done everything they could to raise a good boy. Taught me right from wrong. Took me to church on Sundays...well, *Mom* did anyway.

Why was I such an *ass*?

We rolled to a stop in the lot, the cop killing his lights. I'd been to the police station before, on a field trip in fourth grade. They'd given us candy and toy badges. Tonight, I expected neither. Officer Graves marched us inside—"Sit down!"—typing a report as we wrote down our numbers. The clock read 1:40, the room smelling of Formula 409. One by one, he called our parents, Crandall twitching, 'Stretch' giggling nervously, and Barry staring at the wall. I was nervous, too, but not petrified. My father rarely disciplined me. Then again, he rarely got a call from the cops at two in the morning.

A short time later, Officer Graves left the room, returning with our parents. From the looks on their faces, he'd told them what happened, 'Stretch's' mom crying, Barry's dad frowning, and Crandall's dad the color of his blood-red windbreaker. "Cutie pie!" he spoke through gritted teeth, staring at his son's license. Crandall shuddered. 'Stretch' stopped giggling. And Barry remained frozen. *My* father was the last to enter, a veteran, if you will, of moments like this, thanks to my brother. As I tensed, he offered a quick nod but no smile.

"I'll take out the trash," I stammered on the way home. "Sweep the garage, even trim the hedges!" Promising chores was my go-to in moments like these. As I spewed more, Dad steered the Lincoln, eyes on the road. "I know what I did was wrong..." And I meant it, feeling bad about the 'air assaults', the 'naked jogs', even the 'dwarf harassment'. "...and I deserve punishment," adding, "You and Mom are the best parents in the world!"

A little sucking up couldn't hurt.

Dad cruised down Tweedy, past the crime scene, then turned up Suva, glancing at his idiot son. In life—like in comedy—timing is everything. My father was sixty-two years old. He'd suffered a brutal childhood, survived the jungles of New Guinea, and raised a child with serious health problems. He didn't rattle easily. Nor did he, at this point in life, worry about stuff like this. "Seems like a trip to the police station is punishment enough."

And it was. For a while.

An entire month passed without incident. I drove to school. Went to work. And hung out with friends, at least the ones who weren't on restriction. Everything was going well till 'Bert cruised up in his mom's van. "Hey, assholes!" he shouted, Crandall, 'Stretch', and I looking up. "We're locked and loaded!" He glanced at Benny who hoisted two bombs from the passenger seat. "Care to join us?"

We hesitated, deep in thought. Crandall had just gotten his license back, and 'Stretch' was still on 'probation'. Climbing into that van would be a boneheaded move—*beyond* boneheaded— especially with a tub full of 'grenades' in back. So naturally...

We did.

As we sped up DePalma, we each grabbed a bomb, hands shaking. *Wasn't one trip to jail enough?* The tension was palpable, our confidence weak. "Targets!" Benny yelled, 'Bert closing in on a bus stop. With the wind in our hair, our eyes strained to focus. There, less than fifty feet away, were two Catholic nuns waiting for an RTD. "Prepare to launch!" 'Bert screamed. I looked to Crandall in desperation, his look matching mine. This was *wrong*, we told ourselves, 'Stretch' nodding in agreement.

And that's when I heard it. Five voices fused in sweet, angelic harmony...

"HEY, SISTERS!"

31

SISYPHUS

I admit to one glaring omission in this opus. In chronicling my memories from birth through tenth grade, I've made no mention of dates, girlfriends, or sexual encounters.

There's a good reason for this. There weren't any.

Don't get me wrong, I wanted there to be. In fact, once I entered high school, it was all I thought about. But for reasons beyond my comprehension, I was terrified of the opposite sex. Oh, I could talk to girls. Joke around a bit. Even flirt with them every now and again. But when it came to asking one out...I turned to stone.

This debilitating condition—we'll call it 'femalus geologus'—had been going on for a long time: from the sixth-grade dances, where I skulked in the shadows; to the eighth-grade skating party, where I hid in the bathroom; to the Homecoming balls, where I phoned for a date and hung up a thousand times. There was even an incident in Oklahoma. While swimming in the Cimarron, Odell, Rowan, and I encountered three nubile Girl Scouts from a nearby camp. While the older ones—fourteen or fifteen, based on how they filled out their bikinis—vamped with my cousins, I stared at the twelve-year-old, developing parallel cases of lockjaw and akinesia. Odell and Rowan got phone numbers. I got a sunburn.

This sort of thing happened all the time. When teachers placed us in boy-girl lines. When I had to choose a female lab partner. When I needed a 'wife' for a Drama scene. I understood the petrification when I was young. But I was a junior in high school now, one who'd grown three inches over the summer and finally—*miraculously*—discovered a pubic hair. What the hell was wrong with me? I blamed everything from acne to lack of time on my busy schedule. But they were all excuses, and lame ones at that, made worse by the fact that every guy I knew had been to 'first' or 'second base'. Some had even hit 'home runs'! At least, that's what they told me. I, on the other hand, had never even stepped in the 'batter's box'.

It came to a head at a Friday night dance. Held in the gym after Varsity football games, these requisite events featured DJs, streamers, and a thousand horny teens, ranging in confidence from Todd Baxter, our cocksure class president, to...well, *me*. In my two-plus years at Warren, I'd never missed a dance. I'd also never stepped on the dancefloor. This time, I told myself, things were going to be different. I'd walk straight up to a girl, smile knowingly, and ask for a 'pas de deux'. I'd heard the expression in a movie once and thought it sounded cool. Clearly, it doesn't. And to ensure my success, I'd borrowed Dad's aftershave, blow-dried my hair extra big, and for the first time ever wore my JV football jersey away from the field.

Girls, as I'd come to find out, liked football players, which was the sole reason I signed up, long after quitting Pop Warner. In *my* sport, baseball, there were no cheerleaders. "Football's where it's at!" I barked at the mirror in 'Gipper'-esque fashion, scolding myself later as I struggled through 'two-a-days'. Going out for football was the dumbest thing I ever did. But at least I had the jersey. And I was damn sure going to use it!

"It won't work," one of the Gunderson twins chided. "All a *JV* jersey says..." He paused to pop a mint, sweat pooling in my newly-fuzzed armpits. "...is you didn't make *Varsity!*" I hadn't thought of that, but wearing 'old number sixty' wasn't my only failsafe. To further ensure triumph, I'd threatened myself with consequences. If I didn't ask a girl to dance, I'd have to weed the back yard, an odious task that no one, not even Dad, did of his own accord. In addition, I told the guys—Jim Crandall, Barry Tiller, even Saul Tannenbaum who I hadn't spoken to in years—that tonight...*yes, tonight*...was the night I'd "land a woman"!

As the DJ, a sad, little man with a Fu Manchu, dropped a needle on AC/DC's *Shake a Leg*, I got a feel for the room. It was mostly girls, the Varsity players (still being yelled at or showering in shame) yet to arrive. A perfect time to make my move. Shelly Bertrum and Cindy Taft chatted nearby, as did Tanya Lawrence, Susie Quantrill, and Laura Leigh. I'd known them all for years. Unfortunately, they knew me, too. I glanced at the dancefloor—too empty—finding another excuse to mothball my plans. "I've got all night," I muttered, wandering over to meet Barry and Crandall. They'd just gotten back from a water bomb run, and I suddenly needed every detail. Over the course of the next hour, I listened intently, laughed harder than usual, and watched the gymnasium fill to capacity. It's what I *always* did, huddled with friends away from the action, pretending to be so caught up in a joke or story that I didn't have time to fit in a dance. *Dammit!* Despite all my threats, I was doing it again.

AC/DC turned to Queen, Bowie, Pat Benatar, and Dexys Midnight Runners. Through it all, I watched and listened, begging myself to make a move. Why was this so difficult? I had tons of confidence in the classroom, around my buddies, on the baseball field. Why couldn't I do what every other guy in the world could do—pick out a girl and lead her to the dancefloor? When 'Fu Manchu' swapped REO Speedwagon for the B-52s, I lost even the shyest of cronies, everyone—even Tanenbaum!—grabbing a partner for *Rock Lobster*. There were plenty of girls still available, but I saw none of them, eyes blurred with failure. I knew then and there, as I watched the entire school 'pogo' in unison, that tonight would end like every other, The Vapors' *Turning Japanese* a painful reminder.

At seven minutes to midnight, the familiar riff of an acoustic guitar filled the room, along with flashing lights. Every kid in school knew what it meant, Led Zeppelin's *Stairway to Heaven* our official 'last chance to hook up' anthem. As Robert Plant sang, '*A new day will dawn for those who stand long*,' I doubted every word, my '*stairway*' gone '*on the whispering wind*'.

"Hey, Capps!" I turned to see Dale Lingenfelder and three other meatheads, each having 'bagged' a cheerleader. I froze, suddenly exposed in the harsh fluorescents, the sound of exiting feet replacing the music. "You couldn't get laid in a Chinese whorehouse!"

Turns out, 'Ling' was right. A month later, as I finally got around to weeding the back yard, Crandall and Barry roared up in the Capri. "What are you doing?" It didn't merit a response. "Get in, dude!" Crandall demanded. "We've got a surprise!"

Easily persuaded, I dropped the hoe. Twelve beers later, we stopped at the most uninviting building I'd ever seen. It was dark by then, and we'd snaked our way from the 101 to a grungy back alley off Santa Monica Boulevard. I stared out the window, a neon sign—*OR ENTAL MASS GE*—flickering. "Surprise!"

My ineptitude with women was well-documented, my friends just trying to help. But this was too much. There was no way in hell I was having my first sexual experience in a Hollywood whorehouse! "You ready?" Crandall asked, holding up a twenty.

"Okay," I responded, guzzling the rest of my beer. Peer pressure had beaten me again. We climbed from the car and headed inside, stepping over blobs of coagulating fluid. The door creaked as it shut behind us, the place smelling of sardines and liniment oil. After sixty-four beats of my heart (which took about eight seconds), a young Asian woman appeared, Crandall doing the talking. His brother's friend, 'Doogie', he explained, had gotten the 'Kung-*Pow*' here last week, and he wanted the same for me. As always, Barry remained silent. Nodding, the woman took the money and led me into a six-foot cell, pointing to a table and motioning for me to disrobe. My heart, still leaping in my chest, shot like an elevator to the roof. I was about to have sex. *Before* my first kiss! Not what I'd pictured, or even wanted, but with my friends listening in the next room, there was no turning back.

I unbuttoned my shirt, hands barely-functional, studying the girl. She wasn't *bad* looking, twenty-something with teardrop eyes, rail-thin arms, and straight, black hair, possibly a wig. All things considered, I could've done worse. But as I sat on the table, she handed me a towel and left. A minute later, her three-hundred-pound mother—it might've been her *grand*mother, actually—came back in her place, the cable on my 'elevator' snapping. Over the course of the next twenty minutes, the woman chopped, slapped, and pounded my back, giving me the worst and most painful massage I'd ever receive. I don't know how Lingenfelder knew it, but when I left the 'whorehouse' that night, I was still a virgin.

Over time, the bruises faded, my predictable life returning to normal. I had a crush on a girl in Spanish, doing absolutely 'nada'. I worshiped a girl at church, unable to commit a sin. And I bought tickets to a play, determined to take Heidi Pierce but after hundreds of failed calls, asked 'Gee' LeBlanc instead. Yup, life was back to 'normal', Merriam-Webster defining the word as: '1, *conforming to a certain type or standard;* 2, *regular or average;* 3, *Shannon will **never** get laid!*'

But if I'm being honest, I wasn't looking for sex, not really. I wanted a girlfriend. Someone to *like* me, for Christ's sake! I wanted what Mom and Dad had, though I was nowhere near ready. Living with my parents was a blessing *and* a curse. They were head-over-heels in love, two halves of a perfect whole. Every kiss made them blush. Every hug—I can still see Dad stealing a pinch on Mom's bottom—made them giggle. Indeed, no couple ever looked more right together than Clarence and Berneice.

So why couldn't their son get a simple damn date?

The question haunted me. Till I finally stopped asking it. As I posed for senior pictures in the fall of '81, I was resigned to the fact that I'd graduate high school without 'carnal knowledge'. Without *any* knowledge, really. I was Sisyphus. Rolling a huge boulder up an equally-huge hill, day after day, hour after hour, only to have it roll back down when I neared the top. And, like the condemned king, I'd be doing it for eternity.

But 'eternity', as I was about to find out, was not that far away.

Our senior year included all kinds of perks, the biggest a trip to New York. To be eligible, one need only take Drama, the sole reason we did so. None of us could act, but we could sure as hell drink! And the drinking age in New York was eighteen. Oh, and there was one more thing...our Drama teacher was the *only* chaperone. In charge of thirty feral teens!

No fault of hers, but we saw her just twice, on the flight there and the flight home, the week in between glorious! We were to attend six different plays. Instead, my friends and I visited strip clubs, watched live sex on stage, and became regulars at every bar in Manhattan. When I think back on the trip, I wonder how we survived. We were a bunch of brainless kids, no longer sheltered by the safety of the suburbs, unleashed and under-the-influence in the scariest city on Earth. Andy Zolig bought a fifty-dollar bottle of champagne for a dancer named 'Roxy', only to be jilted for a guy who spent a hundred. Crandall led us into a Peep Show, some of us learning the hard way that 'women' are sometimes men. And Keith Budro, shitfaced by noon every day, rode the Milford Plaza elevator in nothing but his socks.

And those are my *tame* memories!

For the first time ever, we were away from our parents, coming and going as we pleased, and partying like there was no tomorrow, a troupe of naïve Drama students 'acting' like fools. And that included the girls. This wasn't, after all, a 'dudes-only' campaign. Twelve misguided females accompanied us on the trip, most as wild as the males. One, a pretty, young blonde I'd noticed on the plane, seemed to be tracking me. From parties in Budro's room. To dinners at Beefsteak Charlie's. To beers at Eddie Condon's. I thought I was imagining it at first. I mean, no girl, as far as I knew, had ever taken note of me. So I had no idea what to look for. But every time I glanced her way, she was staring back—smiling. I, of course, did what any clueless clod would do...wrung my hands together, checked my teeth for chives, etc. But she continued to stare.

By night three, I'd had enough. We were drinking at a bar on 42nd Street, having blown off a musical of the same name. Most of us were tipsy. *I* was downright sloshed. "I'm outta here," I announced, throwing two fives on the table. As I shambled to the door, a hand touched my elbow. It belonged, not surprisingly, to the pretty, young blonde. She'd left the table when I did, coat buttoned, mittens on. And she was staring again, her smile slightly changed. Hell, even a rube like me could interpret *that* look! Gulping, I took her arm (Cotillion-style) and escorted her back to the hotel.

The six-block walk, combined with the bitter cold of New York, sobered me up fast. By the time we crossed her threshold, I was a stuttering, nervous wreck. Without a word, she powered up the TV, a rerun of *M*A*S*H* the only light in the room. As 'Hawkeye' asked for a scalpel, she led me to the bed, pushing me down on her way to the bathroom. Every inch of my skin burned, not from arousal but from panic. *I had no idea what to do!* When she returned, dressed in an ankle-length nightgown—an odd choice, by the way—I was trembling. She leaned down and kissed me, my first ever. It was incredible but tarnished by fear. It was time to perform!

From that moment on, things were a blur of groping hands, probing tongues, and utter confusion. I was trying to keep up, feeling my way, both literally and figuratively, in the dark, hoping against hope that I wouldn't let her down. But how could I not? I was a rank amateur! A clown on a unicycle with no sense of balance. A blindfolded squirrel in search of...well, you get the idea. And then, like the *M*A*S*H* episode on TV, the whole thing was over, leaving me with one agonizing thought...

I gave that poor girl the worst two minutes of sex she'd *ever* experience!

Despite my abysmal performance, I had the gall, like every other seventeen-year-old, to brag, telling my friends about the encounter and embellishing the details. "*No*, I don't like her!" I chuffed, a compulsory response to the age-old question (and one pulled directly from the *Men Are Jerks* manual). In truth, I didn't know if I liked her or not. I didn't even know her. And she didn't know me. So I did what every other jackass from the dawn of man through the writing of this sentence has done. I ignored her. And for that, I feel awful.

"You opened the floodgates, dude!" Crandall said on the flight home. "When we get back to Downey, you'll get laid all the time!" I nodded and smiled but knew it was pretense. I felt more uncertain than ever. Yes, I'd finally pushed the 'boulder' over the hill, but in a weird way, I missed that rock, knowing I'd never see it again. And I missed the feeling that went with it. The feeling of being a simple, starry-eyed kid.

Turns out the 'floodgates' remained closed. I'd experience no more sex in high school and just one more kiss, with my prom date who found love a year later when she married someone else. *I* wouldn't find love for nearly a decade. And I'm grateful for that. High school is about foolish adventures, misguided activities, and dimwitted mistakes, all with the best friends you'll ever find, friends who'd 'take a bullet for you' or 'throw you under a bus'. Often in the same day.

But as I sit here, forty years later, I realize it's more than that. It's about feelings, many unique to those moments in time. And memories, good, bad, and everything in between. For as long as I live, I'll remember New York. From the soaring skyscrapers and bustling streets to the smell of the hot dogs and crisp winter air. But when I think of the sounds—the wailing sirens, the shouting vendors, the endless horns—they *all* pale in comparison...

To the voice of Alan Alda. And the drum of my beating heart.

32

POMP & CIRCUMSPECT

Time's a funny thing. It can zoom along at Mach speed, like it does on great vacations. Or crawl at a sloth's pace, like it did for my vasectomy—that was the longest twenty minutes of my life! Funnier still, it can sometimes do both, the last half of my senior year a prime example.

With the 'Big Apple' behind us, we embarked on our farewell semester, our twenty-sixth if you're counting. Like most high school seniors, we knew the clock was ticking but didn't lose sleep over it. The final bell meant the end of public education. Of homework and pop quizzes. Of teachers and principals telling us what to do. Of course, it also meant the end of predictability. Of seeing our friends every day. Of the only life we knew, really, our futures now uncertain.

Jim Crandall and I spent most of our final semester in the principal's office. We'd been elected, by relatively-fair referendum, to the student council, serving as public announcers for the spring of '82. This was a huge mistake, as it gave us unsupervised access to the school's sound system and ten minutes of guaranteed airtime a day. We used it to make fun of classmates —"Free cake is available; please form a line behind Bobo

Grabowski at snack"—conduct hard-hitting interviews—"So, Bobby, big game tonight...what's your favorite color?"—and issue urgent proclamations—"Today at lunch, all students *must* imitate Flip Wilson." As a result, Mr. Spudner threatened us daily and in the end, changed our positions in the school canon from 'elected' to 'appointed'. But not before we announced Italian Club meetings using thick New Jersey accents and observed thirty seconds of silence for a student who hadn't died.

Today, even one of these infractions would merit expulsion, as would planting marijuana in the school flower bed, posting Bob Cobb's locker combo on a giant banner, or holding a bake sale for charity, only to use the proceeds for a weekend keg party. We accomplished all this and more while the 'sands of the hourglass' continued to fall. Like the seniors before us, we clung to our childhoods the only way we knew how. By acting like children. But the 'train of adulthood' was chugging our way, the last few months of high school turning to weeks, the last few weeks turning to days, with one 'final stop'...the Southern California Service Symposium.

Almost every male at Warren belonged to one of two service clubs. If you wanted to help your community and connect with other civic-minded individuals, you joined Key Club, sponsored by Kiwanis. If you wanted to fuck off and drink beer (at least at our school), you joined Interact, sponsored by the Rotary Club. As I'm sure you've already guessed, my friends and I belonged to the latter and as proud members were invited, like every other Interact group in the southland, to the annual Symposium in Buena Park. We were excited about the event. Not for the workshops on 'team building' but for the lodging arrangements—two adjoining rooms at the Knott's Berry Farm Hotel. There were four beds for forty of us, but no one planned to sleep, not with another outmanned chaperone in charge, this poor guy a member of the local Rotaries who had no idea what he'd signed up for. I'll give him credit, though. He was smart enough to book a room on the other side of the hotel.

"Pardoooooo!" Crandall screamed, the rest of us dropping our bags. As Benny Sherman and Keith Budro wheeled a keg into the room, Vinnie Bonetti fired up the stereo, The Dickies' *Gigantor* shaking the walls. Our president, Todd Baxter, handed out schedules, the last order of business he'd remember that weekend, the rest of us converting them to airplanes. It was ten a.m. on Saturday morning, the Budweiser flowing, the music pumping. And to borrow a phrase from four decades later, 'We were living our best lives!'

A knock at the door stopped us. Vinnie killed the stereo. Budro covered the keg. And the rest of us ditched our cups. As we retrieved our mangled schedules, Barry Tiller opened the door. "What in the name of—" Sid Dankworth stopped himself, adjusting his Rotary Club sweater and waggling his nose. It was clear he smelled alcohol, maybe even pot, though he didn't look certain. As he stared at the assemblage, face turning crimson, his Harry Caray glasses fogged. "You guys missed the first workshop! The one on the schedules we printed!" 'Stretch' Wurtz smoothed his self-consciously, a couple of juniors staring at the rug. "We're not here for fun and games!" he berated us. "We're here to represent Interact, Warren High School, and the Downey Rotary Club! Do I make myself clear?" Someone belched, but he ignored it, producing his own itinerary. "I expect every one of you at the two o'clock workshop, showered, dressed, and ready to participate!" He let his statement hang for a moment, then exited the room.

A full five seconds passed, no one speaking. As our president stood, all eyes were on him. "Gentlemen..." He walked to the center of the room, picking up a schedule. "...we came here for a purpose. And that purpose..." He wadded it up and fired it off the balcony. "...is to party our asses off!" The place went nuts,

Vinnie hitting the stereo, Budro manning the keg. As Crandall and I high-fived, Barry filled a beer bong, Russ Banaway rolling a joint the size of Bob Marley's arm. I don't remember much about the next few hours. But I do know we didn't make the two o'clock workshop on 'brotherhood'. There was no need. We *were* brothers, raised in the same town, at the same time, by the same blue-collar parents. Over the years, we'd played together and fought with each other. 'Brotherhood' was more than a lecture topic to us. It was a way of life. But I think we knew, even then, that this was our denouement.

"Who farted?" Andy Zolig yelled, everyone laughing as 'Bert Barker claimed it. Now's as good a time as any to point out, for those who've never experienced life as a teenage boy, the three universal touchstones of high school male humor. They are, in no particular order: farts, wieners, and poop. Come to think of it, these are the same three things we howled at in third grade! But I digress. While thirty-nine of us worked to empty the keg, Barry snuck off to the bathroom, 'making a deposit', not in the toilet but in one of the hotel ice buckets. Unfortunately for the rest of us, the now-sullied vessel made its way around both rooms over the next twelve hours, turning multiple stomachs and ending up in the hall at six a.m.

"Good morning, sir," Barry whispered into the phone. It was one of the few times we'd ever heard him speak. "Your morning biscuits are ready." A groggy voice responded, followed by the creak of a door, then a violent slamming noise. Those of us who hadn't passed out thought this was hilarious! But the poor yokel who'd saved all year to take his family to Knott's Berry Farm, only to find feces in a bucket outside his room, probably thought differently. That being said, we pulled off the gag five more times before parking the pail next to 'President Baxter'. He fired it over the same balcony that claimed his schedule.

The action rousted several guys from slumber, the knock

that followed waking everyone else. Half-dozing drunks, as a general rule, do a lousy job destroying evidence. We didn't even try, our chaperone walking through a minefield of beer-soaked cups. "Goddammit!" Dankworth screamed, redder than his first visit. "You missed opening ceremonies, skipped every seminar, blew off the fellowship dinner." He paused, grimacing. The smell alone must've weakened his knees. "And now *this!* One of the bellhops just got hit with *human shit!*" Crandall giggled first, followed by Budro, Andy, and the Gunderson twins. In no time at all, we were all doubled over, howling like spaniels. But no one, as it turned out, howled louder (or longer) than Sid Dankworth, proving 'poop humor' doesn't end at seventeen.

"When's the award luncheon?" Crandall spoke up, the rest of us wiping back tears. As Dankworth gathered himself, Vinnie and Budro canvassed the room, finding a schedule and handing it off. "It says here," Crandall read, "that 'festivities start at eleven'." We glanced at the clock, feeling a sudden kinship with our still-giggling chaperone.

"We'll be there!" Barry promised—another rare utterance— the rest of us nodding.

We threw on soiled ties and made our way to the ballroom, where thousands of fine, young men already filled the seats. Two rows were reserved for us in back. We made our way down them and sat. The guest speaker, a guy who owned a Midas muffler shop in Pacoima, was halfway through his speech, a huge bronze trophy on the table behind him. When finished, to a weak smattering of applause, he yielded the mic to the district governor. It was time to announce the 'Club of the Year' but not till each chapter had a chance to plead its case. We sat through speech after speech, heads aching, stomachs churning. The Reseda consortium "visited kids in the hospital". The boys from Bellflower "held a Shingles fundraiser". The El Segundo coalition "painted benches in a park". Every club sounded better than the last, their deeds recounted from intricate notes. Not surprisingly, Warren's band of blockheads was introduced last, our commander-in-chief (no notes anywhere) standing. But before he could move, Barry shot past him, making his way to the podium.

The maneuver was completely out of character. Barry, as mentioned, was an introvert, never once seeking the spotlight in four years of high school. But something was happening that weekend, maybe to all of us. "My fellow Americans," he began, surveying the crowd. "I could outline the projects we've finished, the charities we've supported, and the organizations we've helped." He paused for effect, scanning the fidgety faces. "But I'm not going to do that."

"Where's he going with this?" I whispered to Crandall. He shook his head.

"Instead, I'm going to tell you a story." He yanked the mic from the podium and began working the stage. "A few months ago, my friends and I were on our way to a fundraiser."

"*What* 'fundraiser'?" Budro mouthed. I shrugged.

"We noticed a boy. On the side of the road. Wearing tattered clothes. And weeping." The crowd of five thousand no longer fidgeted, each moving forward in his seat. "We stopped to help. All forty of us, working as one. For as Thomas Paine once said, 'It's not in numbers but in unity that our greatest strength lies.'"

I glanced down our row, shocked at Barry's disquisition and staring at my friends—Benny, Budro, 'Bert, and more—eyes wide, mouths agape. And they weren't the only ones. The entire congregation was in the palm of Barry's hand.

"He was 'lost', the boy told us. Separated from his family. Alone on the streets." Barry choked up, the district governor doing the same. "We took him under our wings. Developed a plan. And went door to door in search of his folks."

None of this was true. But we were starting to believe it ourselves.

"Minutes ticked by. Then hours. We missed the fundraiser, but what did that matter? *This* was service, in its purist form. We had a job to do, an important job. And we asked ourselves one question, 'If not us, *who*?'"

He walked back to the podium and replaced the mic, the audience spellbound.

Barry looked out on the masses. "Most of us are about to graduate. To head into the world. Alone." My stomach gurgled. "Well, I'm here to tell you, gentlemen, it's not about who goes to the best college. Or makes the most money. Or drives the nicest car." He shook his head, the rest of us unconsciously doing the same. "It's about friendship. And family. And finding our way home." He grabbed both sides of the podium and leaned into the microphone. "We worked from dusk till dawn that night. Scouring every neighborhood. Knocking on every door. It wasn't easy. No one said it would be. But *by God*..." He looked to the ceiling and tapped his chest, then collected himself for one final salvo. "...we—got—that—boy— home!"

As he walked offstage, I could hear a pin drop.

Till the walls of the ballroom quaked with applause.

What happened next, I'll freely admit, is hard to believe. In fact, it's so implausible I'd never put it in a novel. But as God is my witness, I watched the district governor walk to the podium, glance at his notes, and make the most unthinkable announcement in Rotary Club history. "It's my distinct honor to present the 'Club of the Year' award to...Warren High School!"

I'll never forget Dankworth's face when he held up the trophy.

It was the last time we saw either of them.

Two weeks later, we graduated from high school, the day sneaking up on us. As I stared at the mirror, a half-kid/half-man stared back—six feet tall, 170 pounds drenched, and with enough acne to star in an Oxy 10 commercial. My face was still flat as parchment, but I'd accepted my curls, finally wearing them like God (and my birth parents) made them. Photos of the ceremony would've been nice, but our camera malfunctioned, Mom forever apologizing.

She and Dad were there, of course. But they were *always* there. For ballgames, teacher conferences, for everything, really, the two best parents (adoptive or otherwise) a kid could ask for. Time, however, was chasing them both. Eighteen years had passed since they walked out of that hospital, carrying the burden of an obdurate son. Mom had lost a step or two, having survived a difficult hysterectomy. Undaunted, she worked full-time at a yardage store to save for my tuition, Dad (almost sixty-five now) watching his coal-black hair turn gray. He was quick to point out, however, that he could still kick my ass!

Most of my lifelong friends were there, too, though some had moved on. Sean and Seamus O'Leary lived in Burbank now, having switched schools and moved in with their dad. I pictured them at Seamus' commencement, Sean stealing his brother's diploma, Seamus clobbering him with a chair. Other friends had left in different ways, Arthur C. Fitch finding a home in Band, 'Stretch' Wurtz growing his hair out to become a very tall 'wow', and Willie Haskins forging a weird and winding path of his own. But that's what life is, an endless stream of people coming and going. Of moments that mean nothing and those that mean everything. With *change* the only constant.

"You changin', dude?" someone asked. I turned to the voice, a siren in the fog. Crandall, wearing shorts and a T-shirt, stood nearby, his graduation robe a memory. "Don't get me wrong, it's a sweet hat and all." I reached for my mortarboard, careful not to lose the tassel. Most of our classmates had already gone, some on their way to Disneyland, others at the country club, where the school pot dealer had rented the ballroom.

After saying goodbye to our folks, Crandall and I headed there, along with most of our friends, and later the Downey PD! We knew *all* the officers by name, the 'boys in blue' busting every shindig we ever threw. In their defense, there wasn't much else to do in Downey. When they broke up the grad party, my pals and I scattered in fifty different directions.

I didn't know it then, but it was the last time I'd see them all together.

"Where to, dude?" Crandall asked as we jumped in the Celica. The question caught me off guard. I'd been asking it for months. Since getting my SAT score. While applying to colleges on the other side of the country. When putting a pen to my last-ever yearbook. As I cranked the engine, Billy Friedhoffer's words came back to me, *'Buckle up, bitches!'*

I smiled, then turned to Crandall, offering the truest words I'd ever spoken.

"I have no idea."

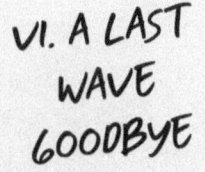

VI. A LAST WAVE GOODBYE

33

HOME AGAIN

The last day of high school wasn't the end of my childhood. Nor was the last day of college. My childhood ended on April 25, 1988. On the third floor of Mercy Hospital in Oklahoma City. That's where Mom died, after a ten-year battle with cancer. She fought like a warrior, but it razed her body anyway. Even stole that sweet, little voice, fake Hungarian accent and all.

We'd moved to Oklahoma nine months earlier, me to take a job as a reporter in Ardmore, my parents to buy a house thirteen miles from the one Mom grew up in. She'd dreamed of living near her sisters again, Dad of hunting and fishing with his brothers in Missouri.

Both thought they had more time.

I have no recollection of Mom's final breath, my brain, as a defense mechanism, filing it away. But I do remember the last time she looked at me. She hadn't spoken in hours, her grip nonexistent, her eyes on the ceiling—the same eyes that glistened on Route 66, that twinkled each time she stared up at Dad, that filled with pride when she held either son. Those eyes were glazed now, doctors saying it was only a matter of time. "Go make the arrangements," they insisted, Dad and I, with great reluctance, leaving her side. As we got to the door, we paused to look back. Mom hadn't moved, her stare still fixed, her breathing labored.

"So long, Mom," I recited out of habit. With the greatest of efforts, she turned our way, then raised her little hand in a last wave goodbye.

She died eight hours later.

On the way home that night, I clutched her glasses and robe, Dad squeezing the wedding band he'd given her forty-five years earlier. I don't know what he was thinking—I can only guess— but thoughts flashed at me like the pulse of passing lights. I saw Mom on Christmas morning, climbing on my rocking horse while I pushed her new vacuum. I saw me on Dad's shoulders, Mom and Dennis cackling as we galloped around the room. I saw the four of us at North Woods Inn, Dad's chin covered in butter, Mom dabbing it with a napkin. Funny how the mind works. In times of unbearable grief, we latch onto memories like life preservers. The snowman we built in Big Bear. Dad's '53 Mercury up on blocks. The acrylic grapes on our dining room table—why would I think of that?

But it's the memories that sustain us. And our love for one another. Both got me through the death of my mother. As did 'time', our unyielding companion. It doesn't, as the saying goes, 'heal all wounds'. Not completely anyway. What it does, is make them bearable. A blessing in some respects. A curse in others.

But life, with no ability to pause or rewind, pushes on. I went back to work, spending the next few years in the newsroom before heading back to California to start a business. Dennis, in declining health, moved from one assisted living facility to the next. And Dad eventually remarried, buying a log home on Grand Lake, where he chopped wood, tinkered in the garage, and fed the wild ducks. I asked him once, on one of my many visits to Oklahoma, if he was happy. He stared at the line he'd just cast, then turned to look at me. "Not without your mother." As he spoke, his eyes shined like glass, the hair on his crown white as 'Cotton' (the nickname his father had given him eight decades earlier). He peered across the water, managing a wan smile. "She was everything."

Yes, she was.

I met *my* everything around the same time, at a wedding in Orange County. Therese was the maid of honor. I was working on the video crew, something I did on weekends for extra cash. Flirting with clients, I'd been told, was "strictly forbidden". So naturally I asked her out. When we tied the knot two years later, most of my childhood friends were there, as were her nine brothers and sisters (one fewer than Mom had) and both our widowed fathers. It was the one and only time I saw Dad in a tux. Mainly because it was the one and only time he ever wore one.

My brother, Dennis, as mentioned earlier, passed away in '04, our father a year later. But not before he got to know his grandchildren, Michael and Stephanie. Watching Dad toss a baseball to my four-year-old son was one of the happiest moments of my life. And the memory of my baby girl bouncing up and down on his weathered knee still brings a smile.

I only wish they'd known their grandmother.

Mom would've loved watching them grow up, first in California, then in Washington state, where we moved to give them experiences different from our own. But how different were they, really? Our children grew up in a close-knit neighborhood, riding bikes, playing games (albeit *video* mostly), and looking for trouble with friends. Sure, it rained a lot more...and there were no sidewalks...and the riverbed behind our house was a *real* one, but childhood is childhood, whether you grow up in the concrete labyrinth of southern California or the lush, green forests of the Pacific Northwest. Whether you skate the frozen ponds of Minnesota or noodle for catfish in the Cimarron River. Our similarities far outweigh our differences, don't they?

Something we seem to have forgotten in recent years.

Time has a way of doing that, of making us forget the things that matter, and focus on the ones that don't. It also has a way of sneaking past us, even when we see it moving like honey from a spoon. My childhood passed that way, my children's even faster. In the blink of an eye, they went from Little League and dance lessons to buying their own toothpaste and paying rent, all a thousand miles away from their aging parents. Their mother, at least, aged gracefully. Their father...well, let's just say he looks (and acts) like an old man these days.

As I worked to complete this manuscript, I got a call from my daughter. She was packing her things in San Juan Capistrano, having taken a sales job in Portland and needing to stay with us till her apartment was ready. "Up for a little road trip, Dad?" It was the easiest 'sale' of her life. Decades after tossing my last water bomb, I still can't pass up an adventure.

She picked me up at John Wayne Airport, my little girl (whose curls rival her dad's) a woman now. *When the hell did that happen?* After bitching about how much room my overnight bag took up, she cranked the stereo and headed north. The Taylor Swift song playing matched the terrain, drab and forgettable. As it droned on, my eyes moved from the buildings to the blue-brown sky to my chauffeur. She was so like her dad—stubborn, dogmatic, and with a depraved sense of humor. I'd cursed her, all right. Thank God her brother took after his mom! She grabbed her phone and cycled through the playlist, one of *many* things we'd told her not to do while driving. As I shook my head, she chose a Morgan Wallen tune, a remake of Jason Isbell's *Cover Me Up.* "I like it better than the original," she said.

I did, too.

As one melody morphed into another, we crept up the 5, making horrible time as usual. When we puttered through Buena Park, a memory flashed, accompanied by a smile. The same thing happened when we crossed the 605.

"'Downey'!" my daughter read the *EXIT* sign. "Your old stomping grounds."

I smiled again, pointing to the off-ramp. "How about a little detour?" Always up for an adventure herself, she veered off the freeway (without signaling) and turned up Paramount. From there, I guided her to Gallatin, Tweedy, Bangle—and Guatemala. "Park there," I told her, pointing to the Brinkley place. She stopped two houses later, refusing to listen. I have no idea where she gets that from!

We climbed from the car, staring at the cookie-cutter houses, the alternating porches, the now-faded paintjobs. One thing struck me immediately. The entire neighborhood had shrunk, the yards impossibly-small, the houses straight out of 'Munchkin Land'! Was this really the sprawling Elysium I grew up in? Hard to believe, but there *were* signs of familiarity. The Lowes' Mexican fan palm. The busted concrete in front of the Garvers'—that crack had downed many a skater! The Andersons' avocado tree. As we moved up the sidewalk, the one my bare feet knew by heart, the hum of freeway traffic buoyed me, as did the warm autumn air. But the Helms truck was nowhere to be found, nor was the sweet smell of bread—Langendorf Bakery had closed years ago.

"I can't believe you lived here, Dad," my daughter offered between texts.

I couldn't either. It was a lifetime ago. It was also 'yesterday'.

As we passed the Munsons', I almost didn't recognize it, the fence removed, the ivy that claimed so many baseballs replaced by St. Augustine. Ten feet later, my heart began to flutter.

"Well, there it is..." I pointed to the house on the right. The planter Dad bricked was still in place but now void of shrubs, the once-green stucco an ambiguous earth tone. "...still standing." Emotions raw, I thought of all the hours Dad spent on the Dichondra, pictured Mom on the porch, getting us off to church, remembered the games I played with Dennis and my friends.

Could it really be *fifty years* later?

"Selfies!" My daughter tapped her phone, moving into position. She'd seen the house before, of course, but why waste a photo op, her phone storing more images than all my albums combined. "Smile, Dad." I did, my daughter snapping one pic of me, ten more of her. "Well?"

I glanced up the street, first to the O'Learys', where an imaginary Seamus kicked Sean in the balls. I saw eight-year-old me on a yellow Stingray, pedaling up the sidewalk for parts then unknown. I even pictured Mrs. Noid, scolding me as I passed. The thought of peeling rubber on her lawn honestly crossed my mind, but I didn't bring it up. For one thing, I was *pretty* sure she was dead. For another, I was *absolutely* sure my daughter would be up for it!

That's when I heard music, muted but coming from my old house. I turned for a look back. In my mind, and *only* in my mind, the notes fused together, blending to form a familiar old tune—*Moonlight Serenade*, Mom and Dad's favorite.

A realization struck me. In all our years together, I'd never seen them dance. But in that moment, that strange and wonderful moment, I *knew* they were doing just that. Holding each other in the living room, swaying to the sounds of Glenn Miller and his Orchestra. It was a beautiful image—a *perfect* image—and it took everything I had to keep from running to that door and pushing my way inside.

But it was a trap. I knew that. We can't live in the past. We can only visit, the 'good old days' just that. And this visit, like countless others, had come to a close.

"Dad?" I turned from the house to look at my daughter, her expression one of impatience, the same look I'd given *my* parents a million times over.

I nodded and smiled, then put my arm around her.

"Let's go home."

ACKNOWLEDGMENTS

I love to write. Always have. From the Irving Kumquat stories I typed on the Underwood. To this memoir. But my writing career was nearly over before it started. And ironically, a book was to blame. Well, not the book exactly...but the guy who threw it.

That guy was a twelfth-grade doofus with curly hair and acne who thought he'd learned everything there was to learn about writing. And one who was more shocked than anyone to see the book he'd just launched hit his English teacher in the leg.

Mr. Allgood—his look of disappointment rivaled my mother's—was the best teacher I ever had. From sophomore year on, he'd walked my idiot friends and me down a trail of classic literature, Haiku poetry, and onomatopoeias. But he'd reached his limit, sending me to the office, alongside good friend Jon Cockrill (the *intended* target of the book and a teacher himself now), both of us banished from AP English for life.

It was the last lesson Mr. Allgood taught us. And maybe the most important.

I've learned lots of lessons in life, starting with those my mother and father taught me. I could never thank them enough for their patience, understanding, and love. And for nurturing a young writer who for two decades forced them to read every horrible story he churned out. They were the best people I've ever known. And they influenced me in untold ways.

There were other influences as well. Childhood friend Greg

Farmer showed me what good storytelling sounded like. At age nine, he'd 'hold court' at recess, spinning tales of the "Rimshaw Place", a haunted house he'd invented for our entertainment and his. While the other kids played kickball, we sat under the Sweetgum tree, hanging on every word. Years after he moved to Orange County, never to be seen again, we secretly wondered if he'd changed his name to Dean Koontz.

But Greg wasn't the only raconteur to inspire me. When it came to writing prose, lifelong pal Steven Smith set the bar. As a kid, he was a brilliant wordsmith—that would've been a great nickname, actually!—and his writing as a 'grownup', which includes two acclaimed biographies, hundreds of documentaries, and several Emmy nominations, never fails to humble me.

I'm also humbled by the amazing friendships I've been blessed with, every one of them an influence on my writing and life. There are too many names to mention, but they all mean the world to me, from the 'Keith Budros', 'Benny Shermans', and 'Arthur C. Fitches' of my youth to the 'Jim Crandalls' and 'Barry Tillers' of my teens and beyond. And to the friends that were also family. The ones I grew up with: Mom, Dad, and Dennis, may they each rest in peace. And the ones I found later: my wife, Therese, who never stops believing in me; my son, Michael, who loves books and baseball more than I do; and my daughter, Stephanie, who curses like her grandpa and keeps us all in line.

I really am, as Tennyson once wrote, '*a part of all that I have met*'. I first read that quote in Mr. Allgood's class, somewhere between *Silas Marner* and *The Merchant of Venice*. And it stuck, like so many other things the man taught us.

Every writer needs a mentor. And Bill Allgood was mine.

A few years back, I brought him a copy of *A Separate Peace*, a novel we read in class and the first book I truly *loved*. When I asked for an inscription, he thought for a moment, then penned the following, *'I'm glad this book set free the artist in you.'*

At the risk of correcting my teacher, it wasn't the book, Mr. Allgood.

It was the man who assigned it.

ABOUT THE AUTHOR

S.W. Capps grew up on the 'not-so-mean streets' of Downey, California, where he parlayed a childhood of bloody knees, countless spankings, and failed accordion lessons into a writing career.

A one-time TV news reporter—he was nominated for an Oklahoma Broadcasters Award for his 'hard-hitting' piece on Christmas fruit-cake—he's also penned numerous magazine articles and three novels. The Midwest Book Review calls his latest, *Runaway Train*, "a solid, fast-paced action piece".

No One Special is Capps' first foray into nonfiction. A recent empty-nester, he lives with his wife in the Pacific Northwest, currently at work on his next book.

www.ingramcontent.com/pod-product-compliance
Lightning Source LLC
Chambersburg PA
CBHW050854150626
46549CB00013B/1623